# VICE AND VIGILANCE

# Edward J. Bristow

# VICE
# AND VIGILANCE

Purity Movements in Britain since 1700

GILL AND MACMILLAN
ROWMAN AND LITTLEFIELD

First published 1977 by
Gill and Macmillan Ltd
15/17 Eden Quay
Dublin 1
with associated companies in
London and Basingstoke
New York, Melbourne, Delhi, Johannesburg

© Edward J. Bristow 1977

7171 0821 X

First published in the United States by
Rowman and Littlefield
81 Adams Drive, Totowa, N.J.

ISBN 0-8476-6057-5

Printed by Bristol Typesetting Co Ltd,
Barton Manor, St Philips, Bristol

*To Holly*

# Contents

# Acknowledgments

I wish first to thank Dr Kenneth Brown of The Queen's University, Belfast, for encouraging this work in its very early stages. To Mr E. A. Sedgely of the Home Office I owe the opportunity of consulting a series of hitherto closed files on questions of public morality; to Mr Reg Goodwin, Leader of the Greater London Council, I am indebted for having made available the papers of the Public Morality Council.

My thanks are due to the Rev. David Wainwright for permitting me to consult the White Cross Collection in the possession of the Church Board for Social Responsibility; to the Rev. G. A. D. Mann who very kindly made available the records of the Free Church Federal Council; to Sister J. M. Wilbourne, Church Army Archivist, who directed me to some interesting sources and to the officials of the West London Mission who allowed me to consult their records.

I owe a debt of gratitude to Sir Cyril Black, J.P., D.L., and to Mrs Margaret Blyth-Scrutton for having spent a considerable amount of time sharing their reminiscences with me. The unpublished papers made available by Dr Robert Storch of the University of Wisconsin and Ms Penny Summerfield, on street prostitution and the music halls respectively, were much appreciated, as was the information on the Victorian vice squad supplied by the Publicity Branch of New Scotland Yard and material on contemporary white slavery supplied by Colonel Patrick Montgomery of the Anti-Slavery Society.

I wish to thank Ms Mildred Surrey, formerly librarian at the Fawcett Society, for facilitating my research, and Mr Hunter Cordaiy, my colleague at New England College, for overcoming formidable technical problems in reproducing a number of the illustrations. I am also grateful to a number of scholars for their helpful suggestions and references : Dr Judith Walkowitz of Rutgers University; Dr Deborah Gorham of Carleton University; Ms Jean L'Esperance; Dr Don Smith of Grinnel College, Mr Raphael Samuel of Ruskin College and Mr Clement Crisp of the Royal Ballet. I should like to stress that they bear no responsibility for matters of interpretation or any possible errors.

EDWARD BRISTOW, April 1977

# List of Illustrations

Between pages 132 and 133

feature on venereal disease, *Damaged Lives*. Reproduced by kind permission of the Trustees of the Fawcett Society.

15. The Seldons, victims of the 1907 crackdown on living statuary.

16. The popular 'La Milo', another victim.

17. The music halls retaliate with satire : 'The Vigilance Committee', at the Duke of York's Theatre, 1895. All reproduced by the kind permission of the Raymond Mander and Joe Mitchenson Theatre Collection.

18. The controversial poster of Zæo, for her acrobatic act of 1890 at the Royal Aquarium. Taken from the only known copy, in *Honi Soit Qui Mal Y Pense. The Life of Zæo* (London 1891). Reproduced by kind permission of the Theatre Museum, Victoria and Albert Museum.

19. The suffragists and white slavery : 'The Appeal of Womanhood', 1912. Reproduced by kind permission of the Museum of London.

# Introduction

MACAULAY once observed that there was 'no spectacle so ridiculous as the British public in one of its periodic fits of morality'. He was talking about the occasional expiatory sacrifice of an establishment son for violating the code of respectable sexual behaviour; Lord Byron's ostracism and exile in 1816, following allegations against him of incest with his half sister, was Macaulay's case in point. The subject of this study is the related but more historically significant and continuous moral impulse: anti-vice crusading on behalf of pure standards of public morality and chaste private sexual behaviour.

Anti-vice workers utilised a variety of tactics. They prosecuted the perpetrators of sexually related offences, including those involving prostitution, obscenity, homosexuality and rape; they pressed parliament to strengthen the law; they reclaimed prostitutes and even their clients from sin and they sought to educate the public to a purer standard of behaviour.

Campaigns against sexual vice and erotic expression in the arts and entertainment have sometimes appeared as ridiculous as the fits Macaulay decried. The forgotten but powerful William Coote, the more human counterpart of his famous and frenzied American contemporary, Comstock, once started an agitation to clothe the nude statues astride the British Medical Association offices in the Strand. That was in 1908 at the height of insistent Edwardian agitation against the obscene. Victorian rescue workers courted violence taking the message of the gospels into brothels. Alfred Dyer, the Quaker journalist whose revelations in 1880 about British girls allegedly ensnared in Belgium's municipally regulated brothels ignited one of the century's most bitter scandals, tried to tear prostitutes from Satan's grasp regardless of their own wishes. Allies of Coote and Dyer patrolled with lanterns on 'midnight missions' to identify and humiliate brothel clients and in unruly Georgian London devoted workers were sometimes killed when trying to arrest prostitutes.

While such colourful examples of prudery and militant right-eousness abound and are interesting in their own right, the whole history of what has sometimes appeared to be the most peculiar of the many forms of voluntary effort that have flourished in British society is worth recording for what it reveals about the influence purity work has exerted. It has left its mark on law enforcement, the evolution of the statute book, standards for sex expression in the arts and entertainment and even on the nature of private attitudes to sexuality. From the 1690s until after the First World War purity work was an im-portant force in pushing the erotic in its many forms out of the public sphere and relegating it to the dark. Mrs Whitehouse, Lord Longford and the Festival of Light were preceded by purity movements and institutions whose influence, grounded in the Christian revivals of the past, far exceeded what could be accomplished in their own post-Christian Britain.

There were four peaks of anti-vice agitation : the 1690s, the late eighteenth and early nineteenth centuries, the 1880s and the early twentieth century. Each was fed by religious revivals that converted young men and channelled waves of sublimated anti-sexual energy against the erotic. Each left behind an important institutional legacy to carry on the struggle against sexual vice after the original fever had died down.

In the 1690s the remarkably pervasive Societies for the Reformation of Manners spread through London and the provinces. While much of their early membership was drawn from circles of young churchmen who had come together as part of the late-seventeenth-century revival in Anglican spirituality, the Societies endured for nearly a half-century, prosecuting moral transgressors who included violators of the sabbath and profane swearers as well as prostitutes, keepers of bawdy houses, actors in indecent plays and homosexuals. As with the later outbreaks of purity fever, revivalism alone was not sufficient to make the Societies for the Reformation of Manners significant. There were additional factors at work to transform the anti-sexual energy of the revivals into important *public* forces. In the case of the Societies, we shall see that they appeared at a crucial point in the history of public order, after the old medieval ecclesiastical jurisdiction over moral offences had broken down and before the secular authorities were capable of filling the breach. Public officials and the royal court encouraged the Societies as an important contribution to the woefully inadequate police.

When in the late eighteenth century William Wilberforce, the great anti-slavery advocate and spokesman in high places for the evangelical revival, felt called upon to reform the nation's morals, an account of the earlier Societies set him on his way to obtain a royal proclamation against immorality and to establish the institutions to enforce it. Anti-vice crusading had become and was to remain a self-conscious tradition, with the spiritually elevated reformers of the original Societies celebrated as the pioneers in the field.

The evangelical leaders of Wilberforce's generation and the one following established a whole industry for moral reform that had a profound influence on the tone of British life. Once again it was the problem of order, this time the spectre of social revolution across the Channel, that made the establishment so receptive to the moralists' efforts. For in the aftermath of the French Revolution it was commonplace to assume that irreligion, immorality and sexual licence were the harbingers of social dissolution. Evangelical approaches to doing good and to spreading vital religion ranged from Hannah More's popular Cheap Repository Tracts to the more obscure National Truss Society for the Relief of the Ruptured Poor. To confront sexual vice the evangelicals established penitentiaries for the redemption of prostitutes. Their Society for the Suppression of Vice, founded in 1802 and universally known as the Vice Society, began with the same wide range of vicious opponents as had the reformation of manners. This was an 'age of societies', however, and in the luxuriant growth of voluntary institutions those for moral reform became differentiated according to transgression. The Vice Society came to specialise in sexual vice. Until absorbed by the leaders of the 1880s outbreak of purity fever, it remained the Victorians' basic legal force against the obscene; allied with the penitentiaries and rescue committees, the Vice Society participated, before the great turning point in the 1880s, in what we shall see was a particularly lonely and daunting task: that of trying to curb prostitution.

Part One of this narrative traces the early efforts against sexual vice. It discusses the reformation of manners, the discovery and pursuit of the obscene, and the origins and development of the rescue movement and of the frustrating struggle against prostitution up to the moral watershed of the 1880s. The heart of the study is in Part Two, which explains the emergence of the self-styled 'social-purity movement' of that decade, and in Part Three, which discusses its busy but until now uncharted career that actually carried on until the 1950s.

In a way analagous to the earlier high points in the struggle against vice, Christians reborn in the revivalist missions of the 1860s and 1870s supplied much of the leadership for the social-purity movement. William Coote, who plays a central role in what follows, went through a typical adolescent conversion experience in these years, as did W. T. Stead, the famous muck-raking editor of the *Pall Mall Gazette*, whose *exposé* of child prostitution gave so much impetus to social purity. Stead described himself as 'a child of the revival of 1859–60' which had swept across the Atlantic and won over 100,000 converts in Ulster alone.[1] Many of the colleagues of Stead and Coote received their inspiration in the lively musical missions of the famous American visitors of the 1870s, Moody and Sankey. The fourth and final episode of rage against sexual vice forms part of the same pattern. This outbreak came in the Edwardian period, shortly after the Free Church Council in 1901 and 1902 sponsored the last great series of revival missions in Britain. These not only added thousands of new communicants to the nonconformist denominations but also revitalised social-purity institutions around the country.

There were, of course, special factors which transformed the crusading Christian purity workers of the 1880s and the Edwardian years into an important public force. We shall see that after the turn of the century it was a species of national fear that once again triggered purity and repression. However, the original dynamism of the social-purity movement in the 1880s derived from its nature as a militant holy alliance. Christian feminists like the legendary Josephine Butler and the forgotten but important Ellice Hopkins, brought large sections of the women's movement into coalition with latter-day puritans of chapel and church. This was an alliance forged in outrage and guilt against the 'double standard', with its acceptance of male sexual incontinence and its division of womanhood into rigid categories of pure and fallen.

When parliament gave its legal sanction to the double standard in the Contagious Diseases Acts of 1864, 1866 and 1869, the immensely capable and brave Mrs Butler was handed the perfect issue for dramatising the immorality of this standard and for demonstrating how it resulted in the exploitation and dehumanisation of prostitutes. By compelling women who were alleged to be prostitutes in any of the eighteen scheduled garrison or seaport towns to be examined internally for venereal disease, this legislation brought the continental protection of men's vice to Britain. While Mrs Butler was challenging the Contagious Diseases Acts with one of the century's most notable protest movements, Ellice Hopkins was doing almost as much on her own to undermine the respectability of the double standard. Beginning a strenuous ten-year tour of the British Isles in 1875, she addressed innumerable audiences and in the process founded some two hundred ladies' rescue committees and men's chastity leagues.

The leaders of this two-pronged assault on the double standard ultimately fastened on to the highly emotive twin issues of enforced and juvenile prostitution. These abuses still persisted in the 1880s and the year 1885, the most remarkable in the history of sexual politics, is the focal point of Part Two. It was then, after a ferocious campaign, that the enraged latter-day puritans of both sexes obtained the Criminal Law Amendment Act. This raised the age of consent to sixteen, where it has remained, and made it easier to bring procurers and brothel-keepers to justice.

The agitation succeeded largely because of W. T. Stead's sensational and classic exercise in the new investigative journalism, 'The Maiden Tribute of Modern Babylon'. While all accounts of 'The Maiden Tribute' end with the events of 1885, the legislative victory of that year was as much a beginning as an end. An infrastructure of purity institutions had emerged to obtain the new legislation and even more, to work on for a single standard of chastity for both sexes. This was the self-styled 'social-purity movement' and it long remained a legacy of the 1885 triumph. William Coote's National Vigilance Association was at the centre of the movement, which came to include many of the groups first mobilised by Josephine Butler and Ellice Hopkins. Hundreds of institutions ranging from local vigilance committees to rescue societies and chastity leagues blanketed Britain.

After the 1885 impulse weakened, there was the final indignant outburst that once more corresponded with the cycle of revivals and which strengthened social purity in the Edwardian years. The factor promoting the attack on vice at the turn of the century was a new variety of national anxiety. The Edwardians were concerned about the degeneration of the race in an age of escalating international rivalry. With the birth rate falling, experts alarmed about the quality of the population, Victorian family mores under attack and indecent publications available to a mass audience, many leaders came to see purity as a precondition for national preparedness. Puritanical divines were joined by eugenicists, imperialists and militant feminists eager to attack males, in an assault on sexual incontinence, obscenity and prostitution. This was one agitation that was not limited to Britain; throughout the western world the equation of purity and national power led to popular movements and to new legislation against vice.

Anti-vice work was styled 'the reformation of manners' in the 1690s and called 'social purity' nearly two hundred years later. Naturally there were differences of outlook, emphasis and organisation in the various stages of so enduring a phenomenon. Some have been mentioned already. Yet the opponents of vice usually settled on similar tactics. Legal action and the legal threat were primary. Quite often threats were enough to persuade brothel keepers to close their doors, publishers to withdraw objectionable books or to move whole industries, like the Edwardian bill posters, film makers and postcard manufacturers, to rush into self-censorship.

By the 1880s this private application of both law and backstairs pressure became known as vigilance work and was carried out by self-styled vigilance committees. The terminology was new, adopted from frontier America where so-called vigilance committees sometimes took the initiative in enforcing a rough-and-ready law and order. Yet concerted legal activism over moral matters in England was centuries old, and had been encouraged by common law as well as the ineffectiveness of police. The Societies for the Reformation of Manners and the Vice Society fielded their own vigilantes. Such workers either bore the burden of enforcing the laws against prostitution and obscenity or gave critical assistance to the authorities.

As well as engaging in their vigilance work, many of the institutions we shall describe acted as pressure groups. The British Parliament has traditionally been subject to 'pressure from without'. Some of these 'out-of-doors' efforts, such as those on behalf of the factory code and women's suffrage or against the slave trade, are well known. Purity reformers were no less active in exerting pressure and their explosive campaigns and steady efforts deserve to be chronicled. This particular variety of pressure from without was responsible for much of the statute law on the protection of girls and women; on the selling, display and posting of obscene wares; and for many of the strictures against procuring, brothel-keeping and living off immoral earnings.

In human terms all this intrusiveness into the sexual behaviour, literary tastes and leisure activities of others had a very mixed legacy. Part Three, the history of social purity after 'The Maiden Tribute', reveals a worthy effort to protect women from the dangers, real and imagined, to which they were exposed in the early stages of emancipation. Travellers' aid work at railway termini and ports appeared in this climate of feeling, as did new measures against commercialised vice and an influential international movement, guided by the indefatigable Coote, whose goal was to obliterate juvenile and enforced prostitution throughout the world.

On the other hand, social purity came to mean the legal repression of prostitutes and the harassing of serious writers, their publishers and popular entertainers. It meant the terrifying of two generations of adolescents with a deluge of information on the evil of masturbation that in fact helped to initiate the sex-education movement. In such an environment the public demanded a new moral probity of their public men. Charles Parnell, the Irish leader, was destroyed and Charles Dilke, the radical politician, had his career ruined. The discredited punishment of flogging was resurrected for homosexuals and pimps. Unsettling white-slave panics of international scope and medieval irrationality were generated. When 'virtue becomes outrageous', as Macaulay put it, the results are indeed explosive.[2]

# PART ONE

# VICE AND VIGILANCE—
# THE BACKGROUND, 1690–1880

# The Pioneers: The Societies for the Reformation of Manners

THE appearance of reforming societies of vigilantes in the 1690s had a double significance. These pioneering and surprisingly pervasive experiments in private initiative for public benefit stand at the beginning of two traditions: that of the whole family of voluntary reform movements so important through later British history; and, more specifically, that of anti-vice movements. With the former contribution in mind, the Societies have been called 'the most notable social change of their time'.[1] Writing of the men of the 1690s as the original 'Vigilance Workers', Alfred Dyer, one of the leading militants two centuries later, said, 'There is no doubt that Englishmen owe much of that spirit of individual responsibility for the nation, which marks us as a people, to those faithful workers of ancient days.'[2]

During the prehistory of our subject, before its ancient history unfolded in the reformation of manners, there was little need for concerted private initiatives against immorality. From soon after the Norman Conquest until their decline in the seventeenth century, the so-called bawdy courts bore the major responsibility for enforcing good morals.[3] It was the demise of these courts, the hopeless inadequacy of state institutions and the realisation that policing vice was a social necessity which provided the rationale for the first wave of vigilantism.

The epithet 'bawdy court', coined by their opponents, is most appropriate for these church tribunals. Not only did they exercise jurisdiction over religious infractions, like misbehaving during divine services; they dealt with such abuses as fornication, bastardy, adultery, incest, homosexuality, brothel-keeping and even the occasional case of white slavery. There were limits to their effectiveness. The privileged were hardly touched and despite the fact that prenuptial fornication was the most common offence presented before them, the pregnant bride remained a more or less legitimate figure in the culture of the pre-industrial poor. The church's legal arm could do little to stem the development of commercialised vice after 1545, when Henry VIII abolished the Southwark stews, legal brothels curiously located on church land south of the City of London.

Yet in a largely rural and traditional society, the bawdy courts were a real enough force against misbehaviour. All defendants had to pay costs and they could be ordered to appear bare-legged, in the white sheet of contrition, for humiliating penances in the church or marketplace. As London more than doubled in population to over 300,000 during the first half of the seventeenth century, the courts were overwhelmed by the disorder that followed in the migrants' wake. They were abolished by the puritans, who favoured secular authority, and were re-established by Charles II without the compulsion of the *ex-officio* oath. This meant that individuals could no longer be made to testify against themselves in mortal fear of perjury. Soon the courts were more an antiquarian curiosity than a legal force.

The state now fully inherited the function of punishing religious and moral offences—a task considered vital for social stability, indeed, for social survival. It was held that vices fed upon one another and weakened society. Profane swearing, for example, led to perjury and the breakdown of law while fornication robbed the commonweal as well as the fornicator by causing physical and financial ruin. Elaborate disputations on these themes reflect how the breakdown of traditional paternalistic institutions, like the guilds in the labour market and the bawdy courts, reinforced anxieties about social disorder.

Even worse, since vices were sins and insurrections against God, a vicious people was in danger of divine retribution. Leaders responsible for society shared with moral reformers a concept of God the immanent and vengeful judge rather than God the retired engineer with a frontal lobotomy, as the supreme being of late seventeenth-century deism has been described. A typical example of the former mentality is King William III's 1698 Royal Proclamation for Preventing and Punishing Immorality and Profaneness, which begins in the apprehension that 'the open and avowed Practice of Vice' might 'provoke

God to withdraw his Mercy and Blessings from Us, and instead
thereof to inflict heavy and severe Judgments. . . .' Issued in a
mood of supplication brought on by the Treaty of Ryswick, in
which Louis XIV recognised King William's right to the British
throne, the Proclamation was an important aid to the
moralists.

Despite the consensus about the dangers of vice, the civil
authorities had neither the will nor the personnel to organise a
morals police. By the seventeenth century the state had come to
share jurisdiction with the church over a long list of moral
crimes, from Sunday trading to drunkenness, gaming and night
walking, as street soliciting was described at the time. While
action was taken on felonies like rape and buggery, however,
the code of moral laws that had grown up under the Tudors
and Stuarts was unenforced.

There are a number of reasons for this, including the nature
of the police force. It was one of the great anomalies of the age.
There were virtually no professional police and London's streets
were guarded largely by reluctant and corrupt parish constables.
Their deportment is hardly surprising, since the post was an unpaid annual imposition, an 'insupportable hardship' for some unlucky resident, as Daniel Defoe put it. Constables seldom bothered
to arrest moral miscreants caught in the act and they commonly
collected their 'gin money', as such bribes were known when
gin became the rage after 1690, for permitting night walkers to
parade in the streets.

The whole system was based on the decaying premise that
there was a collective responsibility for individual sin. Public-
spirited informers were expected to come forward and obtain
warrants from magistrates that constables would have to serve.
But informing had become very unpopular. Once again it was
Defoe who pointed out that 'A Rougue and an Informer are
Synonymous in the Vulgar Acceptation'.⁴ The defects of the
system were compounded by the notorious dishonesty of the
magistrates. Some justices of the peace were virtually on bawdy-
house payrolls, extorting protection money from the bawds. One
early eighteenth-century magistrate in Wapping was known to
rent space in his own home to prostitutes. After the reformation
of manners was under way, John Disney, one of its spokesmen,
hardly needed to emphasise, 'This whole Undertaking of ex-

ecuting the penal laws against Profaneness and Debauchery is *new* and *looks odd*'.[5]

What prompted the Herculean effort? While there is some mystery and controversy about the origins of the Societies for the Reformation of Manners, the basic factors are clear enough and have already been suggested. This initial outbreak of anti-vice crusading emerged when local and national leaders harnessed the militance of a religious revival to fill the gap in police. The crucial impetus from above was provided by Queen Mary in 1691. The Christian awakening was that of the so-called Religious Societies, circles of young Anglicans which first emerged in the 1670s for private devotions and spiritual exercises.[6]

The Religious Societies had a long and fruitful history. They served as a rallying point for Protestant piety during the days of Charles II's lascivious Restoration court and during James II's abortive assault on Anglicanism. They survived to be present at the birth of the great Methodist revival in the 1730s. In between they supplied just the kind of inspired informers and meddlers needed to rehabilitate this crucial aspect of police work. Most members were either skilled craftsmen or tradesmen. These respectable carpenters, shoemakers, grocers, drapers and the like were so poised in the social scale to be particularly sensitive to the crudity and irreligion of the lower orders and resentful of the cultivated immorality of the upper ranks. They pledged themselves to a rule that included prayer seven times daily and self-mortification. The degree of moral corruption at large is but one factor in the recurrence of revivalism. Yet the men of the Religious Societies had their awakening against a social background particularly notorious for its gross and open immorality.

In the later days of the Religious Societies the gin orgy accelerated vice amongst the lower orders. When the government threw open the distilling and retailing of spirits to free trade in 1690, the intention was to deal a blow to French brandy. The unintended consequences were the proliferation of dram shops, drunkenness and coarse sexuality. In their earlier days there was the self-conscious immorality of Charles II's Restoration court. As a reformation-of-manners tract later explained, until 1685 'It was reckoned Breeding to Swear, Gallantry to be Lewd, Good Humour to be Drunk, and Wit to despise Sacred Things'.[7] Dissoluteness received the positive sanction of the court and this in an age when the imitation of one's superiors was judged to be one of the most important forms of social cement. To emphasise the point it is enough to recall the famous case of Sir Charles Sedley, the King's boon companion, whose conviction in 1663 became an important precedent for using the common law against moral offenders. Sir Charles and illustrious friends, the worse for drink, caused a riot after they had gone onto a balcony in Covent Garden; 'putting down their breeches they excrementized into the street; which being done, Sedley stripped himself naked, and with eloquence preached blasphemy to the people.'[8] The King reputedly paid the £500 fine. For the reborn with their heightened sense of sin it was like being amongst pagans.

The revolution of 1688 provided moralists with new opportunities for reform. Vice could now be tarred with the Stuart brush and the corruption of manners blamed on the discredited dynasty. But just how could moral reform be accomplished? The problem of strategy faced by the reformers is illustrated by the struggle of Edward Stephens. One of the movement's pioneers, Stephens was a Gloucestershire squire who took holy orders, became a well-known anti-Catholic controversialist and prolific pamphleteer before converting to, of all things, Greek Orthodoxy.

Between 1688 and the launching of the Societies in 1690 Stephens poured forth plan after plan.[9] He urged national fasts and mass public confessions. He pestered King William about issuing declarations demanding that magistrates enforce the law and officers purify the army, and in fact on the day after William and Mary accepted their crowns, the King sent letters to the two archbishops and to the Bishop of London encouraging a 'general reformation of manners'. (This was hardly more than a customary gesture, as Charles II had issued no less than four royal proclamations on the subject.) When a group of bishops asked Stephens to draw up legislation against the vices mentioned by the King, he produced a bill that was more than a match for anything decreed in Calvin's Geneva. It would have introduced the death penalty for adultery, transportation for bawdy-house keepers and stiff fines for practitioners of the popular pastime of drinking healths.

Not surprisingly, the Bishop of London was unable to find much support for this draconian addition to the moral code. In fact the reformation of manners was getting nowhere. New legislation was useless. The concept of a state police force was not yet born and that of a concerted voluntary effort to achieve a moral or social objective would appear only with the Societies for the Reformation of Manners. In the absence of new institutions, the customary royal initiatives calling for more sermons or better police were like pushing on string. It would take spontaneous action from below combined with paternal support to sustain the breakthrough.

A partly extraneous factor led to the new departure. London was in the midst of a crime wave and was already plagued by the mixture of serious crime and prostitution that was to remain an infamous feature of the Georgian capital. In 1690 when King William issued a proclamation encouraging the punishment of robbers and highwaymen, the parish officers and leading citizens of the Tower Hamlets, to the east of London, responded by forming a society to suppress bawdy houses, which they described as 'Dens of Notorious Thieves, Robbers, Traytors and other Criminals'. This was the pioneering venture in extra-parochial police which ultimately evoked the enthusiastic support of the Religious Societies from below and national and local leaders from above.

The Tower Hamlets Society had a variety of grievances against brothels. Their broadside continues:

> Here 'tis that Impudent Harlots by their Antick Dresses, Painted Faces and Whorish Insinuations allure and tempt our Sons and Servants to Debauchery, and consequently to embezel and steal from us, to maintain their strumpets. Here 'tis that Bodies are Poxt and Pockets are picked of considerable sums, the Revenge of which Injuries have frequently occasioned Quarrellings, Fightings, Bloodshed, Clamours of Murther (and that sometimes at midnight), pulling down of signs and parts of houses, breaking of windows, also other tumultuous Routs, Riots and Uproars . . . Here 'tis that many a Housekeeper is infected with a venomous Plague, which he communicates to his Honest and Innocent Wife . . . Here 'tis that Multitudes of Soldiers and Seamen get such bane that effeminates their spirits and soon rots their bodies. . . .[10]

There was nothing new about any of these complaints. The belief that the unsupervised recreation of London's apprentices naturally evolved from whoring to thieving had a venerable history and had been enunciated by Chaucer as early as the fourteenth century. Three hundred years later, as apprenticeship regulations were overwhelmed by the free market and urban growth, and the masterless worker came into his own, there seemed genuine cause for alarm. The brothel riot had already taken its place as one of the varieties of chronic civil disorder that troubled the authorities. On one occasion in 1668 eight men were convicted of high treason for leading an armed mob, with standards flying, against some of London's bawdy houses on the Easter holiday.[11] King William's proclamation ignited lingering resentment against these nuisances. In this climate of reform the Tower Hamlets Society broadened its own objectives to include the disorderly drunk and profane swearers and became the prototype vigilance committee.

By 1691 a second Society emerged in the Strand, one that Edward Stephens claimed to have founded. The influential Bishop Stillingfleet then called the attention of Queen Mary to these developments and the result was crucial assistance from above. As a ruler who lived in fear of divine retribution for her own and her country's misdeeds, she was interested in the experiments. As the first ruling queen since Elizabeth she enjoyed the full attention of the nation. In July 1691 while the King was fighting in the low countries she issued a letter to the Middlesex bench of justices, requesting they do everything possible to get the parish police to enforce the moral laws. Not only did the Middlesex Quarter Sessions and ultimately many local benches through the country issue such directives; groups of magistrates and constables began joining or forming their own Societies for the Reformation of Manners.

The fact that the membership of the movement remained largely secret is as discomforting to the historian as it was to its 100,000 or more victims. There is less evidence extant on this initial outbreak of anti-vice crusading than on its sequels; but there is enough to answer some of the general questions about the organisation and dimensions of the phenomenon as well as the nature of its support.

In terms of organisation the Societies created a morals police to mesh with the inadequate machinery of order. The hubs of the new network were local agencies where paid agents were supplied with blank warrants covering the crimes to be suppressed. Informers would go along to the nearest agency, provide details of the offence and take away a completed warrant for signing by a magistrate. They were then delivered to constables for serving on the offenders. By 1692 there were a score of agents in Society offices through London.[12]

The Societies were differentiated by function, social class and neighbourhood, at least in the capital. The whole operation there ultimately came to be directed by a central body of lawyers, MPs and other eminent gentlemen who made policy and subscribed towards the expenses.[13] Some of the Religious Societies formed themselves into groups of informers. Whipped into a frenzy of indignation at prayer meetings and armed with a handbook describing, among other things, what it looked like to be drunk, they showed little mercy to the poor. A task force of fifty tradesmen specialised in suppressing street debauchery, while Societies of magistrates and constables, organised to improve law enforcement.

Some of these constables seem to have been semi-permanent 'constables by proxy', paid annually by persons for whom they were standing in. This was probably the case with the unlucky John Dent, who was stabbed to death by a troop of soldiers when assisting in the arrest of a prostitute in 1709. At his funeral, where some thirty fellow constables were among the thousand mourners he was eulogised as a pioneer in the movement who had aided in the 'apprehension and prosecution of several thousands lewd and profligate persons, besides a vast number of sabbath breakers, swearers and drunkards'.[14] The Societies provided these early professionals with a sense of vocation.

The reformation of manners made a leap into the provinces and abroad in 1698, assisted by the support of the Archbishop of Canterbury and one of those royal proclamations from King William, who had temporarily turned to domestic issues following the Treaty of Ryswick. The redoubled interest in fighting vice was partly a response to John Toland's threatening landmark of deism, *Christianity Not Mysterious*. With the gospels being debunked Christians rushed to reinforce the bulwarks against the expected wave of immorality. By the beginning of the new century the movement reached its limits, with at least twenty Societies in London and a minimum of forty-two in the provinces as well as another thirteen in Edinburgh. Accounts of these activities in translation led to the formation of Societies through Protestant northern Europe and the idea was carried to Jamaica and British North America.

This initial effort in voluntary reform thus enjoyed a diverse social membership, from the indispensable troops of awakened tradesmen to the socially prominent leadership. While members of local and national elites continued to play a role in fighting vice, their importance was to be considerably less in the social purity movement of the 1880s. In the early days of voluntary movements, however, it not only took the royal court and leading church dignitaries to provide impetus; mayors and aldermen were needed to bring the Societies to Bristol, Carlisle, Chester, Durham, Portsmouth, Newcastle and undoubtedly to other cities where they appeared.[15]

In addition to the active membership, known to include Sir Richard Steele, the journalist whose contributions to the *Tatler* and *Spectator* did so much to promote civility and morality, there was substantial sympathy from the low church party, including such luminaries as Bishop Burnet of Salisbury. Their high church opponents were estranged by the influx of dissenters into the movement and by puritanical informing and prying. In 1709, a few months before the sermon against the Whig ministry that led to his celebrated trial for impeachment, Dr Sacheverell, the high church champion, turned his vitriol on the Societies, which he accused of 'Reformation by Lying, Slandering, Whispering, Backbiting and Tale Bearing'.[16] Sacheverell's posture as an early Tory democrat, a champion of the rights of the poor against the busybody reformers, was one of the factors later leading the London mob into the streets for the famous riots on his behalf.

The movement had enemies in high places and its fortunes depended on the vagaries of the conflict in high politics between Whigs and Tories. The poor were violently opposed to it and Constable Dent was not the only worker to be killed in action. Ultimately these political and social forces brought down the Societies. Before that happened in 1738, they were responsible for seven convictions per day, Sundays excluded, over nearly half a century of vigilantism.

The reformation of manners was about more than sex, as

voluntary institutions for moral reform did not begin to specialise in particular abuses until the nineteenth century. The Societies' blacklists include the names of profane swearers, drunkards and sabbath violators as well as bawds and prostitutes. As consideration of both the moral ideas of the time and the Societies' activities demonstrate, however, carnal sin was a central concern of the enterprise.

*     *     *

For conventional moralists of the late seventeenth and early eighteenth centuries, sexual misconduct was a serious matter; but there was no reason to single it out as the ultimate in wickedness. The ranking of the sins offered by the Vicar of St Sepulchre's, in his 1732 contribution to the Societies' long series of sermons, provides a useful insight into the reformation of manners' hierarchy of demons. According to the learned speaker 'apostacy from revealed truth' was the first problem and 'Uncleanness' was the 'Second Sin of the Age'.[17]

Irreligion itself, in the form of wrong dogma or violation of observances, was considered the principal danger, the open door to all the vices. This was to be expected in an age so uncomfortable with heterodox beliefs that it was argued deism caused prostitution, and so violent that even deists like Voltaire and atheists like Gibbon argued for the importance of 'religion as policeman'. Typically, Edmund Gibson, Bishop of London and great friend of the Societies, cast 'religious observance of the Lord's Day as the best preservative for virtue and religion, and the neglect and profanation of it as the most general inlet to vice and wickedness'.[18]

This belief that right religion was the key to morality led in 1698 to the formation of the Society for Promoting Christian Knowledge. Still active today, this was the most enduring agency of the late-seventeenth-century religious revival. While the vigilantes 'pluck up the weeds and prepare the ground', the SPCK 'sows the good Seed'. This was how the Rev. Josiah Woodward, the moral movements's most articulate spokesman, explained the division of labour. Before turning completely to education, the SPCK helped promote the reforming Societies in the provinces; in the present context, though, the SPCK is important for what it tells us about the revival's attitude to the vices.

Along with its bibles, psalters and testaments, the SPCK distributed great quantities of admonitions, among them the austere works of Josiah Woodward. His *Rebuke to the Sin of Uncleanness* was very severe with fornicators. 'The greatest punishments of humane laws to affright people from this vice are the greatest kindness', according to Woodward, who concludes by offering suggestions from asceticism to help his readers 'keep down the heat of your inclinations'.[19] Here is an early purity tract which anticipates the flood of Victorian literature on the same subject. But something is missing. Woodward on incontinence is not nearly as fraught as contributors a century or two later. For one thing, he is nearly as severe with drunkenness and swearing. For another, while he is concerned here and elsewhere with the dreadful traps that awaited impressionable youths of fifteen or so, he manifests none of the obsessive concern with masturbation that was about to sweep Europe. The reformation of manners just predated the two-century-long conviction that masturbation had lethal consequences. Woodward's traditional aids to continence—bread, water and the like—are indeed benign when compared with the bizarre tortures later devised to keep the young from gradually killing themselves. Yet it should be kept in mind that the reformation of manners helped create the state of moral opinion in which anti-masturbatory ideas could spread very rapidly.

Spokesmen like Woodward thus enunciated the traditional unadorned Christian arguments against sexual sin. When we turn to the actual legal work, however, a particular preoccupation becomes clear, that of cleansing public places of the erotic and forcing sex underground. Of the 101,683 recorded convictions, the largest category is for lewd and disorderly practices, much of it street soliciting, indecent exposure and intercourse in the open.[20] The attacks on bawdy houses, frequently located in taverns, and on the theatre, were aspects of the same struggle. These institutions were very much part of public rather than private space.

Why the concern with public lewdness? To cite John Disney again, 'Vice when it is private is not attended with those provoking circumstances as when it revels in your streets and in your markets. . . .' All open vice was dangerous and the second largest number of convictions involved the provocative act of sabbath

B

breaking, much of it trading to supply the poor with their Sunday dinner. In the case of open lewdness, however, there are special factors to consider. The reflex of shame, which first suffused the middle classes and then spread through society, was becoming attached to the bodily processes. Thus in 1725 Bernard Mandeville, the *emigré* Dutch social philosopher, attacked the Societies because he believed that their repressive methods extinguished rather than nurtured the natural shame of 'street prostitutes', the worst of the species.[21]

The propensity of social groups to distance themselves from their inferiors by adopting good manners also helped to push the lewd out of sight. This was the case with the upper bourgeoisie and aristocracy, who developed what has been called a 'cult of decorum' to reinforce their social authority. Powdered wigs, hauteur, and drawing a veil over the bodily functions all went together. In his classic *Letters to his Son*, Lord Chesterfield explained in 1747 that 'a real man of fashion', if he had vices, 'gratifies them with choice, delicacy and secrecy.'[22] Concerned with civilising his coarse converts, John Wesley advised them, amongst other things, not to urinate in public.

Anti-vice movements became an important force in the trend towards keeping sexual matters private. They helped cleanse the theatre, abolish the singing of bawdy ballads and the display of obscene wares; finally late in the nineteenth century they helped destroy the brothel and tame the street whore. The task was a slow one. As one social class after another adopted a code of private sexual respectability, a countervailing force was created; the sphere of public activity emerged as a compensatory 'immoral domain . . . where moral violation occurred and was tolerated'.[23] Hence part of the difficulty reformers had in removing the tribes of prostitutes from the streets and from the theatres.

\* \* \*

In its struggle with prostitution, the reformation of manners was confronting a phenomenon which had become as endemic to the metropolis as drinking healths, selling meat on Sunday or uttering blasphemous oaths. In the City and Middlesex the secular authorities had made sporadic and unsuccessful attempts to suppress prostitution since the sixteenth century. The criminal classes were not the only social sector to know them. Indeed, the likelihood that a significant proportion of prostitutes plied their trade part-time or on a casual basis placed them squarely in the community of the labouring poor. Labourers and apprentices discomforted their employers by consorting with them. Sailors and soldiers were their companions, protectors and sometimes their common-law partners. In Holland, prostitutes committed to workhouses by magistrates were, with luck, recycled right back into the community. Jonas Hanway, the great Georgian philanthropist, reported that for years it had been the custom to promenade the inmates, with the result that 'Sailors just landed, and who have neither time nor inclination for a long courtship often marry them. . . .'[24]

Prostitution for the respectable was also part of London life by the 1690s, though the institutional development was to go a lot farther in the following century with the appearance of brothels to cater for every taste and perversion and even aids to debauchery in the form of celebrated advertising sheets like *Harris's List of Covent Garden Ladies* and *The Man of Measure's Kalendar for the Year*. The Societies warned the literate and respectable of the dangers of consorting with whores. There might be more than venereal disease lurking in the shadows; in 1689 and 1690 there were some particularly gruesome 'ripper' murders. First the Queen Dowager's butler was murdered and it was generally assumed the incident had something to do with his friendship with Sarah Hodges, a famous brothel-keeper. Then Sarah and two of her girls were found with their throats cut. These incidents were widely publicised by the reformers. But the attitude taken to the pleasures of the respectable classes is nicely summed up by the Bishop of St Asaph, who said in his 1730 lecture to the Societies that if immorality was impervious to the advantages of education and wealth, there was nothing they could do.[25] The moralists never troubled with high-class brothels.

The series of confrontations with prostitution in these years had some short-term results. The Societies' *Account* for 1699 claims that about five hundred disorderly houses had been recently suppressed and

. . . some Thousands of Lewd Persons have been imprisoned, fined and whipt; so that the Tower-End of the Town, and many of our streets, have been much purged of that pestilent

Generation of Night Walkers that used to infest them . . . forty or fifty of them having been sent in a Week to Bridewell, where they have of late received such Discipline, that a considerable number of them have chose rather to be Transported to our Plantations, to work there for an honest subsistence. . . .

This roundup had its counterparts in Dublin and some of the provincial towns. In London its main impact was felt in the City, where the lord mayor and aldermen worked closely with the Societies, who were thanked for informing on, amongst other characters, one notorious Blackfriars brothel-keeper called 'Widdow Crabbe'.[26]

Constable Dent's murder occurred during the subsequent episode of repression, between 1708 and 1709. Dent is known to have been killed while trying to convey a group of men and women to the Covent Garden watch house. Did the early struggle against prostitution contain the element of equal justice for both sexes so grievously lacking in Victorian times? Apparently not. During the wars with France in 1702 the government had obtained legislation permitting lewd and disorderly manservants to be put into the navy. Dent had been helping to drag off some very unwilling recruits; the normal situation was to let men go free, unless they were caught committing grossly indecent behaviour. In a notably early attack on this double standard Jeremy Collier, one of England's most widely-read moralists, reflected on the practice in 1705: 'Is not this a sign The *Sex* is crept into the Administration and that we live under a *Masculine* government?'[27]

Dent's heroic efforts against vice were not unique, as legal anomalies made it possible for reforming constables to carry out personal campaigns. Such an opportunity arose in 1725 when a complaint was sworn against one Mary Ealey, who kept Robinson's Coffee House, a grossly disorderly establishment at Charing Cross. Two Westminster justices granted a general warrant directing constables to search Mary's bawdy house and others, and to arrest streetwalkers out at 'unseasonable hours'. Over a period of months Sampson Cooke arrested hundreds of prostitutes and 169 of them were sent to Bridewell to serve one month's hard labour beating hemp. When a complaint was made about

Cooke's activities, it was discovered that many of the arrests had been illegal because the warrant stipulated no time limit for its return. The law was hopelessly inadequate and this was not the first time reformers had stretched its cover.[28]

By 1730 the authorities themselves were showing more initiative. Sir John Gonson, the courageous chairman of the Westminster bench, had already led a campaign against gambling houses when in June 1730 he received a petition from the inhabitants of St Martin's-in-the-Fields, near Charing Cross. Sampson Cooke's efforts had accomplished little because bawds and whores had moved back into the neighbourhood. There was so much disorder that the petitioners could neither sleep nor carry on their trades. Gonson first overcame a legal obstacle by obtaining the government's promise to defend those constables sued for illegal brothel searches. He then ran the creaky machinery of order in top gear for a year. But as a report in the 30 July 1730 *Grub Street Journal* indicates, the role of the vigilantes remained crucial: 'Last night about ten lewd men and women of the Town were apprehended by Constables belonging to the Reformation of Manners and being examined before Sir John Gonson, then were committed to Bridewell.' This was the very time the most celebrated madam of the era was apprehended. Mother Needham, immortalised as the procuress in Hogarth's *Harlot's Progress*, was pelted to death in the pillory by an ungrateful London mob.[29] She was not the last fatality of the reformation of manners.

These colourful attempts at repression were a labour of Sisyphus. It took great courage merely to arrest a streetwalker. Seven years before his own end, Dent had gone to the rescue of John Cooper, another reforming constable, who had been sent to 'look for disorderly women and other lewd persons' at the sometimes riotous May Fair. Dent was too late to save Cooper from being killed in a pitched battle with forty soldiers. In 1712 a group of constables were badly mauled by yet another mob of soldiers when they tried to arrest prostitutes in Covent Garden.[30]

The inadequate state of the law was as much a problem as the solidarity of the poor. Prostitution was not and is not illegal in itself. It was a common-law offence to keep a brothel or to engage in grossly indecent behaviour in a public place. As common law was relatively cumbersome and expensive, until

1709 reformers used an old act of Edward III which permitted the arrest of streetwalkers on simple suspicion. Dent's murderers had interfered with such an operation and they successfully appealed against their conviction. Lord Chief Justice Holt, a bitter enemy of the Societies, drove a wedge through the old tactic, ruling 'that it was not lawful, even for a legal constable, to take up a woman upon a bare suspicion only, having been guilty of no breach of the peace, nor any unlawful act'.[31] Arrests for simple soliciting became more difficult. Yet there was no shortage of grossly indecent lawbreakers of both sexes. Amongst those arrested in the 1730 drive were, typically for this coarse age, a whore and client fornicating on one of London's new shop windows, and a group of women 'taken at 12 or 1 o'clock, exposing their nakedness in the open street to all passengers and using most abominable filthy expressions'.[32] One of the latter was Kate Hackabout, the name Hogarth gave to the central figure in his *Harlot's Progress*. But many of those convicted, and this was the final legal loophole, were bailed before they had beaten any hemp or suffered the celebrated floggings, naked from the waist up, that Londoners loved to attend.

It was a problem getting at brothels because the circumscribed possibilities of search made it so difficult to obtain evidence. Of course reformers could partake of the service and then testify. But this was beyond the call of duty. A common tactic then and well into the nineteenth century was to convict brothels on the lesser charge of being disorderly. The bawds did not make things any easier. In 1720 officials complained that bawdy houses in Drury Lane were equipped with 'strong hatches to their street doors and also the doors of their inner rooms, with sharp iron spikes over the said hatches, which hatches are kept fast, locked and are guarded by soldiers'.[33]

Not surprisingly the authorities had little will for the struggle. Constables were continually being presented for either taking bribes from prostitutes or discharging them before bringing them into custody. One of Gonson's colleagues on the Westminster bench was Thomas de Veil, who used his position to arrange meetings with whores, allegedly fathering twenty-five children in the process. The incidence of prostitution was to increase before any effective action was taken.

While the Societies had little luck against prostitutes, they did considerably better reforming a related object of their attentions, the theatre. There was good reason for the long historic association between prostitution and the stage. Just as the Empress Theodora had been an actress and prostitute in the sixth century before her marriage to Justinian, so too did Nell Gwynne move from the stage to Charles II's bed. There was also the popular custom of open assignations in the playhouse, a practice that carried on in the music halls until protests by the social-purity movement finally stopped it in 1916. Back in 1699 during the dragooning of prostitutes in the City of London, the grand jury there vividly described the dangers of one of the whores' favourite haunts:

> Whereas we are informed that severall Persons in this City, especially Apprentices, do frequently resort to the Play Houses —whereby they are corrupted and enticed to wickedness, not only by hearing and seeing diverse lewd representations, but especially by meeting and conversing with many Lewd Persons that boldly attend those places . . . we do think ourselves obliged to represent this to the honourable court, as a matter very worthy of their consideration and care in order to prevent the corruption and ruin of our youth.[34]

The apprentices were not the only ones at risk, however, and a few years later a lecturer to the Societies mentioned the corruption caused at Oxford and Cambridge by touring theatrical troupes.

The plays themselves were enough to win considerable support for Jeremy Collier's popular diatribe of 1698, *A Short View of the Immorality and Profaneness of the English Stage.* As he pointed out, pieces like Wycherley's *The Plain Dealer* and *Country Wife*, or Vanbrugh's *Provoked Wife*, manifest 'Smuttiness of Expression . . . Swearing, Profaneness and Lewd Application of Scripture . . . Abuse of Clergy . . . making of their top characters Libertines and giving them success in their Debauchery. . . .' For Collier, 'The business of plays is to recognize virtue and discountence vice'. This left at least a didactic rationale for drama, but a number of moralists were against the theatre in principle and would have liked to emulate the puritans and close playhouses down. Arthur Bedford, one of the spirits behind the Bristol Society and later chaplain to the Prince of Wales, believed that the opening of the new playhouse in Bath caused the fatal storms in 1703 while the performance of *The Tempest* brought on the freakish squalls of the following year.[35]

Supervision of plays was breaking down and the Societies utilised the same tactics here as in other areas: they pressed the authorities to enforce the law and they tried to plug the gaps themselves. While the licensing of plays had been under the supervision of the Master of the Revels since the reign of Elizabeth, the recent incumbents of the office were simply not bothering to do their job. From 1696 orders came down over and over again from the Lord Chamberlain, another official of the Royal Household, that the Master of the Revels should not only ban new objectionable works, but also revoke the licences of older indecent or profane Restoration plays. The reformation of manners had another royal sympathiser in Queen Anne. Her royal proclamation of 1704 repeated the older orders and made some additional ones reflecting on the conduct of the audiences of the day: No person could go backstage or onstage before or during a performance or wear the masks that were so popular in society; all entrants had to pay and constables were required to attend and enforce the rules.

In the meantime the Societies were undertaking prosecutions of their own. In 1701 they successfully brought an action against eight actors who had set up a common playhouse in Lincoln's Inn Fields and performed *The Provoked Wife*. The judges in King's Bench had the play repeated but 'were so shocked that they obliged the players to leave off in the middle. . . .'[36] At least some of the actors were fined, despite the fact that the play was licensed. Informers even ventured into theatres to gain evidence for prosecutions, thus breaking one of the Societies' cardinal rules, that they never set foot in such places. Public opinion was quick to change on the content of the plays, if not on behaviour in the playhouse. In 1711 Queen Anne could announce that 'The orders we have given for the reformation of the stage by not permitting anything to be acted contrary to religion and good manners have in great measure had the good effect we proposed.'[37] Stage vulgarity was growing unfashionable and for this the Societies and moralists like Collier take much of the credit.

In the Restoration theatre the Societies confronted an institution which openly compounded the profane and the lewd. In homosexuality they faced a practice which seemed a gross insult to God's order. Most contemporaries would have agreed with the Vicar of St Sepulchre's in his lecture when he called 'Unnatural Lust . . . the worst sin of the Lewd Kind'. Most would also have agreed with Jeremy Collier that 'such Monsters ought to be the Detestation of Mankind, pursued by justice, and exterminated [from] the Earth'.[38]

Homosexuals derived no benefit from either the solidarity of the poor or the casualness shown to immorality in public places. Henry VIII's 1533 statute on the subject could hardly have been more severe. The act of sodomy was punished by hanging; the attempt could mean the pillory, and prison if the victim survived. There is one late eighteenth-century case on record of a short convict being hanged to death in the pillory. Milder forms of homosexual embrace were not strictly regarded as illegal until the Criminal Law Amendment Act of 1885 outlawed so-called gross indecency between males, though by the early eighteenth century acts of mutual masturbation or the touching of genitals were being treated as attempted sodomy.[39]

There were few prosecutions of such offenders in the seventeenth century and those that occurred were usually *causes célèbres* involving aristocrats. By the turn of the eighteenth century, however, cases were increasing and the defendants tended to be from the lower orders. Homosexuals followed the custom in this sociable society and began forming clubs and meeting in brothels. This made them vulnerable to detection and the outraged authorities were not reluctant to invoke the full fury of the 1533 statute.

While the Societies were responsible for closing homosexual clubs in 1709, social institutions for homosexuals were already nearly as impervious to repression as ordinary brothels. Convictions for 'sodomitical' practices are mentioned sporadically in the Societies' accounts from that date onward. Then in 1726 the Tyburn executioner was put to work after a virtual bloody assizes at which a milkman, an upholsterer and a woolcomber were capitally convicted on the evidence of Society informers.

More than twenty homosexual brothels, known at the time as 'Molly Houses', were broken up in 1726 and, as the *British Gazetteer* reported, this was 'in addition to nocturnal assemblies in the Royal Exchange, Moorfields, Lincoln's Inn, the south side of St James's Park and Covent Garden Piazza'. Society informers and constables were instrumental in gathering evidence, making arrests and testifying in a number of the cases, though the government deemed the matter important enough to take charge of the prosecutions. The central trials involved one Mother Clap, who ran a 'sodomitical house' that attracted up to forty men nightly and many more on Sundays. In February two reforming constables, Willis and Williams, collected enough evidence to arrest Mother Clap, who was bailed by one of her lodgers, Thomas Newton. Willis and Williams then broke the case by convincing Newton to give lethal evidence against his accomplices. In the subsequent trials the three men were capitally convicted for sodomy with Newton, and Mother Clap was sentenced to a turn in the pillory. Judging from the far more wholesome reputation of Mother Needham, she may not have survived.[40]

These trials and the others in the series were notable for the testimony of informers who insinuated themselves into the brothels and collected evidence in notebooks of how couples went off to 'marry' in bedrooms with doors open. Some of this low work was assisted by jealous homosexual lovers. On one occasion two informers went as a couple to avoid the sexual advances of the sodomites and on another a vigilante defended his honour with a red-hot poker. This was more than they were willing to do to convict ordinary brothels; yet they went even farther in entrapping homosexuals. Later in the year Willis set Newton loose in an alehouse in Moorfields with directions to pick up a suspect. Willis pounced from the dark when the man put his hand on Newton's breeches and the result was one year's imprisonment for attempted sodomy. Homosexuals lived in fear in these years. After another hanging in 1730 two men were convicted of conspiring to charge a third with sodomy unless he paid them ten guineas.[41] This particular witch-hunt lifted, to be followed by others during the evangelical fervour early in the following century and the social-purity agitation at its close. In the meantime, clubs for homosexuals apparently continued their underground existence.

By the 1730s the spirit had gone from the Societies and there may well have been substance to the perennial charge that their

members were corrupt. Using the returns available on convictions for lewd and disorderly practices, we find that 1720–24
shows an annual average of 1,400, while by the 1730s there was
a decline to 170. With the passage of the Gin Act of 1736, which
created a new class of professional informers, more odium was
heaped upon this unpopular species and the Societies may have
found it impossible to operate.

What had they accomplished before their disappearance in
1738? The Bishop of St Asaph concluded that 'If the People of
lower condition are at all reformed, the Societies are justified'.
Using this as a criterion, there is little to justify them. There
is some evidence that the sabbath was being more strictly
observed by the time they departed the scene. But the gin orgy
was at its worst and we can gauge the condition of the streets
from the remarks of one pedestrian about a walk from Charing
Cross to Ludgate in 1737; he was greeted by 'Twitches on the
sleeve, lewd and ogling Salutations; and not infrequently by the
more profligate Impudence of some Ladies who boldly dare to
seize a man by the Elbow . . . in spight of our Reforming Society
we are more scandalously lewd. . . .'[42]

Yet the Societies had an important dual legacy. They initiated
the tradition of concerted voluntary moral reform. Later movements in the tradition had more success getting the poor to adopt
the new respectable norms of behaviour. They also created the
climate of opinion in which government and administration
began to mobilise behind the new values of civility and respectability in sexual behaviour and expression. There were immediate
concrete gains. In 1724 the Bishop of Lichfield applauded the
Societies because 'The plays are writ with more modesty, and
acted with more decency'.[43] In the following year the Attorney
General achieved the landmark decision in *Rex v Curll* which
made the common law available against obscene publications.
Gradually the obscene became a major preoccupation with
moralists; during the subsequent episode of purity fever vigilantes had the weapon of obscene libel forged in the reformation of manners.

# The Vice Society and Fear of the Obscene

THE obscene was among the lesser demons during the reformation of manners. By the time the next episode of anti-vice crusading broke out in the late eighteenth century, exorcising erotic expression was central to the whole enterprise of reform. Through the eighteenth century obscenity spread from books, prints, cartoons, joke books and street ballads to such objects as snuff boxes and playing cards. Underworld gangs imported indecent wares from the Continent and hawked them through the countryside. Pornography, in the sense of material not merely sexually arousing, but describing regressive and infantile fixations like sadism and masochism, made its appearance.[1]

The sensitivity of moralists to this form of abuse increased apace, for reasons to be explored below. A few basic factors, however, should be kept in mind. The obscene and fear of it were locked in a vicious cycle. That is to say, as prudery came to inform standards for drama early in the eighteenth century, standards for literature in the middle of the century and codes of personal behaviour in one social class after another, the erotic was pushed underground into distorted forms like pornography and peculiar objects like naughty snuffboxes. This in turn exacerbated fears of the obscene. Yet nothing systematic was done about the problem until the new moral vigilantes organised two years before the French Revolution; and little of significance was accomplished until after 1789, when Britain's first pack of smuthounds took advantage of a repressive climate in which invitations to sexual indiscipline were equated with invitations to political rebellion.

These early smuthounds were children of the great chain of religious awakenings known as the evangelical revival. In 1738, the year that the Societies for the Reformation of Manners disappeared, John Wesley had the momentous experience in which he sensed his sins were forgiven in the atoning death of Christ. Over the following decades Wesley and his Methodist field preachers made thousands of conversions among the poor while the same kind of 'vital religion' began to spread more slowly in higher places. By the 1780s the most socially prominent concentration of evangelicals, the 'Clapham Sect' in South London, was poised for activity. William Wilberforce, then a young MP for Yorkshire, was the central figure among the 'Saints' of Clapham and was to channel the heightened religious impulses of the time into a new reformation of manners, one of whose primary targets was obscenity. The Vice Society was the institution the evangelicals built to purify Britain. Long after the heat was out of their revival and the fear of revolution had subsided, in fact until 1880, this voluntary agency remained the Victorians' chief legal deterrent against the demon smut.

*    *    *

During the original reformation of manners the indecent extended far beyond the Restoration stage. Even in the age before widespread literacy the poor enjoyed a medium that communicated indecency, the street ballad. Yet the reforming Societies showed little interest in the singers and hawkers of the popular songs; and this despite attempts in the sixteenth century by the state to regulate their publication and by the church to spiritualise them by substituting religious lyrics for the bawdy. Such seventeenth-century standards as *Advice to Young Gentlemen, or An Answer to the Ladies of London*, which offered good-natured advice on seduction; or *Virginity Grown Troublesome*; or *The School of Venus*, with its crude woodcut of exposed breasts, and their successors, were in wide distribution in the following century until this form of expression was suppressed by a more prudish and embattled establishment after the French Revolution.[2]

Nor was there any shortage of erotic books and illustrations. By the late seventeenth century there were enduring European imports like the Venetian Pietro Aretino's 'postures', a set of sixteenth-century engravings illustrating the positions of sexual intercourse; or Michel Millot's irrepressible *L'Escole des Filles*, which more than titillated Samuel Pepys. This *School of Venus*, as it was translated, bore little relation to the ballad of the same

title : the bawdry of the poor was as adulterated as their food.
There was also the beginning of a native tradition, with Lord
Rochester's *Poems* and *Sodom*, his scatological play aptly sub-
titled *The Quintessence of Debauchery*. At the turn of the eighteenth century few protested when Francis Osborne dispensed
such wisdom in his popular *Advice to His Son* as, 'I have heard
a well-built woman compared in her motion to a ship under
sail. Yet I would advise no wise man to be her owner, if her
freight be nothing but what she carries between wind and
water.' This was not quite as respectable as the advice offered
by Lord Chesterfield and William Cobbett in their later contributions to this form of letters.

Before the repeal of the Licensing Act in 1695 government
agents, the 'messengers of the press', were responsible for tracking down and prosecuting unauthorised works of all kinds,
including occasional obscene books. But with the ending of
licensing the state was left with no effective weapon against
obscenity in print—a situation it faced with plays as theatre
censorship degenerated. The Societies for the Reformation of
Manners may have been responsible for some of the common-law
prosecutions for obscenity that cropped up after 1695. The state
of the law, however, was imperfect and when the publishers of
*Sodom, The School of Love* and a series of poems called *The
Fifteen Plagues of a Maidenhead* appealed against their conviction in 1707, Lord Chief Justice Holt ruled, 'There are ecclesiastical courts, why may not this be punished there? If we have no
precedent we cannot punish. Shew me any precedent.'[3] The
Lord Chief Justice erected a road-block against literary prudery
just before wrecking the Societies' strategy against street-walkers.

Such works circulated freely until 1725 when the Attorney
General convinced a more sympathetic Court of Kings Bench
that publishing an obscene libel was in fact an offence in common law. He successfully argued that the 1663 conviction of
Sir Charles Sedley for immorality was precedent enough for the
court to protect public morals by scrutinising books for obscene
expression; and that 'libel' in the context of obscenity did
not require defamation, but was simply the English equivalent of the Latin for 'little book'. This legal coup was carried
off at the expense of an unpopular London publisher, Edmund
Curll. The government obtained the crucial Curll judgment at

a moment when the reformation of manners had rendered the moral climate particularly intolerant. The Attorney General was about to go back into court to prosecute the homosexuals; newspaper *exposés* of the time, one written by the angry 'Philogynus', were uncovering the organised practice of sado-masochistic perversions.[4] While the Societies may not have fielded any smut-hounds themselves, they certainly contributed indirectly to the emergence of the concept of obscene libel.

If the legal legerdemain of 1725 seemed to signal a new initiative by government, officialdom soon sank back into its customary lassitude. There were scattered prosecutions for obscene libel through the 1780s, but nothing systematic enough to threaten the distribution of the old erotic classics or new ones like *Fanny Hill*, first published in 1749; nor new collections of prints and articles like naughty playing cards. Yet the easy availability of all these materials increasingly troubled respectable opinion, and for a number of interrelated reasons.

As the size of the reading public increased there were new groups to protect. Long before middle-class ladies came to dominate the market for fiction, Jeremy Collier had observed, 'Obscenity in any Company is a rustick uncreditable Talent, but among Women 'tis particularly rude.'[5] By the middle of the eighteenth century that domination was a fact, through the membership of women in the new circulating libraries. Recognition of this fact contributed to an alteration in literary norms and in the 1750s Samuel Johnson could say of Henry Fielding's *Tom Jones* that he 'scarcely knew a more corrupt work'. The erotic was banned from respectable literature.

There was also a growing number of young readers, many of them poor. Charity schools founded early in the century and generously supported by the Society for Promoting Christian Knowledge were supplemented in the 1780s by the Sunday school movement. The era was noted for its discovery of the special needs of the child and an interest in child development. Rousseau's *Emile*, first published in 1762, was the definitive expression of this departure, which in the sexual sphere meant a shift away from the traditional practices of exposing children to sexual allusion, sexual play and sexual abuse. Now there was a growing propensity to shield children and even adolescents from the world of adult sexuality. Since 'continence is the law of

nature' until the age of twenty, according to Rousseau, his carefully nurtured Emile is protected from knowledge of sex until
then.[6]

The sensational diffusion of propaganda to stop masturbation
was part of the new pursuit of purity for the young and, naturally, removing the provocation of the obscene became of central
importance. Bishop Porteus of London, one of the leaders of
the new reformation of manners, dramatically claimed in the
1780s that 'The contagion of a licentious publication . . . [was]
. . . particularly fatal to the unsuspecting and unguarded minds
of the youth of both sexes; and to them, its breath is poison, and
its touch is death.'[7]

Growing disquiet about the open display of indecent wares of
all kinds was related to the new attitudes to the young and also
to the developing sense of shame that we have mentioned. John
Fielding, who replaced his half-brother Henry as Bow Street
Magistrate in 1754 and then succeeded to the chairmanship of
the Westminster Quarter Sessions, was as troubled by the 'exposing to sale of indecent books and prints' and by the songs of the
allegedly growing horde of street balladeers as he was by open
fornication.[8] The impulse to keep sex out of sight grew during
the century but the law lagged behind. Not until after the
French Revolution were the balladeers and open obscene displays dealt with. In the meantime, strollers through London
could peruse the grossly detailed *Harris's List of Covent Garden
Ladies* displayed by booksellers next to the Book of Common
Prayer.

Along with women and the young, there were also the literate
poor to consider. Bishop Porteus, with his usual sense of urgency,
feared that the obscene 'knows no bounds; it flies to the remotest
corners of the earth—it penetrates the obscure and retired
habitations of simplicity and innocence, it makes its way into
the cottage of the peasant, into the hut of the shepherd, and the
shop of the mechanic'. Certainly the poor papered their homes
with old ballads, bawdy or not. Porteus was a bit of a crank on
the subject. Yet William Paley, the more detached theologian,
concluded in 1785 that 'few crimes within the reach of private
wickedness have more to answer for' than the circulating of
obscene songs, pictures and books.[9] Society was poised to act and
the lead was supplied by the evangelicals.

* * *

With the religious conversion of the young, energetic and well-connected William Wilberforce, the new anti-vice movement was born. While a young MP for Yorkshire, Wilberforce returned from a European tour in 1785 with Isaac Milner, one of the pioneers of the evangelical revival, as 'another man in his inner being'.[10] Little more than a year later he recorded in his journal, 'God has set before me as my object the reformation of [my country's] manners'. Above all he wanted to bring the nation true Christianity and towards this end the evangelical party in the Church of England created a phalanx of institutions for disseminating vital religion and for doing good. There was a basic distinction between real conversion and outward observance. But the former could be expedited by repressing the kinds of evils from which he had escaped, such as gambling and carousing with his friend Charles James Fox.

Wilberforce's self-proclaimed mission was to be a Wesley in high places; but he did suggest that it was only charitable and public spirited to suppress the vices of the poor. After all, they could not afford immorality and their indulgence led to personal hardship and crime. This struck a resonant note with the propertied classes. Even before the French Revolution they were engaging in the kind of sporadic and vicious legal repression that indicated that the new reformation of manners, in its legal sphere, would be directed once again at the poor. In response to the vagrancy and higher poor rates during the demobilisation after the American War, the criminal law was enforced severely in the 1780s. The number of executions in 1785 and 1787 are among the highest in the century; vagrants suffered from whipping epidemics and the relatively enlightened William Paley suggested that capitally convicted felons be thrown into dens of wild animals.[11]

At just this time in the towns of the West Riding of Yorkshire, where evangelicalism was particularly strong, magistrates were forming vigilance committees to assist in detecting criminal and immoral behaviour. Typical was the association created by William Hey, the Mayor of Leeds and a leading evangelical. The fact that he spent much of his professional life working on the problem of congenital syphilis reminds one of D. H. Lawrence's belief that there was a connection between puritan sexual attitudes and the sixteenth-century invasion of Europe by venereal disease. Hey's clean-up was greeted with a violent reception. His horse was stabbed and his wife nearly killed; he was only able to defend his constables in regular lawsuits for false arrest brought by profane swearers and prostitutes with financial help from his good friend Wilberforce.

In 1787 Wilberforce read about the old Societies for the Reformation of Manners and decided that the voluntary movement could be broadened. Suggesting that the defunct messengers of the press could be replaced by vigilantes, he recorded, 'In our free state it is needful to obtain these ends by the agency of some voluntary associations for thus only can those moral principles be guarded, which of old were under the immediate protection of the government. It thus becomes to us, like the ancient censorship, the guardian of the religion and morals of the people.'

He interested the court in moral reform and elicited from George III in June 1787 a 'Proclamation for the Encouragement of Piety and Virtue, and for the Preventing and Punishing of Vice, Profaneness and Immorality'. Horace Walpole recorded that it was 'no more minded in town that St Swithin's Day'.[12] Wilberforce set to work forming a Proclamation Society to enforce it, and on a local level the King's intervention stimulated the kind of developments that had begun in the West Riding. There was a new determination on the part of the authorities to enforce the old moral laws. But the limits of the movement are indicated by William Hey's continuing troubles. At the Spring Assizes in York in 1788 his constables were successfully sued for false arrest by a profane swearer when the judge told the jury, 'These constables are of the reforming kind. Reformation generally produces greater evils than those it attempts to redress... I don't know that damned my eyes and limbs is swearing.'[13]

The legal reformation was short-lived but for two significant developments. The licensing magistrates attacked a major source of working-class enjoyment and disorder by adopting a much stricter policy toward public houses. The Proclamation Society helped by obtaining legislation making it illegal for bawdy houses to obtain a wine licence after being refused a regular one. This was the first attempt to destroy the bond between prostitution and drink. While it was not nearly successful, it has been claimed that the tighter licensing policy generally was the very basis for the increased working-class respectability evident by the early nineteenth century.[14] The second enduring result of the new reformation of manners was the attack on the obscene. While Wilberforce never established the kind of vigilance network that existed earlier, his Proclamation Society was highly influential and it initiated Britain's first sustained campaign against smut.

Wilberforce, who stayed in the background, gathered in the Proclamation Society a membership that included the two archbishops, seventeen bishops, five dukes and the Speaker of the House of Commons. The committee met at the Whitehall home of the first president, the Duke of Montagu, and it is symptomatic of the changing mores of the aristocracy that the old rake and former prime minister, the Duke of Grafton, joined as well. Almost immediately it was decided to start prosecuting. In 1788 and 1790 there were four convictions in Kings Bench against the publishers of a variety of works including those old favourites, *The School of Venus* and *Fanny Hill*. Bishop Porteus commented about another case in 1790 against two shopkeepers that 'Westminster boys frequented those shops, and bought the most shocking prints—two of those pests were convicted and punished in a most exemplary manner'. With such miscreants being pilloried and imprisoned, it was only appropriate that the Society established a sub-committee on prison reform and sent Thomas Bowdler, the famous expurgator of Shakespeare and Gibbon, on a tour to popularise solitary confinement.[15]

Over the next decade the upholders of the proclamation had some temporary success against a new and most promising commercial venture, the naughty periodical. Typical was *The Ranger's Magazine, or The Man of Fashion's Companion*. It was spiced with quite legal reports on adultery and 'crim-con' cases, those curious lawsuits for adultery which engendered such juicy testimony. As one of the last outlets for public erotic detail, these reports were the bane of purity reformers well into the next century. Numbers of *The Ranger's Magazine* were not usually legally obscene, though they sailed close to the wind and were sporadically suppressed. Basically they were irrepressible: ban one and others popped up, sometimes under the same editor. Yet it is interesting to note that in the wake of the French Revolu-

tion *The Rambler* and then *The New Rambler* succumbed to
the Proclamation Society, as did the venerable *Harris's List of
Covent Garden Ladies.*

After 1789 it was as risky to publish, display or recite an
immoral work as a seditious one. Sexual indiscipline was widely
equated with disloyalty. At a deep psychological level, it has been
argued by such radical Freudians as Herbert Marcuse and
Wilhelm Reich, that, to cite the second, 'sexual repression
cripples the power to rebel'.[16] While the men of the 1790s did not
think in these terms, they believed that sexual laxity was socially
dangerous. Their arguments were historical and social. The
British had long projected their fears of sexual immorality across
the Channel—the so-called French pox is one example—and
now the political fruits of French lasciviousness and irreligion
were being demonstrated. In this climate *Harris's List* was considered as dangerous as the meanest bawdy ballad, for the
morality and loyalty of the lower orders was seen as a product
of social imitation and reform had to start from above. In 1797
John Bowdler, Thomas's older brother, had pointed out in his
influential *Reform or Ruin* that moral improvement had to begin
with the King and Queen driving 'from their councils and their
court all adulterers and adulteresses; all gamblers; all, in short,
whose characters are notoriously bad. . . .'[17]

The link between immorality and expropriation was reinforced
by the fact that sexual abuses were seen to be the consequence
as well as the cause of revolution. After all, there were such
revolutionary excesses as the rapes of aristocratic ladies, mutila-
tions of clergy and Carrier's notorious 'republican marriages' in
which couples were tied together naked and drowned. Prostitution became more open and by 1791 Parisian whores were seen
standing nude in their windows and imitating copulation. From
1794 the *merveilleuses,* the Thermidorian women of fashion, wore
light and very revealing muslin and sometimes drenched themselves before going out so that their clothes would cling to their
bodies. In fact there was no sexual upheaval in France. The
Parisian whores were temporarily free of supervision because
state regulation had broken down and the more reckless of the
*merveilleuses* were killed off by tuberculosis. But such incidents
became part of the ideology of counter-revolution and some endured to be cited by a leading London physician in the 1830s

as examples of 'the extent to which abuses and excesses of the reproductive function may be carried when religion and the laws founded on its principles are abolished'.[18]

Political repression in Britain ended neither with the termination of the social upheaval in France nor with the defeat of Napoleon in 1815. The suspension and abuse of civil rights and the use of *agents provocateurs* continued intermittently through the age of popular radicalism culminating in the Reform Act of 1832. The anti-vice workers thrived in this environment, first utilising the Proclamation Society. Bishop Porteus, who became president in 1793, loathed vice and once caused a riot at the King's Theatre by forcing the manager to drop the curtain at Saturday midnight in the middle of a ballet. But the burden of his pastoral duties was great and progressively his spare time went into Wilberforce's anti-slavery crusade. By the late 1790s cases were being badly prepared and, as in some of the great political trials of the time, English juries were failing to convict.

The situation was remedied when the Vice Society, established as an auxiliary of the Proclamation Society, simply superseded its defunct parent in 1802. Its impressive membership included leading evangelicals like Wilberforce, the Bowdlers, Hannah More and Zachary Macaulay, the historian's father; officials like Patrick Colquhoun, the reforming magistrate; the Lord Mayor of London; and a respectable sample of the aristocracy. Government money may have been involved. The author of the Vice Society's first *Address* was John Bowles, a professional anti-Jacobin hack whose political work was rewarded by the Prime Minister, William Pitt.[19]

Bowles's *Address of 1803*, slavishly imitative of Edmund Burke's counter-revolutionary philosophy, is a good index of the Vice Society's priorities. History had dispensed with the Elizabethan laws requiring church attendance and so the Society would not attempt to resurrect them. This was the only concession to change. Since 'violation of religious principles' was the origin of all vices, they would enforce the laws against work and travel on the sabbath. It was particularly important to uproot new vices before they enjoyed 'the inveteracy of custom', so obscene publications would be hunted down.

The Society began with three sub-committees, one on obscene and blasphemous publications, another on the sabbath and a third relating to a miscellany of working-class modes of disorder, including blood sports and bawdy houses. At first all these objectives were pursued. The London and dozen or so provincial chapters relentlessly struck at Sunday traders, and the fact that their agents did not start work until 10 am, to give the poor a chance to buy necessities for dinner, hardly made these vigilantes any more popular. By about 1820, however, virtually all functions except the scrutinising of the printed page had devolved onto other specialised groups. The Vice Society became a powerful prosecuting agency located in Lincoln's Inn Fields, and a membership of 1,200 in 1804 shrank and became dominated by a legal committee employing spies to hunt out smut and blasphemy.[20]

The first phase of the Vice Society's work lasted until the formation of the professional police in 1829. Until then it was virtually on its own against obscenity; parish officers rarely helped because no rewards accrued from apprehending the publishers and sellers of obscene articles. It is true that the vigilantes recorded some real gains. But the obvious pattern that marked the long history of the Vice Society, what we might call the 'finger in the dyke' syndrome, established itself early. Suppress one medium for erotic expression or one criminal gang and sex broke through somewhere else.

Initial investigations in 1802 unravelled a major network for the manufacture and distribution of articles including books, prints, drawings, toys, snuff boxes and looking glasses. Libidinous expression takes many forms when linked to the prospect of profit and in 1812 one vendor was convicted for 'publishing' an obscene toothpick case. The 1802 ring employed two artists to design engravings and sculpture and also imported from Europe to supply its wholesalers at least thirty itinerant Italian pedlars and keepers of ballad stalls. All told, six hundred people were said to be involved, and the most alarming feature was that female agents posed as old-clothes merchants in order to gain entry to girls' boarding schools where they did a brisk business.[21]

The Vice Society set to work and by 1805 it had disrupted Britain's first commercial pornography ring and imprisoned a number of the smaller operators. Usually only the more serious cases were prosecuted, and in the expensive but well-reported Kings Bench. The case of Baptista Bertazzi, who got six months for selling obscene prints in a girls' school, is notable for Lord Chief Justice Ellenborough's defence of the vigilantes against their many detractors. They were criticised by Whigs and Tories alike for interfering with the culture of the poor, and one reactionary backwoodsman went so far as to insist that it had been 'proved incontestably that bear baiting was the great support of the constitution in church and state'. Their work against indecency was less controversial and the radical Joseph Hume said it was the only decent thing they ever did. Yet there were those who held that their prosecutions infringed on government prerogative. Ellenborough spoke for the repressive Tory government and insisted that 'they have done very properly in taking an interest in the morals and happiness of society, and in exerting themselves to prevent the contagion of these infamous publications. It appears to me they have deserved the thanks of all men. . . .'[22]

With the end of the Napoleonic Wars came easier importing, a resurgence in the criminal trade and new repressive measures. By 1817 George Prichard, the long-serving secretary of the Vice Society, claimed that 'A very common answer now returned to approaches made for such articles is, that it is very difficult to procure them in consequence of the prosecutions of the Society for the Suppression of Vice; the very name of which proves of considerable efficacy in spreading dismay among the trade. . . .'[23] This achievement came in the face of substantial disadvantages. Obscene articles were displayed in shop windows through town and hawked by pedlars. Yet not only did the law call for warrants and indictments; during the celebrated Wilkes affair of the 1760s general warrants had been outlawed. This meant the specific name of an obscure itinerant like Baptista Bertazzi had to be obtained. The difficulty was resolved in 1824 when the Vice Society obtained clauses in the Vagrancy Act making obscene displays subject to summary conviction.

This was an early victory for clean streets. In addition to forcing obscene displays out of sight, it made the purveying of bawdy ballads impossible. The hearty balladeers had been harassed and put to work for the establishment after 1789. In his important *Treatise on the Police of the Metropolis* of 1795, Colquhoun noted how these pests could be controlled : 'Even the common ballad singers in the streets might be rendered instruments useful under the control of a well-regulated police, in giving a better turn to the minds of the lowest classes of people.' He suggested they be put to work singing of 'loyalty to the Sovereign, love to their country and obedience to the laws'.[24] The anti-Jacobin Association for Preserving Liberty and Property, which fielded 2,000 vigilantes to check on the loyalty of their countrymen, was already intimidating balladeers into singing and selling just such patriotic tunes. In 1795 the evangelical Hannah More began her moralistic Cheap Repository Tracts and used balladeers to help distribute them. In its early years the Vice Society prosecuted them, especially if they purveyed indecent prints with their songs. All this hurt and the threat of summary conviction finished them off.

Thus working-class bawdry was driven from the streets. In the 1820s Francis Place noted, 'We no longer see groups of servant girls standing in the streets to hear songs which the prostitutes themselves would now pelt those who attempted to sing them.'[25] But the erotic resurfaced in concert taverns and 'free and easies', where entertainment was first recruited from the audience. These evolved into the Victorian music halls, whose naughty turns were later policed by the social-purity movement for over thirty years.

\* \* \*

The cycle in which repression was followed by the reassertion or reformulation of erotic expression continued at all levels of society; as the great utopian Charles Fourier observed of his century, 'nature driven through the door comes back through the window'. This is evident not only in working-class entertainment but in the sexual subculture contrived by the classes above, who provided most of the demand for pornography. Literary prudery; delayed middle-class marriages and the need for an alternative sexual outlet; the tendency for sexual repression in the Victorian milieu to create a propensity for depersonalised or regressive and infantile sexuality: all these factors fed the demand for pornography and most contributed to its twin, the taste for prostitutes.

Officialdom struck a compromise with prostitution, as we shall see in the next chapter. But the obscene was held to be corrupting and potentially lethal if it led to masturbation. Havelock Ellis, the pioneering sexologist, compared the fear of the obscene to the older witch craze. It therefore appears striking in our survey of the Vice Society's second phase, after the founding of the modern police in 1829, that officials left the initiative for law enforcement as well as legal reform to the vigilantes. Did the state acquiesce with a cunning understanding of the function obscenity played in the social system, as was the case with prostitution? Perhaps more relevant in explaining official reticence was the availability of a strong voluntary effort, the tradition of private initiative, the unpopularity of using the police to entrap people and the very magnitude of the task.

When the Society launched its next campaign in the late 1830s, at least it could count on police assistance in carrying out raids. This required that its agents make a purchase and take it along to the authorities; thus it meant violating the original promise not to field *agents provocateurs*. These agents were very convincing. They had to be because traders were wary of entrapment. When the rescue journal, *Magdalen's Friend*, tried to expose Holywell Street, centre of the pornography trade, its austere investigators were appropriately stuck every time with books whose pasted covers held only old sermons. But not even regular police cooperation could be taken for granted. Following the late 1830s crackdown, the chief commissioner temporarily disrupted the partnership with the Vice Society; in 1843 he ordered that no seizures should take place unless special directions came from him on each occasion.[26]

In the midst of the campaign in 1838, Prichard claimed that the Society had reduced the number of establishments selling obscene goods in London from ninety to twenty-three. But it was an uphill battle. One expert insisted that 4,000 people were involved in the trade. Pedlars still worked the boarding schools and one prosecution had been undertaken at the instance of Eton, which had subscribed to the Vice Society since the days of Dr Keate, its flagellomaniac headmaster. Vendors also visited racecourses and fairs. Foreign imports were flowing in disguised as prayer books and in working-class areas prices for indecent pamphlets were as low as sixpence.[27] What is more, a group of young and energetic professionals had entered the field. The most notorious was William Dugdale, said to have been involved in the Cato Street conspiracy. After turning from insurrection to indecency in the late 1820s he carried on through at least ten prison sentences to die back in jail in 1868. From the fastness of his fortress-like establishment in Holywell Street, he published a whole library of erotica. Typical of his list in the 1860s was *Betsy Thoughtless*, advertised as 'a most spicey and piquant narrative of a young girl obliged to excoriate her sweetheart's bum before he could ravish her maidenhead'.[28]

Against such professionals the law as it stood was insufficient. In 1857 the Vice Society obtained what was to remain for a century the basic legislative instrument against the sale of dirty wares, the Obscene Publications Act. Its passage demonstrates the close relationship between private vigilance and the public authorities. On 11 May 1857 Lord Chancellor Campbell was outraged by two cases before him.[29] First William Strange, a shopkeeper, was accused of selling two indecent magazines, *Paul Pry* and *Women of London*. Campbell was 'astonished' to learn —it was rather late—that such titles were hawked in the streets and retailed for one penny. The jury instantly found Strange guilty and he was sentenced to three months' imprisonment.

Then William Dugdale was brought into court, apoplectic with rage after having been trapped for the ninth time by the Vice Society. Henry Dodson, a former ivory bone brushmaker employed part-time by the Society at five shillings per day, testified that 'he went on two separate occasions to the defendant's shop' and purchased obscene prints. One set was given to Prichard and the other was given to a policeman who had searched him just before the transaction to make certain the filth could only have come from Dugdale. This was necessary to make the evidence acceptable in court. A second agent then told a similar story. Dugdale raged incoherently about the time a few years earlier when one of Prichard's men had broken into his house and stolen £3,000 worth of books. On that occasion he had sued successfully. But now he pulled a penknife and had to be dragged off to the cells to begin his one-year sentence.

Campbell went from the court determined to investigate, and this meant being briefed by Prichard. It was an opportunity for the Vice Society to obtain another item on its shopping list of legislation. At the same time it was promoting draft bills to repress prostitution on behalf of the overrun West-End vestries. By July the Lord Chancellor introduced a Vice Society bill on obscene publications and in the debates Campbell gave prominent publicity to the fifty-five-year voluntary struggle: 159 prosecutions and only five acquittals. Prichard was referred to as 'a gentleman of great intelligence and of high honour'. Something had to be done, the Lord Chancellor continued, about the cumbersome procedure which encouraged the use of spies and required those absurd personal police searches. The bill was modelled on gaming-house legislation and empowered magistrates to issue search warrants on the receipt of sworn information that premises contained obscene items for sale or distribution. Furthermore, defendants would have to show cause why seized obscene items should not be consigned to the flames. After Campbell assured the hesitant Lords that the measure was not intended for use against serious works of art, like the recent and regrettable *The Lady of the Camellias* which he waved in his hand, it was plain sailing.[30]

In the wake of the 1857 Act Lord Campbell recorded in his diary that 'Holywell St. has capitulated after several assaults. Half the shops are shut up, and the remainder deal in nothing but moral and religious books!' The Metropolitan Police had begun to keep watch and make purchases and in 1863 the first obscene publications squad was established, consisting of a sergeant and two constables.[31] This was just about the time that the term 'pornography' was coming, somewhat belatedly, into common English usage. While the new squad was disbanded and not re-established until demanded by public opinion in the late 1880s, it was available in 1870 for an assault coordinated with the Vice Society on what the vigilantes called the 'low class, cheap, obscene papers hawked by boys'. It was after this that the more enterprising and better capitalised purveyors of erotica departed for the Continent to reorganise at a safe distance from constant harassment.

All this was encouraging. But in 1868 the Vice Society was already reporting on 'a new phase . . . in the history of vice'. The development of the stereoscope and photography opened up new vistas in the erotic. By the 1850s London clubmen were gazing through stereoscopic lenses into machines which depicted vice in '3D'. Later these popular mutoscopes, bearing titles like 'Naughty' or 'How Shocking' and harbouring photographs of semi-clad women, were to provide yet another problem for the social-purity lobby.

Meanwhile, the potential of photography was being discovered by such pioneers as Henry Hayler, who escaped to Berlin in 1874 just ahead of the police. They found thousands of photographs in his studio, many depicting Hayler engaged with his wife and two sons. Long exposures had their advantages.[32] Between 1868 and 1880 the Vice Society seized more than a quarter of a million photographs and prints. While this hastened the exodus of such low life as Hayler, there was little that could be done about distribution from abroad by post. Internationally celebrated dealers like Charles Carrington, with their parcels from Paris, Brussels, Barcelona and elsewhere, would plague William Coote and the authorities into the twentieth century and demonstrate once again the protean nature of the trade.

The Vice Society was true to the Lord Chancellor's promise in 1857 that the Obscene Publications Act would not be used against serious literature. Of course authors censored themselves, with assistance from their publishers, who in turn had to answer to the great lending libraries like Mudies' and W. H. Smith's. These bought fiction in bulk for their respectable middle-class subscribers and wielded great power in the market. The Vice Society assisted by exerting private pressure of its own. For example in 1870 C. H. Collette, Prichard's successor, prevailed upon the new publishers of the popular Bohn Library to withdraw a rather bland edition of Rabelais' writings. As one of Collette's enemies observed, 'So timid are Englishmen where there is a question of being charged with encouraging vice that I fancy the effect upon an average bookseller of a visit from one in Mr Collette's position is like that which would once have been produced by the call of a functionary of the Inquisition upon a Spanish Jew.'[33]

We are informed on the good authority of J. W. Horsley, Chaplain of Clerkenwell Prison and a leader in purity circles, that when another publisher was considering a new translation of Rabelais with illustrations by Gustave Doré, the Vice Society called on G. A. Sala, the well-known journalist, to arbitrate, with the result that the book was held back.[34] Sala was later revealed to be the author of hard-core sado-masochistic pornography. At least Moncton Milnes who housed the era's greatest collection of erotica at his country home, known familiarly as 'Aphrodisiopolis', spoke against the Obscene Publications Bill. By 1875 the

new edition of Rabelais had been published by Chatto and
Windus and Collette was bombarded with letters of complaint.
But it is instructive that when he failed to obtain the withdrawal of the publication, which he called 'disgusting filth', he
did not prosecute.

In 1868 Lord Chief Justice Cockburn had made the seminal
judgment in the case of *Regina v Hicklin* that 'The test of
obscenity is whether the tendency of the matter charged . . . is
to deprave and corrupt those whose minds are open to such
immoral influences and into whose hands a publication of this
sort might fall'.[35] The case had been brought against the Protestant Electoral Union for publishing obscene and cheap anti-
Catholic propaganda and Cockburn made much of the fact that
the Union's *Confessional Unmasked* had been distributed on
street corners. The Vice Society and the police deferred to the
implication that the test for obscenity had to take into account
mode of dissemination and audience. In the heat of the later
social-purity crusades, however, the door would be open for
men and women more angry and prudish than the mid-
Victorians to overcome the Campbell and Cockburn safeguards
and persecute serious art.

That day was not far off. In 1880 a shortage of funds caught
up with the Vice Society. No more was heard of it in court after
that date, though its masthead still included Lord Shaftesbury
and other leading evangelicals. All that was left really was the
Society's treble-locked strongbox containing samples of the libidinous materials that had been condemned.

Between 1834 and 1880 alone those amounted to more than
385,000 obscene prints and photographs; 80,000 books and
pamphlets; five tons of other printed matter; 28,000 sheets of
obscene songs and circulars; stereotypes, copper plates and the
like. In comparison with Anthony Comstock's New York Society
for the Suppression of Vice, which measured its success after
1873 in terms of loaded railway cars, this would have filled a
short suburban train. Such a haul represents hundreds of prosecutions whose deterrent value was obvious to everyone, and
which freed London in the early 1870s from its most determined
pornographers and from its reputation as smut capital of
Europe. In 1879 the Society was exaggerating only slightly when
it claimed that 'The Metropolis has been freed from the scandal

of open and flagrant violations of the law . . . solely as your
Committee venture to assert from the constant supervision given
by its agents'.[36] With no more than sporadic official help the
Vice Society was the chief mechanism for the legal application
of Victorian prudery. When we return later to this aspect of
purity work it should not be surprising to find that its successors
had to start the cleansing process all over again. William
Coote's National Vigilance Association did so with the help of
the Vice Society's £50 bank balance and none of the occasional
restraint it had shown.

# 3

## Repression and Rescue of
## Prostitutes, 1750-1860

THE efforts of the Societies for the Reformation of Manners
had proved that prostitution was impervious to repression.
Through the eighteenth century the phenomenon became more
intractable. Common lodging houses letting beds at three pence
per couple were notorious. Brothel riots of alarming proportions
plagued the keepers of the peace. As bawdy houses for the rich
proliferated and diversified, such concomitants of commercialised
vice as entrapment and juvenile prostitution appeared. In 1763
John Fielding was telling the Westminster grand jury that at
least street fornication was waning: 'as this offence belongs to
none but the most abandoned mind, I thank God it is not common
. . . as to the bawdy houses, they are the receptacles of those who
still have some sense of shame left. . . .'¹ But public space was still
an 'immoral domain'; this was the very time James Boswell was
recording how he enjoyed whores in a court off the Strand, in
St James's Park and on Westminster Bridge 'with the Thames
rolling below us'.²

Faced with the difficulties of repression, reformers looked to
alternatives and state regulation was an obvious one. Legalised
prostitution was being practised in parts of Europe and had
lasted for 375 years in pre-Reformation London. In 1724
Bernard Mandeville's *Modest Defense of Public Stews* offered
the first modern argument for maintaining prostitution under
the control and surveillance of the authorities. His early utili-
tarianism, however, and his defence of the brothel as 'a Bog-
house in a garden', were odious to his contemporaries. There
was a discrepancy in his age between the acceptable in practice
and in theory. Arguments about the virtues of prostitution would
not become respectable until the next century and state regula-

tion was introduced on a limited scale only with the Contagious Diseases Acts of the 1860s.

In the meantime, reformers and moralists followed two main approaches. In 1758 they extended the hand of redemptive Christian charity to prostitutes by founding the Magdalen Hospital, the prototype for the more than three hundred rescue homes that were to be established over the following 150 years. They also pressed for legal reforms to repress the most objectionable aspects of prostitution: provocative street soliciting, disorderly and dangerous brothels, and the cruel recruitment of the young and unwilling.

Before Josephine Butler's campaign against the Contagious Diseases Acts and the white-slavery *exposés* of the 1880s brought the double standard for sexual behaviour into ill repute, both the rescue and repression of prostitutes were dogged with opposition. The harlot was a deeply stigmatised figure, tolerated as a bedmate but widely considered polluting in any other relationship, including the one of soulmate implied in Christian rescue work. As we shall see, rescue workers were driven for reasons of their own to help prostitutes while the respectable public largely mistrusted their efforts.

Since the harlot was also an integral part of the life of the late-eighteenth and nineteenth centuries, there is no paradox in the fact that the respectable public also opposed repression. As the anomaly of Georgian administration, the anarchy of its police and the casual nature of its sexual attitudes were overcome, a generous legal compromise with prostitutes was arrived at. The custom of middle-class men to defer marriage until they were well-established led them to seek a commercial sexual outlet. Doctors were divided on whether fornication was necessary but they were almost unanimous that it was preferable to masturbation. Sir James Paget, the eminent physician whose arguments for chastity were widely publicised by social-purity forces towards the end of the century, complained that 'patients ask you about sexual intercourse and expect you to prescribe fornication'.[3]

There was also an important psychological syndrome at work promoting the prostitute and keeping her in moral limbo. Mandeville's 'Bog-house in a garden', Aquinas's 'cesspool in a palace' and similar vivid images formulated over the centuries reveal a recurrent disparity that has been shown to have dominated the Victorians in particular: the disparity Freud discovered between love and sex. It was manifested in the idealisation and sexual anaesthetisation of middle-class women and the projection of the erotic on to prostitutes. One of the greatest historians of the century, W. E. H. Lecky, did violence to his reputation by articulating the classic Victorian statement embodying this attitude; for Lecky and many of his contemporary gentlemen, the prostitute 'is ultimately the most efficient guardian of virtue. But for her the unchallenged purity of countless happy homes would be polluted. ...'[4]

The official Victorian mind reflected these attitudes to prostitution. When the Vice Society approached the Home Office in 1857 on behalf of the West-End vestries struggling with an invasion of streetwalkers, this bureaucratic minute found its way onto the memorial: 'An attempt to suppress these things in London by legislation would be quite absurd.'[5] Anti-vice workers could enforce some of the laws themselves; by elevating public opinion they could influence the authorities to move on the more notorious abuses. But they worked within formidable constraints.

\* \* \*

The evolution of the law on street prostitution demonstrates how Georgian laxity gave way to nineteenth-century compromise. Harlots constituted part of the class of social refuse and the Vagrancy Act of 1744 provided a simple procedure for punishing disorderly persons, rogues and vagabonds. Moral reformers soon discovered to their dismay that it could not be applied to the London streetwalkers whom Jonas Hanway, the well-travelled philanthropist, called the most disorderly and indecent in the world. Reformers pressed for an amendment of the law. When soliciting became particularly troublesome at the end of the Napoleonic Wars, evangelicals and officials of the City of London formed the Guardian Society to clean up the City streets and press for legal reform. Under the presidency of the Lord Mayor, they advocated that prostitutes 'offending public decorum by indecent language or solicitation' should be subject to the Vagrancy Acts.[6]

In 1824 the Guardian Society achieved one of its aims when common prostitutes found 'wandering ... and behaving in a

C

riotous or indecent manner' were in fact brought under the vagrancy laws. Fifteen years later the Metropolitan Police Act provided what was to remain for 120 years the basic legal weapon against street prostitutes. They were made subject to a month's imprisonment or a fine if they annoyed passers-by. But 'annoyance' and 'indecent manner' were subject to varying judicial interpretations. Enforcement could be severe when the social-purity lobby mobilised public opinion later in the century. Until then prostitutes would have to do a lot more than proposition a man in gross language to commit indecent behaviour and persons annoyed would have to corroborate police evidence by appearing in court themselves—a step very few gentlemen were willing to take.

A false start and compromise also emerged over brothels. The tenure of Henry Fielding at Bow Street, so fruitful for law enforcement, is interesting in our context because of the steps the great police pioneer took to suppress bawdy houses. Fielding is celebrated for recruiting a famous flying squad of hand-picked constables and placing them under Saunders Welch, the High Constable of Holborn, whom he called 'one of the best officers who was ever concerned in the execution of justice'.[7] After promoting the effective Gin Act of 1751, Fielding was largely responsible for the Disorderly Houses Act of the following year. By requiring the licensing of places offering music and dancing, it closed some of London's popular tea gardens, the notorious haunts of prostitutes. The brothel clauses remained basic to the law for 133 years. Until 1752 private individuals or parish authorities were free to prosecute bawdy houses if they liked. From this point two ratepayers with evidence could get those authorities bound over by a justice to prosecute.

Saunders Welch attributed this departure to a terrible brothel riot that nearly got out of control in 1749. While a group of sailors from the *Grafton* man-o'-war were enjoying leave at the notorious Star Tavern in the Strand, they discovered their pockets had been pilfered by the whores. After being thrown into the street by the bullies they returned with their mates, wrecked the tavern and proceeded to work their way through the neighbouring bawdy houses. With a bonfire fuelled by the furnishings signalling the London mob, attacks on brothels broke out elsewhere and order was restored only with the aid of the military. One Bosavern Penlez, son of a clergyman and a passive member of the crowd, was unlucky enough to be capitally convicted before Fielding on the evidence of a brothel keeper. There was a national outcry and at Tyburn, where 'the multitude of spectators was infinite', another riot was only narrowly averted.[8]

Public opinion largely sided with the sailors as well as Penlez. One correspondent to the *Gentleman's Magazine* was outraged that when 'an honest devotee to Neptune is seduced to pay his vows to the altar of Venus, he should be robbed in the midst of his devotion, while his attention is engaged in the honour of the goddess'.[9] He suggested brothels publicly regulated, on the European model. In the aftermath of the riot there was a serious public debate on prostitution in which a variety of remedies were suggested, including Magdalen homes, another European expedient. But the immediate outcome was the clauses to facilitate the suppression of brothels.

In fact the new provisions did not go as far as Fielding had hoped. He failed to obtain a prohibition on bailing brothel keepers, their common mode of escape. Saunders Welch, who wanted to transport these offenders, reported that within a few years informers had virtually stopped coming forward. Their victims were free to intimidate them. When a group of Methodists began an association in 1757 modelled on the Societies for the Reformation of Manners, John Fielding encouraged their inspired informing against both lewd ladies and brothels. But the movement was short-lived and succumbed to a lawsuit a few years later.[10]

When the Guardian Society launched its attack on prostitution bawdy houses were as intractable as ever. Its survey turned up 360 brothels and 2,000 prostitutes in three East-End parishes alone. From church wardens in Shoreditch and Shadwell came complaints of 'the deficiency of a summary mode of proceeding ...the difficulty of proof...the uncertainty of success and the certainty of enormous expense...the parties frequently changed their abode, and it is difficult to get at the real occupier'. It was not until the legislation of 1885 that a summary and effective procedure against brothels became available. In the meantime, moral reformers pressed for legal reform, urged the parishes to prosecute and undertook the task themselves.

The rescue and preventive movement was deeply involved in repression. By 1860 the London Society for the Protection of Young Females claimed alone to have suppressed more than five hundred brothels and indirectly closed a larger number in its quarter-century of activity. The omnipresent Earl of Shaftesbury presided over a National Association for the Suppression of Public Immorality in the 1860s, allied to London's evangelical Magdalen homes, which closed another hundred brothels.[11] The role of the police in London was limited to calling the attention of the responsible parish vestries to notorious brothels, and keeping watch to collect the required legal evidence on the movements of clients where the vestries requested it. Generally there were few requests and some parishes tried simply to localise brothels in what Americans called segregated districts. In the 1880s Chief Commissioner Warren admitted all this was 'tantamount to licensing and regulating them'.[12] Private vigilance was the main force in the field against the mid-Victorian brothel. But the state of the law and opinion made it a losing battle.

By the 1850s the West End was so overrun with prostitutes that the local authorities and purity lobby, consisting of the Vice Society and rescue homes, joined forces to press for stricter police control of the streets and suppression of the prostitutes' favourite haunts. The results are instructive as an example of the kind of tortuous progress that could be made when public opinion was aroused.[13] The problem was centred on the Haymarket which George R. Sims, the great balladeer and acute social observer, evoked as 'the street of midnight adventure. It was packed with riotous revellers till the small hours, and the revellers were of all classes and conditions. More than one heir to a title met his *mésalliance* under the gas lamps of the Haymarket or in the cafés, night houses or dancing rooms that were in it or adjacent to it.'

For local residents this carnival meant loss of trade and tranquillity. In 1858 Prichard pointed out to Sir George Grey, the Home Secretary, that there were 137 recent cases in which respectable tradesmen had been driven out and their houses converted to night houses. These were the celebrated all-night drinking establishments which catered for prostitutes and their clients when the dancing emporia, like the Argyll Rooms, and the music halls closed. A comical account of how the Piccadilly

Saloon avoided the controls of the licensing laws is provided by Montagu Williams, later to defend Mrs Jeffries, one of the most notorious procuresses of the age, in her fixed trial of 1885 :

> What used to take place here—for I have seen it with my own eyes—was simply a ludicrous farce. A knock was given at the outer door by the visiting inspector, whereupon the word was passed : 'police !' Some two or three minutes were allowed to elapse and then the inspector, accompanied by one or two subordinates, entered the building, lantern in hand. Coffee and lemonade had replaced spirits and musicians were hidden in the cupboard.

While the protesters wanted broad reforms, they focused their attention on these night houses; and here lies a vexed tale of Home Office delay, badly drafted legislation, unfavourable judicial rulings and police corruption. It was not until 1874 that crusading Supt Dunlop was able to report that the last and most infamous of all the night houses had been closed: 'Kate Hamilton was present when police entered with a warrant, and was crying bitterly, saying that she supposed there was nothing for her now but the workhouse'. Prostitutes could be dislodged from one habitat, but everyone agreed that the dispossessed took to the streets and the music halls. If this was frustrating to repressionists, the absence of progress against the nastiest concomitants of commercialised vice, entrapment and juvenile prostitution was even more so.

* * *

There is little reliable evidence on the age distribution of prostitutes or on the numbers recruited to the trade or detained in it by force or deceit. But these evils were at least as extensive in Fielding's and Henry Mayhew's London as in W. T. Stead's. Involuntary prostitution is as old as the profession itself and so is the correlation between entrapment and the youth of the victim. By the eleventh century there was a brisk sale of slaves into prostitution and a century later markets for young girls appeared through the continent. They were finally abolished during the Reformation, the last one being eliminated at Nuremberg in 1562.[14]

With forcible prostitution then going underground the historian must tread very warily. For this is a symbolically super-charged topic about which the most extraordinary claims have been made by alleged victims, reformers and journalists. Adolescent girls, after all, may be subject to fantasies about surrender and rape. Reformers like Josephine Butler and William Coote discovered it could be tactically expedient to put such symbolic issues to the fore to achieve more basic goals. Besides, it is easier to decry the peripheral concomitants of an entrenched institution like prostitution than to advocate the radical social changes necessary to uproot the institution itself. There is no doubt that there were cases of white slavery. But the force of circumstances, of abysmal ignorance and grinding poverty, were much more important than the wiles of the white-slave trader in keeping the brothels filled. White slavery was hardly the most prevalent form of brutal sexual coercion. Engels observed in 1844 that 'factory servitude, like any other, and to an even higher degree, confers the *jus primae noctis* upon the master.' This was no idle exaggeration in the early days of the factory system. Even later in the century field girls sometimes remained the prerogative of their gang masters and in 1887 the National Vigilance Association typically complained, 'Servants are only too often the prey of their masters and their masters' friends'.[15]

In England where there were no legal markets, a common procurer was brought before the bawdy court in 1489 after he had 'carried away by stealth and violence and against her will' a London girl and sold her.[16] Undoubtedly there were other early cases. Then by the eighteenth century the steady stream of young women on the move from country to city provided an opportunity for organised and systematic entrapment. They were vulnerable while travelling and after they arrived in the overwhelming urban environment. However, their very fear of the city also sparked off hysterical fantasies of abduction and seduction. From this time until the Second World War England's cities were never free for long of the inner demon of white-slave stories. They also surfaced with great force in the spreading towns of Europe and North America, especially during the great trans-Atlantic migrations before 1914. The problem is to determine how much white slavery actually existed.

There is evidence that entrapment was a fact of life in Georgian London. Hogarth's classic *A Harlot's Progress* shows the real Mother Needham at work meeting the wagons arriving from the provinces and carrying off a country girl with promises of lodging and employment. Also represented in the first frame of the progress is Colonel Francis Charteris, whose career of despoiling just such country girls achieved great notoriety when he was capitally convicted of rape in 1730 and then pardoned. In 1747 a procuress whom the *Gentleman's Magazine* called 'the second Mother Needham' was pilloried. Testimony before Henry Fielding in 1752 revealed a common trick used to detain girls, one not rooted out until Stead's campaign. A sixteen-year-old hatter's daughter was decoyed into a bawdy house and persuaded to take up the calling. Once there, she was issued with the tools of the trade, flimsy clothing, for which she signed a £5 note. If she walked off in it the bawd could have her imprisoned. Saunders Welch claimed hundreds of girls were trapped in this way.[17]

While there were plenty of accounts like this about, the sensational and puzzling case of Elizabeth Canning burst on the scene in 1753. This eighteen-year-old resident of the city disappeared on the way home from her aunt's house in Middlesex. She turned up in a shocking state four weeks later, insisting she had been forcibly taken to a brothel where an old gypsy and two whores tried to starve her into submission. After her escape she was apparently able to identify her place of captivity, a notorious house run by one Mother Wells. The Canning family managed to get the culprits tried before a sympathetic Henry Fielding and one defendant was capitally convicted for stealing Elizabeth's clothing, while Mother Wells was found guilty as an accomplice. But this was not the end of the story. The Lord Mayor had been attending the trial and he was struck by discrepancies in Elizabeth's testimony. The ensuing investigation led to pardons for the defendants and a perjury conviction and transportation for Miss Canning.[18] Fielding continued to believe she had been telling the truth. The case, however, stands as an early warning that white slavery must be seen in its full perspective.

Yet there were the Mother Needhams and there was John Fielding's despair about the two evils coinciding in the notorious practice of mothers selling their daughters to procurers, as in pre-revolutionary China. Fielding's experience of this and of the

natural drift of vagrant girls into prostitution led him to claim
that the majority on the street were under eighteen. Already
there were brothels like the Temple of Aurora supplying girls as
young as eleven to the rich. But the greater source of demand for
young girls probably still came from the poor. There was a
terrible legacy of sexual child abuse amongst them. The report
of the Lock Hospital for 1752 revealed that since its opening six
years earlier, more than fifty children had been admitted for
treatment of venereal disease. They were infected 'from a
received opinion among the lower people, both male and female,
that if they have commerce with a sound person, they will get
rid of the disease'.[19] The Georgians had few solutions to these
problems. Jonas Hanway, who was not short of ideas on how to
help chimney sweeps or parish infants, suggested that whores
should keep strict accounts to avoid going into debt to their
keepers. John Fielding took some modest steps to help the
vagrant girls of London. Yet while child abandonment and
migrations continued to supply recruits and victims, these evils
were bound to persist.

The early nineteenth-century investigations of the Guardian
Society and of the London Society for the Protection of Young
Females uncovered methods of entrapment very similar to those
revealed by Stead. The London Society was begun in 1835 in
response to an alleged case in which a Norfolk girl came to
London to visit her father, was lured into a brothel by two
women and subsequently died. J. B. Talbot, the secretary,
claimed there were over four hundred such agents at work in
town and others supplying the metropolis from the country and
abroad. His credibility is put in doubt by his bizarre assertion
regarding prostitution that there were '7,400 Jews engaged in
this traffick who are living on the degradation of Christian girls'.
Such fears of racial violation were behind some of the later white-
slave scares. Talbot overlooked the evidence of his own case-
book, which showed that some recruitment was a family matter.
One Mile End brothel-keeper had thirteen daughters and all
were on the street or keeping their own houses. But the work
of the two Societies does reveal procuresses taking girls from
workhouses and working in league with stagecoach drivers;
and it shows them engaging in the kind of deceit that Stead
claimed was still endemic in his day, placing false notices in

country newspapers and using fake registries for domestics.[20]

The London Society filled its asylum with rescue cases and one of its travelling secretaries started up half-a-dozen branches. The earliest of its brothel prosecutions were assisted by information from the police. However, little progress could be made against the procuring of juveniles without a radical change in the law. The age of consent stood at twelve and there was virtually no way of extricating girls over that age once they were swept up into vice. It was illegal to take a child under sixteen from its parents or guardian; but the Society succeeded in applying this provision only once. The meagre results of the campaign for reform demonstrate once again the limits of what could be achieved before the social-purity movement altered public opinion about prostitution and the double standard.

From 1838, when Lord Ashley, as Shaftesbury was known at the time, first brought the Commons' attention to the issue of protecting girls, it was eleven difficult years before the London rescue world obtained a measure which everyone agreed would fail.[21] This was the 'Act to Protect Women Under Twenty-One From Fraudulent Practices to Procure Their Defilement'. It was rarely used and the Attorney General called it 'a homeopathic dose for a great problem'. The rescue societies wanted an absolute ban on the procuring of girls aged fifteen or younger and a simpler weapon against brothels, goals similar to those of the Stead campaign. While there was some support from the bishops and the anti-slavery movement, the Associate Institute formed to generate a national agitation fell flat on its face. Successive governments, the clergy and the Commons were all indifferent and the public backed off, believing an attempt was afoot to repress prostitutes. When the Bishop of Exeter denied this in 1844 when introducing a 'Bill for the More Effectual Suppression of Brothels and of Trading in Seduction and Prostitution', the Lords responded with shouts of 'madness, impossible'.

By then the moral reformers had given up on their attempt to obtain protection for girls under fifteen. The impulse to make special provision for the young was growing in these years but it was not as strong as it was to become by the 1880s. The Factory Acts regulated the labour of children under thirteen and the 1854 Juvenile Offenders Act would authorise the creation of reformatories. Work and crime apart, the legal age of mar-

riage stood with the age of consent at twelve and the mid-
Victorians were not ready to create an anomalous legal category
of marriageable but unprocurable females. Nor was there any
discussion in these years about raising the age of consent. Even
the contemporary meaning of 'white slavery' indicates how far
the moralists had to go. In the 1830s its primary connotation
was the wage slavery of northern factory girls. The term was
widely employed in this context by reformers like Richard
Oastler and only rarely used before Josephine Butler's campaign
in the sexual context.

This campaign to protect girls failed to exploit the issue of
white slavery and combine it with the age of consent, the explosive mixture of the 1880s, largely because women were still
not prepared to take action. The Josephine Butler generation of
feminists politicised the whole issue of protecting women and
used it as a weapon against the double standard. In the 1840s,
however, it was virtually impossible to attract women to a movement whose focus was prostitution. Victorian ladies exhibited
the same distancing from harlots as did their husbands. W. R.
Greg observed in his celebrated articles on prostitution in the
*Westminster Review* of 1850 that, 'It is discreditable to a
woman even to be supposed to know of their existence'. In 1843
the Associate Institute launched a plan to form female auxiliaries, albeit with male secretaries. It was hoped they would
initiate 'a movement of the women of England' and that the
legislation on prostitution would 'only be the commencement
of a more general improvement in the laws for the benefit of
women'. The scheme was premature. Before feminism could
make prostitution a paradigm for the condition of women, it
took Josephine Butler and Ellice Hopkins to demonstrate to their
sex that, in the words of Miss Hopkins, the fallen were 'martyrs
of purity'.

\* \* \*

The voluntary confinement of prostitutes in rescue homes grew
out of the ever-widening circle of Georgian humanitarianism.
Through the next century the impressive expansion of this
'peculiar form of philanthropy', as it was called by one of its
many enemies, was largely a manifestation of the Christian
workers' struggle with sexual sin. While the double standard

drove some men to prostitutes, fear and trembling about lust moved others, and women as well, to patrol the streets and even enter brothels to rescue harlots from Satan's grasp. Some might call rescue work peculiar; but it was as Victorian as prostitution itself.

William Gladstone's forty-four years of sporadic but compulsive street rescue, a career nearly as long as his political life, is the most celebrated case of its kind. Yet Gladstone was probably typical of other men in the field. Associating with prostitutes was a means of testing his own salvation. His candid *Diaries* reveal a tortured struggle with 'the sins of wrath, impurity and spiritual sloth'. If he could rescue just a few of the pretty and appealing girls whom he particularly sought out without succumbing to their charms it would be a presumptive test of his own salvation. One sleepless night in 1854 he reckoned that he had conversed with eighty or ninety:

> Among these there is but one of whom I know that the miserable life has been abandoned *and* that I can fairly join that fact with influence of mine. Yet this were much more than enough for all the labour and the time, had it been purely spent on my part. But the case is far otherwise....[22]

This was probably about the average success rate with girls approached in the streets at mid-century, when virtually all the workers were men. The campaigns of Josephine Butler and Ellice Hopkins lowered the barriers for ladies to come into rescue work. Whether from sympathy with their victimised sisters, an impulse to associate vicariously with sin or the desire to destroy it, or from a variety of motives, ladies entered the field in substantial numbers. Under them this Victorian vocation reached its limits of expansion.

Rescue work requires the submission, deracination and reconditioning of prostitutes. But it implies at least enough individuality for spiritual redemption and it was a step forward from the standard round-ups of the reforming constables. By the 1740s sympathy with the miserable physical plight of most whores and the sentimental view that many were reduced to their condition as a result of seduction were becoming widespread. Smollet's *Roderick Random* of 1748 manifests this attitude and the new sympathy was given official sanction in the same year when the chaplain-in-ordinary to George II delivered a widely-reported mawkish sermon on the subject at St James's Palace. Rescue work was the logical next step in Christian social charity. There were the charity schools, the Foundling Hospital, Jonas Hanway's Marine Society of 1756 to send vagrant boys to sea, hospitals for the ill and innumerable other institutions. As John Fielding noted in his promotional pamphlet in 1757, 'unfortunate females seem the only objects that have not yet catched the attention of public Benevolence'.[23]

The British were the last Europeans to undertake rescue work and the delay is related to its popular association with Roman Catholicism. When the idea was first mooted in 1749, there were protests in the *Gentleman's Magazine* against 'popish convents' and 'sacred prisons'.[24] Judging by the European experience, there was as little to recommend rescue as there was to recommend regulation. The institutions established after Pope Innocent III's call to the faithful to undertake the task in 1198 virtually all degenerated, whether the inmates took religious vows or not. In Vienna, a home established in 1384 was suppressed in the next century when it was discovered that the women had taken up their old profession. The same thing happened repeatedly in France, where there was the additional abuse of husbands and fathers using the notorious *lettres de cachet* to immure wives and daughters in Magdalen convents.

In 1660 the Parlement of Paris suppressed virtually all these houses. When the Bon Pasteur convent was finally established as the popular new prototype, with the help of Louis XIV's mistress, Madame de Maintenon, its regime was so forbidding it quickly became 'the terror of women of bad life'.[25] Robert Dingley, the merchant and philanthropist who did most to found the Magdalen Hospital, sought to institute 'the utmost care and delicacy, humanity and tenderness'. But British rescue homes were little more popular with their clients than French convents were.

After discussions and plans by John Fielding, Hanway, Dingley and other public-spirited Georgians through the 1750s, the Magdalen Hospital was founded in 1758. Since it remained a model for a century, it is worth looking at its organisation. The goal was the conversion of outcast poor into respectable and disciplined Christian poor; and as Hanway stated, 'It would be an Utopean scheme to expect to make converts upon any other principle than that of confinement'.[26] Europe was still in the midst of a great age of confinement in which vagrants, lunatics and other undesirables were being locked away for moral re-education. But a month in Bridewell was hardly uplifting. Confinement in the Magdalen was longer, up to three years, and more carefully controlled. To maximise the chance for success the age limit was set at thirty, and women had to petition for entry and pass through a probationary ward.

Reconditioning was accomplished by rigid control of time, hard work and religious instruction. While the relative importance of these elements differed amongst later homes, they always constituted the basic ingredients of reclamation. At the Magdalen the day lasted from six am to ten pm in summer and from seven am to nine pm in winter. Every minute was monitored and much of it was spent at work. A number of staple occupations had been suggested for the inmates, from weaving Turkish carpets, which after all kept harems happily occupied, to the manufacture of lace to hurt the French, to Dresden china, soldiers' clothing and laundry work. When the house opened the inmates were set to work making their own clothes and such small items for sale as toys, gloves and artificial flowers. They could keep part of the proceeds and thus learn the diligence and thrift they would need in their new lives as domestic servants.

In the early days this grim Magdalen regime was tempered by common sense and sociability. Under the rules of Dingley and Hanway punishment involved short periods of solitary confinement and forfeiture of meals and wages. Progressively for the time, there was no corporal punishment. The daily ration of beer was two-and-a-half pints. While inmates could not go out without special permission, they were joined in chapel each Sunday by parties of respectable gentlemen out for a morning's amusement. William Dodd, the part-time chaplain, was a well-known figure in town and tickets were sold for his popular services. Unfortunately for Dodd and the collection plate, his speculation in chapel building landed him in debt and he made the fatal mistake of forging the signature of Lord Chesterfield's son, his pupil, on a bond. But even after his hanging in 1777 the Magdalen chapel remained as regular a stop as Bedlam on the London tourist circuit. It was the evangelical revival that brought a new intensity in its regime. By the end of the century the beer ration was curtailed, a full-time chaplain was employed and that particularly onerous if cleansing form of penance instituted : laundry work. In this form, as a sanctimonious sweat-shop, the Magdalen became widely copied.

Advocates of voluntary rescue work never saw it as a panacea. From the beginning there were suggestions that justices be empowered to commit prostitutes to the Magdalen and that the state help by levying a special rate for rescue homes. Surveying the returns for the Magdalen's first forty years, Colquhoun concluded 'the evil is too great a magnitude to admit of a cure through the medium of private benevolence'. A total of 3,250 females had been processed and 2,217 had either been placed in service or reconciled with their families or friends. The success rate was encouraging but the total was insignificant. By 1816 *The Times* was supporting Colquhoun's plan to establish a network of mandatory publicly-financed rescue homes through London.[27]

While magistrates like Colquhoun began to release whores willing to go into the homes, the public authorities contributed nothing to these institutions until after the First World War, when a subsidy was established for the care of unwed mothers. The Victorian fear of sexual immorality, the scapegoating of fallen women and the state's *laissez-faire* response to personal hardship all contrived to keep the rescue world strictly voluntary. The homes were on their own, exposed to the smouldering middle-class prejudice that prostitutes were beyond redemption.

The movement advanced in three increasingly large steps. Early in the century evangelical philanthropists carried the gospel of forgiveness to the fallen and established at least eight penitentiaries in the provinces and London. While the term was meant to convey the old connotation of penance rather than criminal punishment, the new usage was good ammunition for opponents. The London Female Penitentiary established in 1808 was respectable enough later to boast Queen Victoria as a patron. Like its counterparts in the country it added more prayer and a rule of silence to the basic structure of the Magdalen. Yet it provoked an incredible storm of opposition and abuse. William Hale, a manufactory owner and parish official from Spitalfields, effectively demolished the sentimental belief that prostitutes were the victims of seduction and anxious to repent : 'There is not one instance in a thousand of a virtuous woman who becomes a prostitute in consequence of seduction'.[28] According to Hale, most poor women were potential whores kept off the streets only by the dread of suffering and shame. True, much prostitution was casual and temporary. But in a symptomatic paradox he claimed that the wages of sin were depressed by the flood of women onto the street and so the regulars were being forced to find second jobs. The penitentiaries would swamp the vice market with domestic servants.

Along with the cult of sentimentality, which denied prostitutes free will, this kind of scapegoating was one of the psychological options that followed from the double standard. It became significant during the Napoleonic Wars and the age of popular radicalism that followed, when sexual vice and political revolution were believed to be associated. The new hard line hurt the rescue movement. But the enterprising evangelicals were not deterred. In 1815 they entered into an 'enthusiastical phalanx', as the influential Rev. Rowland Hill called it, to clean up the City of London. This was the Guardian Society, whose blueprint was similar to the one being promoted at the time by Colquhoun. After scores of streetwalkers were hauled off to the specially expanded Bridewell, visitors from the Society went along to offer the captive audience room in their new Whitechapel Asylum. Only thirty-four out of 254 of the women chose the home in preference to jail. But the experiment shows how relations with the magistrates had become firmly established and how the workers were now prepared to venture out from the precincts of their asylum.[29]

At about the same time the intrepid Quakers of Bristol were going into brothels to plead with the fallen and tracking down clients to their homes for dangerous confrontations. A debate developed in rescue circles about the virtues of the petition versus active recruiting. But until the second step forward, at mid-century, the homes hardly had enough space to matter. This boom in rescue institutions was fuelled by religious revivals in both low and high-church circles. The collapse of Chartism with parliament's dismissal of the last petition in 1848 helped by freeing middle-class energies for serious consideration of a variety of social problems. The periodicals were soon promoting the most significant discussion of the social evil in a century. Even before the fiasco at Kennington Common a wealth of literary evidence surfaced to suggest a softening of attitudes to the harlot. With the publication of Mrs Gaskell's *Ruth* in 1853, it has been suggested, 'The fallen woman in fiction . . . was establishing herself as a feminine archetype almost equal to the Madonna, almost equally motherly, pure and inspirational'.[30]

In 1847 Charles Dickens persuaded Baroness Burdett-Coutts, the richest woman in England, to finance a rescue home with as few rules as possible to prepare women for emigration. Dickens drew up the plans, furnished the place and composed an *Appeal to Fallen Women* which begins, 'Do not think I write to you as if I felt very much above you. . . .' Whether he felt so or not, Urania Cottage soon failed. Such endeavours required special perseverance and skill. When hundreds of ladies were being attracted to rescue work in the 1880s, one old professional wrote a manual warning dilettantes to stay away. A decade later training homes were being opened for this special breed of social workers. At mid-century such professionalism was supplied by the new Anglo-Catholic and evangelical workers.

By the 1840s clergymen of the thriving high-church persuasion who were interested in the social evil, like the pioneering John Armstrong, were complaining that the homes were not being run on 'sound church principles'. Doctrine apart, Armstrong's influential promotional pieces of 1848 claimed the very spirit was out of them.[31] There were not even any cells for contemplation. Since Dr Pusey was just preparing the ground for the novel Anglican sisterhoods, it was quite natural that these new orders should provide the 'self-devoted and unpaid ladies' whom Armstrong and others felt were necessary for the redemption of the fallen. Within a year two new sisterhoods devoted themselves to the task. At Wantage the vicar helped establish a teaching order; but a home for penitents was built when the mother superior felt called to work with prostitutes. At Clewer, where there resided a community of whores who worked the nearby Windsor garrison, the Sisters of St John the Baptist took over a small home when the original founder died.[32]

Gladstone supported Clewer from the start and one of the girls he sent there wrote to him after fleeing from it, 'I did not fancy being shut up in such a place as that for perhaps twelve months. I should have committed suicide.'[33] By 1852 the hierarchy established the Church Penitentiary Association to promote the movement. In some of the many homes that became affiliated, lay women supplemented the work of the sisters. But this was before Josephine Butler and Ellice Hopkins tackled prostitution with a new frankness. In the high-church penitentiaries the inmates were forbidden to talk of their sins in order to protect the workers.

In the meantime, encouraged by mid-century revivalism and by new legal and voluntary developments for dealing with juvenile delinquency and vagrancy, the evangelicals were making their own spectacular departures with London's street whores. Lieutenant Blackmore and E. W. Thomas are two more rescue pioneers who underwent youthful conversions, both under the influence of the celebrated Rev. Baptist Noel, and who acted out overwhelming feelings of sexual sin.[34] By 1847 Blackmore had left the navy where he had been deeply troubled by the coarse behaviour of his messmates, and had taken to 'cruises' through the streets during which he bombarded the fallen with invitations to his new home in Euston. A few years later Thomas joined him and on one occasion was nearly killed while venturing into a criminal den in the same neighbourhood. Their efforts paved the way for the enduring London Female Preventive and Reformatory Institution, with its 'family plan' offered as an alternative to the drab dress and cropped hair of the penitentiaries.

A whole flood of evangelical institutions emerged in the 1850s, including the Rescue Society, whose secretary, Daniel Cooper, was to become a close ally of Josephine Butler. In 1859 they banded together in that quintessentially Victorian departure, the Midnight Meeting Movement. The idea was to gather prostitutes together in the early hours to hear the gospel of grace. Workers would first meet for prayer and then scour the streets distributing invitation cards. Baptist Noel took this mission seriously and he could usually reduce his audience to temporary tears:

As by an afterthought, he mentions that since their last meeting, some mother has sent him a photograph of her daughter beseeching him to seek that lost one in this company. In an instant the sealed up fountains are opened, and strong emotion replaces real and feigned indifference. They who heard unmoved of divine love and human help are touched and shaken by the voice of a weeping mother. Some sob audibly in their tempest of awakened memory. Tears run down the cheeks of many. It seems as though every fallen daughter were asking: 'Is it my mother? Is it my picture?'[35]

There was tea, sometimes a nosegay from the Bible Flower Mission, and an invitation to the rescue homes. During the next half-century over 100,000 women attended these mawkish meetings, to say nothing of the spectaculars staged later by the Salvation Army and other agencies.

A fund of wisdom developed over these tactics and found its way over the century into a series of rescue manuals, a little genre that sheds interesting light on the subject.[36] One expert warned male workers never to kneel down with women at midnight meetings, especially behind a pew. He also opposed brothel visits because they might require telling a lie to get by the keeper. Ellice Hopkins' favourite tactic was to enter brothels at noon without knocking. A number of experts agreed with her that midnight meetings were practically useless, since the women were usually passing the time after failing to pick up trade. Sarah Robinson, whom we shall meet later as one of Ellice's inspirations, drove herself to visit Aldershot's brothels in the 1860s and became violently sick after each excursion. On one occasion she was trapped but used her wit to escape by breaking into 'Will you go to the Eden above?' With such dangers in mind, Arthur Maddison, the long-lived secretary of the Female Mission to the Fallen, advised brothel workers never to eat or smell anything, to stand near the door and above all not to look scared.

The mid-Victorian rescue boom left London in 1860 with about two dozen homes accommodating 1,200, and the rest of the country with another forty homes with place for about 1,050.[37] The movement was diversifying and as the various societies expanded some of their homes became specialised and made pioneering efforts in social work. The Rescue Society ran a home for the fallen, another for invalids and a third for girls in danger. The Female Mission to the Fallen, which alone fielded lady missioners to approach prostitutes in the streets and workhouses, helped attempted suicides and uniquely sponsored two homes for unmarried mothers and their babies. Some of these institutions were relatively sanguine. The Rescue Society's fallen were kept in a small cottage at Barnett where the matron dispensed plenty of charitable Christian care.[38] Josephine Butler opened a small refuge in Liverpool where she nursed the most hopelessly ill cases she could find. This family environment was part of the evangelical design but it was not always achieved in practice.

While there were real gains, rescue work was still struggling along in the face of resistance from both public and prostitutes. Leaders like Armstrong, Maddison and Blackmore agreed that poverty, low wages, seasonal work and overcrowded housing all contributed to prostitution. But when the *Magdalen's Friend* ran a series 'Is society responsible for the existence of the social evil?', the rescue experts agreed that the primary cause was personal sin. The homes were arranged accordingly. Armstrong had wanted to alter the balance between religion and work and abolish the laundry because it encouraged conversation! But the laundry became central to virtually all the asylums because it was a money earner. Economic necessity reinforced ideology in the making of the sanctimonious sweatshop.

Considering the regime, it is surprising how many entered. Since the most amenable to discipline and restraint, the upwardly mobile whores, never entered, it is curious that the rate of success always remained above fifty per cent. When the remarkable dual personality, Arthur Munby, met an old acquaintance in the Strand in 1859 she explained she had left the trade: 'I'd been on the streets three years, and saved up—I told you I should get on, you know—and so I thought I'd leave, and I've taken a coffee-house with my earnings'.[39] This was the kind of purposeful prostitute who would never go near an asylum, and whom Dr William Acton, in his important *Prostitution Considered* of 1857, thought was at the core of the phenomenon. Rescue work was offering no solution to the social evil. On its own terms, however, it was far from failing. As the Church Penitentiary Association pointed out in 1862, '...the Mission of the Association is to rescue individual souls; and if, out of the number who annually leave the Penitentiaries, between two hundred and three hundred are permanently rescued, who can dare to say that little is done?'[40]

PART TWO

# THE EMERGENCE OF
# SOCIAL PURITY, 1864–85

# 4

# Against the Double Standard: From the
# Contagious Diseases Acts to White Slavery

IF ever there were acts of state which inadvertently tore away
the veil obscuring a deeply rooted social abuse, they were the
Contagious Diseases (CD) Acts. If ever an individual was suited to
lead a particular protest movement, it was Josephine Butler and
this agitation. In 1871 she delivered an annual address which
illustrates both these points. It pinpoints how this legislation
clarified the meaning of the double standard while providing its
opponents with an indispensable commodity—a concrete but
symbolic issue; and it demonstrates the chiliastic and providential
rhetoric which inspired thousands of men and women:

> That we are, and have been all along contending for more
> than the mere repeal of these unjust and unholy Acts of
> Parliament, is proved by certain signs, which are becoming
> more and more clear and frequent. We were, perhaps, our-
> selves unconscious ... how great is the undertaking upon
> which we have entered. It only very gradually dawned with
> perfect clearness on my mind, that it is the old, the inveterate,
> the deeply rooted evil of prostitution itself against which we
> are destined to make war. Had someone arisen in 1863, or at
> any time before this legislation was enacted, and called upon
> us to arise and join in a great crusade against this national,
> and socially-sanctioned abomination, we should scarcely have
> responded. ... It would have appeared too herculean a task
> to dream of. God knew that He should not then find faith on
> the earth to this extent; and the way for the preparation of
> the needful faith and energy was opened up by the permission
> of an evil, terrible in itself, but out of which good will come.
> The Contagious Diseases Acts were enacted. ... It woke us

up . . . the faithful and uninterrupted efforts of the servants
of God to establish the supremacy of conscience . . . will finally
be crowned by an act of the Divine Will whereby the original
principal of evil itself will be expelled from the earth, and the
reign of righteousness will be established.[1]

Hugh Price Hughes, the most celebrated Methodist divine of
the century, heard a speech like this as a young minister, burst
into tears and had to leave the platform. According to Henry
Scott Holland, the influential Regius Professor of Divinity at
Oxford, 'Men could never be the same again after they had
seen and known Josephine Butler. A new sense of what passionate
pity could mean was brought home to them. . . .'[2] Her leadership mobilised a generation of feminists over prostitution and it
helped bring about an important change amongst religious
leaders as well. The nonconformist conscience was readily
brought into line behind repeal of the Acts. The cause was timely
as a sequel to the anti-slavery crusade and in tandem with temperance. In 1873 the visiting American revivalist, Dwight
Moody, was telling his huge audiences that they were 'mistaken
in supposing that it is intemperance that is the chief sin of
England. What is eating into the heart of your noble country is
the sin of impurity'.[3]

The Church was slower to respond. At the 1872 Church
Congress, the Rev. George Butler, Josephine's supportive husband, alluded to the Acts in a paper on 'The Duty of the Church
of England in Moral Questions'. He was howled down and
asked by the chairman to give up the paper. The Church was as
reticent as society at large about sex. The long national debate,
however, and the stunning presentation of the issues helped to
break down the taboo amongst the hierarchy and a portion of
the clergy. So too, in a Church increasingly concerned with a
social gospel, did the perception that purity reform was a species
of social reform.

While the Church never flocked to Josephine's repeal movement, it was deeply stirred by the campaign that grew out of
that agitation, namely, the one to protect girls from white slavery.
The next chapter will explore the central role of Ellice Hopkins
in interesting Anglicans of both sexes in this question. Under the
lead of the sympathetic Archbishop Benson of Canterbury the

Church addressed itself more seriously to the problem of sexual vice by the 1880s than it had since the days of the Societies for the Reformation of Manners.

What is more, Anglicans joined with nonconformists to make the attack on sexual vice interdenominational, as had been the case with some of those pioneering Societies. Cooperation in the social-purity movement was one of the forms of joint effort between evangelicals of Church and chapel that had been stimulated by Dwight Moody's triumphant missions.[4] Social purity, however, was wider than evangelicalism. From the Quakers to the Salvationists to the Catholic hierarchy and the cerebral Lux Mundi group, represented by Scott Holland, Christian leaders joined with feminists against sexual vice and the double standard.

The outcome was not exactly what Josephine Butler had in mind. Well before the repeal of the CD Acts in 1886, she had lost control of the spreading and diversifying movement and social purity had begun to lose sight of her ideal of 'the supremacy of conscience', with its non-repressionist implications. Purity reform came to mean the harassing of prostitutes and systematic blind repression in the arts and entertainment. In 1888 W. T. Stead told the Edinburgh Vigilance Association, 'Hitherto they had had two distinct standards of morality in relation to all questions governing the sexes. . . . In face of the progressive elevation and emancipation of women, they had to face this fact, that in their ideas of sexual morality, they had either to level up or to level down. They had either to raise the standard of the male to the standard of the female, or they had to make up their minds as best they could to see the female standard levelled down to the male standard'.[5] The social-purity movement helped discredit the double standard. But its attempt to enforce a single standard of chastity meant war against Josephine Butler's beloved prostitutes and a long life-after-death for Victorian prudery.

\* \* \*

While Josephine Butler saw the evidence of God's design in the passage of the CD Acts, the War Office, Admiralty and increasingly priestly medical profession had more to do with it. The preparation of the ground is clear enough, though the first regulatory act was processed with such stealth that Gladstone, then a member of the government, later claimed he had little idea who prepared or piloted it. Some 319 years after Henry VIII abolished the Southwark stews state-regulated vice was brought back camouflaged in the legislative language used for foot-and-mouth disease.

The means of passage and the scope of regulation made the British system different from those which had proliferated through Europe after Napoleon had provided the primary modern impetus. As the self-styled 'new abolitionists' pointed out, Britain was virtually the only place where regulation had legislative sanction. Elsewhere it was a question of administrative law and of local option. This shamed the British but it facilitated repeal through the characteristic use of 'pressure from without', the campaign to change law-making opinion. After Josephine formed the British, Continental and General Federation in 1875, James Stansfeld, her prominent liberal parliamentary general, wrote to Aimé Humbert, the Swiss statesman and secretary of the Federation, 'Speaking for my own country I have neither doubt nor fear of the issue in conflict. There is no case in the history of England of the failure of any movement based upon the moral and religious sense of the community in which any considerable number of men and women have had the courage and faith to persist'.[6] The Swiss new abolitionists had a more frustrating time proceeding canton by canton and the Dutch and Germans town by town; the administrative regulations in France remained impervious to public opinion until after the Second World War.

The CD Acts applied only to certain garrison and seaport towns. Through much of Europe, however, regulation was designed to protect the civilian population along with the armed forces. With the new interest in public health around the middle of the century and the continuing intractability of street soliciting, considerable opinion surfaced in favour of regulation. William Acton's influential book of 1857 was a clue to the sentiments of the medical profession; even the pioneering Dr Elizabeth Garrett supported the Acts. By 1862 *The Times* was advocating the idea. But the introduction of compulsory examination and treatment for venereal disease throughout the country would have been a tremendous political and economic undertaking. The armed forces wanted such protection badly. In the Crimean

War, William Howard Russell's celebrated dispatches had enlightened the public to the fact that the British army's most implacable opponent was disease. In the aftermath the army created a statistical section in its Medical Department which demonstrated that the incidence of all forms of infection except venereal disease was being brought under control.

The War Office and Admiralty both appointed committees to investigate in the early 1860s and neither recommended compulsory examination nor detention of prostitutes. Florence Nightingale was tremendously relieved and wrote to Harriet Martineau, 'Better a thousand times our hideous exposure of vice than the French legalised protected vice. . . .'[7] But the top brass and their advisers were not to be denied. They pushed aside arguments that continental regulation was far from being proven a success, and that it would be even harder to achieve good results with the professional British army than with foreign conscript bodies. In 1864 the Secretary to the Admiralty introduced the pilot measure, limited in operation to three years, and it passed without debate. There were two extensions of police powers and geographical jurisdictions before the code reached its final form in 1869. Ununiformed officers sent by the Metropolitan Police to any of the eighteen districts could swear before a magistrate that they had reason to believe a particular woman was a common prostitute. The justice could then order periodic medical examination for up to a year, unless the suspect agreed to a voluntary submission. If diseased she would be detained in hospital for up to nine months. Resistance to examination or the hospital regime could mean imprisonment.[8]

Constitutional, legal, medical, sexual and class objections all arose over this legislation and it was Josephine Butler's achievement to articulate the arguments imaginatively and form a coalition behind abolition. She was as reluctant to begin as Florence Nightingale, who wrote to Harriet Martineau in 1862 that this was one taboo she could not break: 'It is not a subject on which I can have such special knowledge as to head an opposition. . . .'[9] While engaged with her sick prostitutes in Liverpool, Josephine read the brief debates of the 1866 Act. As the excerpt at the beginning of the chapter indicates, the barriers seemed insurmountable. It was improper for a lady to make a public speech. To speak out against the sexual norms that informed the social structure was to provoke terrible abuse and even violence. After beginning she wrote, 'The charge of immodesty is, perhaps, harder for us to bear than many other imputations. The pitiful appeal of some of the Christian Martyrs who shared the fate of the gentle St Agnes is one which we can well understand. "Give us up to wild beasts," they said, "or to death by slow burning or famine or the rack, but leave us our garments." '[10]

The opposition of a handful of physicians and the rescue world was at an impasse in 1869 when Daniel Cooper wrote he was 'rejoiced beyond measure' at Josephine's formation of the Ladies' National Association for the Repeal of the Contagious Diseases Acts (LNA).[11] She had been trained up to the task. Her father, John Grey, had been important in the anti-slavery, parliamentary reform and free-trade movements. From him she imbued a hatred of injustice and an interest in politics. From her remarkable paternal grandmother, who managed the family estate, and from an aunt with a passion for politics and education, she was provided with models of female activity. An adolescent religious crisis left her with a deep faith. Living at Oxford in the 1850s, where her husband taught, she was already demonstrating disgust at the double standard and social hypocrisy. According to her own memoirs and an intimate biography by Stead, it was a terrible personal tragedy that turned her into the prostitutes' champion. In 1863, when George Butler was vice-principal of Cheltenham College, their five-year-old Evangeline toppled over a balustrade and was dashed to death at her mother's feet. A move to Liverpool in the next year provided her with the opportunity to work through her grief. She took to workhouse visiting and opened up her House of Rest for incurably ill prostitutes. Stead wrote that 'other labours in this most difficult field have been impelled thither by a desire to save souls, or to rescue women. Mrs Butler always wanted to save daughters'.[12]

There was something of interest in the new abolitionism for every possible kind of libertarian and radical, as well as for haters of sexual sin. Repeal was supported corporately by the Quakers and the nonconformist sects; by 50,000 working men in the Working Men's League of 1875; by physicians in the National Medical Association for Repeal of the same year, as the balance of medical opinion began to alter; by old Chartists

like Benjamin Lucraft and old abolitionists like Samuel Gurney
and Robert Charleton; by individualist opponents of medical
tyranny like the MPs Charles Hopwood and P. A. Taylor, who
also led the fight against compulsory vaccination; by those
affected by the overcentralisation of government, like Francis
Newman, the Cardinal's brother; by friends of Mazzini, like
James Stansfeld and Madame Venturi; by supporters of
Garibaldi, like Josephine's sister Harriet.

This is not to say that the supporters of the CD Acts were
cold-blooded sanitary experts, misogynist doctors and callous
officers. The vice-chancellors of Oxford and Cambridge and
many other men of note supported them in the beginning. However, they could not stand up to close scrutiny and more and
more people of good faith were converted to repeal. In medical
terms, we now know regulation was hopeless. The requisite
medical information was not available for adequate diagnosis or
treatment of the venereal diseases. Diagnosis of gonorrhoea
requires microscopic rather than local investigation and syphilis
often went undetected before the development of the Wasserman
test in 1907. Even cooperative women could slip through the surgical examination. It was then understood that women were being
released from hospital after primary syphilitic symptoms had
cleared but before a cure had been effected. It was also clear that
no class of prostitutes had ever complied willingly. Regulation
always encouraged the activities of women whose craft was to
help get infected whores through the examination. Prostitutes in
Egypt went so far as to have syphilitic disfigurements hidden by
tattoos and later the Nazis failed to extinguish clandestine prostitution with the threat of the concentration camp.[13] Moreover,
apprehended women were prized by soldiers when released. What
was to prevent reinfection?

The new abolitionists fought a statistical battle with the
government to show the Acts were not working. In 1881, however, Stansfeld admitted, 'I have always said, and I repeat it
here, that to my mind, the most damning evidence against the
Acts would be the proof of their complete hygienic success'.[14]
While the wish to maintain the providential link between sin
and suffering horrified many, the long technical dispute probably cast enough doubt on the working of the system to enable
moral and political arguments to decide the issue. Here the

repealers could hardly have found a more articulate spokes-woman than Josephine Butler.

She taught women to feel outrage at the treatment of public prostitutes. To a Parisian audience of 1875 :

> ... two words from the mouth of a woman, speaking in the name of all women, and these two words are—
> We rebel!
> ... Oppressed women have needed to find this voice in one of their own sex. She is here and she comes to proclaim up-rising and deliverance. ... The degradation of these poor unhappy women is not degradation for them alone; it is a blow to the dignity of every virtuous woman too, it is dis-honour done to *me*, it is the shaming of every woman in every country in the world.[15]

There was cause for outrage. Alleged prostitutes had no rights against ununiformed police who could arrest and humiliate them on whim. The English *police des moeurs* did not sink to the corruption and gratuitous cruelty of their French counterparts, whose grasp Zola's Nana was so anxious to escape that she chose to jump from a window. England nevertheless had men like Inspector Annis, the demonic figure from the Devonport district who enters into every account of the subject. Annis believed all women were potential whores; unfortunately he had the chance to act on his ideas by arresting girls who simply stopped to talk to men and others out for a stroll with a boyfriend.[16] Domestic servants in the controlled areas had to be very careful and part-time prostitutes were liable to be arrested and transformed into professionals.

While arguments against the blatant violation of traditional liberties were useful, the issue of physical violation was crucial. Compulsory examination was symbolic rape. More than anything else it enabled Josephine Butler to make repeal the central feminist concern of the time. The LNA meticulously kept track of the number of examinations in which no venereal disease was discovered; by 1886 it came to nearly half-a-million. This was an age in which Elizabeth Blackwell became a doctor partly because a lady friend had died after refusing to be treated by a man. The spirit of St Agnes was very much alive. Regulation sanctioned rape and the LNA sometimes admitted 'the central iniquity' of the Acts was the surgical examination.[17] Stead also criticised 'instrumental rape' though ironically one of the most controversial aspects of his abduction of Eliza Armstrong in 1885 was her subjection to an examination to prove her *virgo intacta*.

The working classes were reminded of the inherent discriminatory nature of the Acts. After all, the authorities were intimidating poor women into signing voluntary submissions they did not understand and then were humiliating them. At the advice of her close friend James Stuart, later called in the Commons 'the honourable member whose life was one long public meeting', Josephine launched her public campaign in 1870 with addresses to working-class audiences, including one at the Crewe locomotive works. The results were encouraging and within three years of its founding in 1875 the Working Men's League enrolled over five hundred local trade-union secretaries.[18]

Finally the message for all men was the wickedness of the double standard. As Josephine insisted, 'Vain Sophistry! Sirs, you *cannot* hold *us* in honour so long as you drag our sisters in the mire. As you are unjust and cruel to them, you will become unjust and cruel to us . . . we . . . turn away in disgust from the thought of a family life whose purity is preserved at the price of her degradation. . . .' The repealers believed that the double standard was perpetuated by the isolation of males in their own institutions whether they be schools, colleges or barracks, where they promoted their own corrupted standard of morality. The demand for prostitution was then reinforced by the mistaken notion that unchastity was necessary for good health. There were a number of suggestions to rectify the problem. Some repealers supported co-education. Josephine talked of 'The purification of the medical profession . . . and the exposure and defeat of those deadly materialist doctrines respecting the necessity of unchastity'. Acting on the notion that sexual desire was a moral and intellectual error with tragic social implications, and believing that it could be controlled by reason and will, like the taste for drink, she founded the Social Purity Alliance in 1873. It clubbed young men together for mutual self help at maintaining chastity. By 1886 this prototype of the men's purity leagues had over three thousand members in forty stations, including the universities.[19]

In plain arithmetical terms the new abolitionist message, with its central criticism of the double standard, was set forth at over a thousand public meetings. Within the first few years there were thirty regional and national organisations and by 1877 there were over eight hundred provincial groups. This means the total might ultimately have come close to the 1,200 auxiliaries mobilised by the movement which it mirrored in spirit and rhetoric, anti-slavery. As early as 1870 the LNA was reaching the village level. Stead recalled his mother then collecting signatures for a repeal petition in rural Northumberland. Before the conclusion in 1886 there were 2.6 million signatures on more than eighteen thousand petitions. There were electoral unions through the country to influence liberal MPs and a prominent men's National Association for Repeal in London to plot strategy. Tactics were similar to those of the free trade and abolitionist campaigns : educate, win MPs and exert electoral influence.[20]

This paid off in 1883 when the executive of the National Liberal Federation voted for repeal, to be followed three weeks later by the carrying of Stansfeld's resolution in the Commons that 'This House disapproves of the compulsory examination of women under the Contagious Diseases Acts'. From then on, examination was no longer compulsory but final repeal took another three years. One old MP said in 1883 that the pressure was 'unprecedented in the history of any legislation'.[21]

Josephine Butler was a non-repressive puritan. She once put herself in the tradition of Calvin, Knox, Wesley, Whitefield and Wilberforce, who saw it as 'a most important object to make the institutions of the State virtuous, and to purify social custom'.[22] But while these forebears advocated the use of the state to punish vice and compel virtue, Josephine's puritanism was tempered by an anti-statist ideology that was as radical as Herbert Spencer's. Her beliefs in the supremacy of conscience and in the propensity of laws to make people bad were reinforced by some very sophisticated arguments against overcentralisation and the growth of arbitrary administrative law. With her empathy for prostitutes and absolute belief in the equality of the law, she wrote of attempts to harass them, 'As well might you attempt to do away with the slave trade by making it penal to *be* a slave.'[23]

Such members of her personal entourage as James Stuart and Mrs Tanner, the Bristol Quaker who helped run the LNA, shared this individualism and some of the movement formed a Personal Rights Association in 1871 which ultimately fell into the hands of individualist anarchists.[24] One would hardly expect this sympathetic libertarianism to have dominated, especially as social purity diversified from the single issue of the Acts. The success of the LNA in getting the public to think about prostitution re-awakened the repressionists, especially when the state was stripped of its policy of regulation. In the meantime, when the Liberals introduced an abortive bill in 1872 to replace regulation with new police powers, including the right to arrest prostitutes without proving annoyance, the men's National Association refused to condemn the whole measure. This presaged things to come. Soon H. J. Wilson, the Sheffield MP and founder of the Northern Counties Electoral League for Repeal, was toying with a plan for outlawing fornication.[25] By 1885 Wilson became one of Coote's main supporters in the powerful and repressionist National Vigilance Association. For with the white-slave revelations of the 1880s the purity impulse began to assert itself in ways that Josephine was not always pleased about.

* * *

The new abolitionists were well aware of the devious traps of the procurer and of the migrations of prostitutes. They always argued that protected vice markets so stimulated demand that regulation was the basic cause of the traffic in girls and women. Twentieth-century experts have agreed. Josephine Butler knew of entrapment from her earliest days in rescue work. Her associates in Liverpool were the Quaker temperance and anti-slavery workers, James Cropper and his wife; in 1857 the Croppers were responsible for the conviction of one 'Madame Anna' and her agents for sending girls from Liverpool workhouse schools to Hamburg brothels and in turn importing German girls.[26]

Almost immediately after the European repealers organised in 1875 they began providing the earliest reports about the commerce in females that was developing between central Europe and South America. The Swedish branch of the British, Continental and General Federation posted warnings for girls and women migrating to Stockholm each autumn for employment. The Swiss branch, under M. Aimé Humbert, helped

D

obtain an intercantonal agreement in 1877 that became a model for later international conventions on white slavery. The cantons agreed, amongst other things, to license employment agencies and bar the emigration of girls under the age of twenty-one without parental consent. In the same year Madame Humbert launched 'L'Union Internationale des Amis de la Jeune Fille', the prototype for the travellers' aid work that became a rage and covered Europe and America by 1914.[27]

The secondary nature of this work in the struggle against state regulation is emphasised by the usage of the term 'white slavery'. By the 1870s it was widely employed in the context of prostitution. However, Josephine Butler typically used it to refer to prostitution itself, regulation or the migration of prostitutes. In reference to state regulation, Victor Hugo wrote to her at the beginning of the campaign in 1870, 'The slavery of black women is abolished in America, but the slavery of white women continues in Europe'.[28] With the explosive revelation in late 1879 that English girls were being held captive in Brussels brothels, 'white slavery' firmly and permanently took on the connotation of the abductor and the hypodermic syringe. Reformers sometimes meant by it the taking of professional prostitutes to foreign parts where they were subject to gross exploitation. They were never interested in making this distinction clear, however, for public support depended upon fear of the fiendish slaver rather than sympathy for professionals marooned abroad.

The new abolitionists were delighted to fasten on the white-slave revelations to revive their rank and file and mesmerise the public. By late 1879 Disraeli's government was running down and a new issue could be expected to accelerate the gains that would come under the Liberals. The Europeans were particularly enthusiastic. After the most optimistic predictions in 1875, they had got nowhere. Belgium was always praised 'as the Paradise of regulation', as Josephine wrote to H. J. Wilson. To blacken its reputation would deal the whole system a blow. In the wake of the Brussels brothel affair the scholarly and statesmanlike Aimé Humbert claimed that 'the gross barbarities and the stupid cruelties of negro slavery grow pale by the side of these horrible revelations'.[29] What could be expected of less sober workers?

Alfred Dyer's *exposé* was set in train when a fellow Quaker told him, in 1879, that a third party had been approached for help by a nineteen-year-old English girl being held captive in a Brussels brothel. By this time Dyer had achieved some prominence in repeal circles, as an officer in the Friends' Association for Abolition; as editor of the *National League Journal*, the organ of the Working Men's League; and as publisher of a good quantity of repeal literature. Dyer and William Coote both struggled through childhood with widowed mothers in families whose status had dropped when the fathers died prematurely. Both worked their way up through the Working Men's League, to which Dyer was attracted after hearing one of Josephine Butler's speeches. They were amongst the most effective members of a fascinating species that grew to maturity in the 1870s, the working-class radical puritan.

While Coote was a prude Dyer was an obsessed fanatic. A police report of 1880 gives us a glimpse of him at his headquarters at Amen Corner, Paternoster Row, where he occupied a room 'partitioned off into divisions, two of which are occupied for domestic purposes by his wife and family while the third part is used as shop and office'. To the undoubted relief of many, Dyer spent much of the time between 1888 and 1911 in India doing mission and purity work. His great fear was that obscene photos would set off another mutiny in which all the white women would be ravaged. After his return to England his fundamentalism over scriptural interpretation prompted him to leave the Quakers.[30]

Dyer's immediate response to the allegation was to have Josephine Butler make enquiries through her Brussels contacts. These included Pastor Anet, who as early as the 1860s had sent her English girls rescued from Brussels houses. Dyer's charges were no revelation in purity circles. On this occasion Anet turned up a victim who had been lured from Brighton with a promise of marriage, only to end up in a licensed house. Dyer launched a correspondence in the London press and interested the luminaries of the City of London Committee for Repeal. They formed a London Committee for Suppressing the Traffic in British Girls and sent Dyer and George Gillet, another Quaker, off to Brussels to investigate.

They could expect no help from the corrupt Brussels *police des moeurs* and a great deal of abuse from the Belgian bullies. In Gillet, though, Dyer had a colleague with a family tradition to uphold. Forty years earlier and quite remarkably for the time, George's older sister had visited bad houses in Banbury with her father's blessing. Dyer and Gillet found what they were looking for. There was the pathetic Adeline Tanner, who turned up in a venereal ward. This country girl of twenty had also been trapped in a brothel after leaving home expecting to be married. For seventeen days clients attempted sexual intercourse with her; but she had a congenital deformation of the vagina which made it impossible. She was then sent off to the hospital suffering from vaginal abscesses and the two Quakers found her after surgeons had enlarged her vagina. A sickened Josephine Butler wrote that the case would be 'most useful for *us*', and it was.[31] However, few of the cases were as cruel and clear-cut as this.

On their first excursion, for example, Dyer and Gillet met Louisa Bond in the public room of a brothel and over glasses of wine, which they avoided drinking, she told them a desperate story of seduction and betrayal. When the police and British diplomatic mission proved uncooperative, they returned next day to spirit her away in a raincoat, only to have her refuse their offer. Dyer later admitted that Louisa was a professional prostitute but insisted she was too intimidated to come away with them. She was a white slave to her rescuers but just a whore to the British diplomats who refused to intervene because she was over the legal age of twenty-one and had lodged no complaint about forcible detention.

The British public soon knew about the alleged official complicity and the case of Louisa Bond found its way into the diplomatic mails. An embarrassed Sir Saville Lumley, British Minister in Brussels, explained to Lord Salisbury at the Foreign Office why she had not been helped.[32] The British Embassy and community there had not been idle. In the decade before Dyer and Gillet arrived about two hundred girls had been assisted home. While a few were innocent victims, most seem to have been professionals who did not know they would be kept in more severe circumstances than prevailed in the world of English vice. The fact that they came forward disproves Dyer's assertion that the inmates were held in an 'actual condition of slavery'.

In an important way the British officials were either complicit or criminally complacent; this is the implication of Mr Jeffes's testimony before the important Lords' enquiry of 1881 on the subject. Jeffes was vice proconsul and responsible for this rescue work. In reference to Adeline Tanner he claimed that until the public scandal he had 'been able to get the girls out of the country quietly and to keep them from going to prison'. This referred to the fact that a number of English girls including Adeline were illegally registered under false names with the aid of birth certificates easily obtained at Somerset House. The procurers contrived this in order to bring in girls under twenty-one and to compromise their charges by having them break the law. More than the doors that opened only from the street, the confiscation of street clothes or the inevitable debts, the threat of turning a girl over to the police for illegally registering was the pimp's main weapon. Jeffes must have known the inmates could not have arranged this themselves. He did nothing to upset the system because, as he told the Lords, he believed no virtuous girl could ever end up in a Brussels brothel.[33]

Soon after Dyer and Gillet returned from Brussels, Josephine Butler luckily obtained the kind of evidence about police corruption there that enabled the investigators to seize the initiative. One of the subordinates of the chief of the morals police met her in Paris and revealed how officials were in league with brothel-keepers to cover up the registration of underage girls. This revelation, supported by an official deposition that Mrs Butler risked under the extradition treaty, forced the government to look into just what was happening to British girls across the Channel.

Officials were sick and tired of the new abolitionists and expected that a thorough investigation would, as a Home Office official noted in December, 'put an end to an agitation however ill-founded, within and out of parliament'.[34] There were grounds for believing that one last mission would end the controversy. On the heels of Dyer and Gillet Scotland Yard's Inspector Greenham had undertaken what in fact had been a carefully laundered tour of regulated houses through northern Europe and reported back that nothing was amiss. Now Howard Vincent, the director of the CID and one of Josephine's bitterest enemies, made the mistake of recommending for the new mission T. W. Snagge, a London barrister whose chief qualifications were his eight children and his ability to speak French.

Snagge came back with enough evidence to confirm that there

was systematic entrapment of young British girls. With this report in hand, with the convictions of the leading officials of the Brussels *police des moeurs* for registering underage girls and with a petition for improved legal protection for girls signed by a thousand 'ladies of the higher class', Gladstone's government appointed a Select Committee of the Lords in May 1881 'to inquire into the law for the protection of young girls from artifices to induce them to lead a corrupt life, and into the means of amending the same'.

How much white slavery did Snagge and the Lords turn up? Snagge reported on a small rogue's gallery of traffickers, most already well-known. The Home Office had helped the Antwerp police capture the notorious Klyberg in 1877. There was an admittedly incomplete list of thirty-three cases in which English girls under the age of twenty-one had been illegally registered through Belgium, Holland and northern France. Snagge reported that police protection for the unwilling was 'illusory'. The Lords concluded that most of the British inmates abroad were professionals before they embarked. But they had heard enough about entrapment of the innocent and exploitation of everyone to recommend in 1882 that it be made criminal to procure any woman to leave her usual place of abode to go abroad for prostitution.

The Lords' investigation of juvenile prostitution was much more dramatic. Police officials like Howard Vincent and Inspector Dunlop testified that this was the real problem and it was at home. Ellice Hopkins was called as a well-travelled expert on the subject. In 1880, when she was just half-way through a frenetic decade's activity for social purity, she had obtained an amendment of the Industrial Schools Act enabling children found residing with prostitutes to be committed to these certified schools. She now claimed there were 10,000 brothel children across the country, to say nothing of the tribes of juvenile prostitutes. Considering the family nature of some recruitment, the so-called Ellice Hopkins Act was a potentially powerful weapon against the trade. J. W. Horsley, Chaplain at Clerkenwell prison, testified to the 'animalism in the East and the diabolism in the West'. He produced a sample of 3,074 imprisoned prostitutes, nearly a quarter of whom were seventeen or younger.

The Lords were impressed enough to recommend that the age

of consent be raised from thirteen, where it had been set in 1875, to sixteen, and that it be made possible for the police to search private premises for suspected juvenile prostitutes; they also recommended that the age of abduction for immoral purposes be raised from sixteen to twenty-one and that the Ellice Hopkins Act be given teeth by empowering the police to enforce it.[35]

. The Lords' departure on the age of consent was very bold. In 1871 a Lords' Committee on the CD Acts had reported in favour of raising the age to fourteen. But when the new abolitionists tried to redeem this in the 1870s they ran into strenuous opposition. The Attorney General, later Lord Chief Justice Coleridge, produced legal arguments against differentiating the ages of marriage and consent. Josephine Butler complained that in committee in 1874 the bill ran into 'the passionate remonstrances of some gentlemen against any attempt being made to raise the age even to 13, on the ground that *their sons would be placed at a great disadvantage*'.[36] A modest advance to thirteen was obtained in the following year. As late as August 1880 the Home Office supported a measure, written by the repealers' Personal Rights Association, to close a loophole that permitted girls under thirteen to offer consent to indecent assault, a violation lesser than carnal knowledge or rape.[37] There was no discussion about raising the age of consent.

It took a great public scandal before the Lords' committee ventured to ask for sixteen as the age. Not only was the creation of a statutory offence unpopular with gentlemen who wanted to protect their dissolute sons; experts feared widespread entrapment and blackmail by sexually precocious girls. This was the position of Lawson Tait, a well-known Midlands gynaecologist who strenuously resisted any change in the law. After the passage of the Criminal Law Amendment Act in 1885 he was retained by the city of Birmingham to examine alleged rape victims and advise the police on prosecutions. In six years he recommended legal action in only six of a hundred instances and claimed to have uncovered twenty-six cases of poor girls from overcrowded conditions whose imagination or greed led them to fabricate charges. Tait was a misogynist who specialised in performing ovariotomies without using antiseptics. It is worth noting, though, that Albert Moll, the pioneering German sexologist, later wrote that the danger of false accusations by young girls in his country was 'one of the gravest of our present penal system'.[38]

The radical recommendation may be understood as a reflection both of the growing sensitivity to the condition of children and of the rediscovery of poverty. It just anticipated the belated foundation of the Society for the Prevention of Cruelty to Children in 1884 and such revelations of slum conditions as Andrew Mearns's *Bitter Cry of Outcast London*. Mearns, a leading London Congregationalist and soon a founding member of the National Vigilance Association's Council, uncovered 'a vast mass of moral corruption' and made the startling statement that 'incest is common'.[39] When the Royal Commission on Housing began its enquiries in 1884 it devoted considerable attention to the relationship between overcrowding and immorality. Lord Shaftesbury, who sat on the second half of the Lords' white-slavery enquiry as well as on the housing investigation, told the latter about children of ten and eleven engaging in sexual intercourse in back alleys. Horsley had long been interested in housing reform as a cure for vice and Ellice Hopkins was already lecturing widely to working-class mothers on how to avoid incest and immorality in crowded quarters. Interest in raising the age of consent came as much from a desire to civilise the poor and protect them from themselves as from the devils of the West End.

In May 1883 Lord Rosebery introduced a government bill modelled largely on the Lords' recommendations. It passed the upper chamber then and in the following two years but made no further progress on each occasion. The age of consent clause held it up. So too did confusion in the social-purity camp. The new abolitionists, ascendant in 1883, wanted to use any available parliamentary time to repeal the CD Acts outright. There was also controversy in and out of social-purity circles about the extended police powers, for these bills gave the police the sole right to search and close brothels. The Lords had recommended that street soliciting itself should be made illegal. Harcourt, the Home Secretary, would not go quite that far; however, he had the solicitation clauses modelled after the stringent local Act for Glasgow, where it was illegal to loiter or to importune in the streets.

Lord Hartington, the War Secretary, discussed the government's intention and his own reservations in a letter to Rosebery in 1883 : 'If you can carry this Bill, you will provide . . . a complete answer to those who regret the abandonment of the compulsory clauses of the CD Acts, on account of their effects on morality and public order . . . but [the clauses] would give the power to a fanatical local authority to suppress prostitution altogether, either in houses or in the streets, and as it is impossible to suppress the thing itself, it will probably assume some other objectionable form.' James Stuart expressed the dominant opinion of the repealers when he wrote of the 1884 instalment, 'There is too much of the police in it—I mean of absolute police action as apart from and not initiated by citizen action. We want to repress prostitution and I am convinced that cannot be done by the police, but by the action of citizens calling in the aid of the police. The moment you leave the function of repression in the hands of the police, from that moment you fail in the end you aim at, and there arises a modified system of surveillance, regulation and toleration'.[40]

Vigilance work had become the alternative to police tyranny rather than police anarchy. The social-purity forces set to work to get an amended version of the bill and to organise the voluntary agencies to enforce it. The Brussels scandal had activated the highly emotive issues of white slavery and the age of consent. The climate of opinion in late 1881 is revealed by Lord Shaftesbury's observation that white slavery was 'more horribly cruel and detestable than anything in the history of the world'.[41] The subject evoked this kind of surpassing hyperbole from one of the most experienced men of the century. With outrage the governing emotion, the campaign to protect innocents could not be kept separate from the urge to punish vice. Even the libertarian James Stuart talked of repressing prostitution in one way or another. In such a context, rescue and purity committees sprang up all over the country. Many of the new activists had little interest in the CD Acts, like Shaftesbury himself. When the 'Maiden Tribute' bombshell hit in 1885, it did not fall on virgin ground. The expanded social-purity movement was available to create turmoil.

# 5

# The Building of Social Purity:
# From Ellice Hopkins to the
# National Vigilance Association

MORE than any other individual, Ellice Hopkins provided impetus and direction for the new interest in sexual politics. She was central in forging an interdenominational social-purity movement that raised the cry about 'The Maiden Tribute' and remained influential long afterwards. In 1882 Frank Crossley, the bountiful Manchester manufacturer of gas engines who was known as the paymaster general of the Salvation Army, gave Ellice £2,000 to promote the Criminal Law Amendment Bill. She stepped up her own seven-year progress through the country and hired a secretary to help with parliamentary petitions. In the process of promoting the bill she left behind a legacy of over two hundred rescue homes and asylums of all kinds as well as a score of vigilance committees.

Like Florence Nightingale and Josephine Butler she left her sphere and came to be plagued by neurasthenic complaints, in her case insomnia, headaches and sciatica. Unfortunately she enjoyed neither the compensatory public acclaim of the first lady nor the charismatic status with her acolytes of the second. She was so reviled in society that 'the very name of Ellice Hopkins, if anyone dared mention it in a drawing-room, was spoken in a whisper and heard with a shudder'. She once told a friend, a bishop's wife whose child she had sent a birthday poem, 'You didn't know that Nature made me a singing bird, but Grace has made me a sewer-rat!'[1] After a decade's frenetic activity she let go. By 1888 she retired to Brighton to spend her last years in chronic semi-invalidism. Her death in 1904 was largely unnoticed outside rescue and church circles and her memory was lost to posterity. Yet she is one of the most interesting of forgotten Victorians.

Her work was memorable for those who knew her. Bishop

Lightfoot of Durham, who shared with her the founding of the White Cross Movement, said she did 'the work of ten men in ten years—she is the ablest woman I have ever met'. Lightfoot did not meet many. He was an ascetic from the cloistered Cambridge Professorship of Divinity. There is much evidence, however, of her particular strength, a rhetorical ability to move audiences of all kinds. Eliha Burritt, a knowledgeable working-class observer, testified to this:

> We have listened to the most eminent revivalist preachers in America, and to many of the most impressive ministers in this country; but we never heard an address more calculated to meet an audience of common men than hers; and we never saw an audience more deeply moved. In diction and argument it was beautiful and powerful; but in fervour and pathos it was unbelievable.[2]

Ellice was born in 1836 and was the daughter of a prominent Cambridge mathematics tutor. She said they were inseparable, and that 'he made it possible for her to realise the Divine Fatherhood of God'. His impact may also have made it impossible for her to marry, something about which she later expressed regret. The mousy appearance evident in a surviving photograph did not help. Her spellbinding command at the speaker's podium owed nothing to the kind of sexual appeal that radiated from Josephine Butler, who had such an impact on John Addington Symonds that he recorded 'his sexual equipment swelled'. Yet Ellice was a woman of great passion and faith. In 1860 she hit upon an exciting if unconventional outlet for her energies. She decided to begin a mission for working men and prepared by conversing at length with a carpenter, reading Bunyan and studying the great C. H. Spurgeon's oratorical style. Soon her specially built hall in Barnwell, near Cambridge, was attracting hundreds of navvies and costermongers from up to a dozen miles away. This stage of her life ended in 1866 with her father's death. She suffered a breakdown and moved to Brighton to recuperate.

Ellice seems to have preferred work with men. Rescuing prostitutes was a psychological strain and she once wrote that it was only with God's help that she overcame the revulsion it caused. Her decade of activity was a memorial to James Hinton, a revered male friend who sympathised so with the plight of prostitutes and all women that he is said to have died of a broken heart in 1875. Before Ellice came under his spell in 1872, however, she was already an accomplished rescue worker. During the early stages of her seaside convalescence she worked at Mrs Vicars' Albion Hill Home, run on the 'Christian family environment' principle. While on the south coast Ellice also met Sarah Robinson, the 'soldiers' friend', and read her private journals on the agonies of brothel visiting. This encouraged her to form in Brighton a 'Ladies' Association for the Care of the Lost' whose members undertook to spend at least two hours a week visiting prostitutes in their rooms.

Sarah Robinson and Ellice Hopkins were soulmates: sublimated and suffering evangelical spinsters who were driven to do good in unorthodox ways. As a teenager in the 1850s Sarah had undergone a religious conversion and been told by a doctor she could never marry because of a spinal curvature. She burnt her volume of Byron and solaced herself with the thought that 'the unmarried woman careth for the things of the Lord'.[3] An unruly child who had loved soldiers and war games, she went to work in a mission at the Aldershot garrison in the early 1860s. Soon she was involved in the kind of brothel visits described earlier. But her real *métier* was work with soldiers, which she saw as complementary to Josephine Butler's campaign. By the time Ellice came south she was touring British garrisons and lecturing on temperance, purity and the gospel; nothing could stop her and later she took to an invalid's coach and travelled thousands of miles lying face downwards. In 1872 the two women founded a Soldier's Institute in Portsmouth; this was the very time Ellice met James Hinton, whose influence led her back to rescue work.

Few people could claim to have exerted a powerful influence on individuals as different as Ellice Hopkins, the purity worker, and Havelock Ellis, the pioneering sexologist and libertarian. Yet James Hinton's language was just obscure and ambiguous enough to make it possible for Ellice to ignore the radical implications of his work. She wrote his biography without mentioning what made him notorious to his contemporaries, his advocacy of free love. Hinton was the foremost ear specialist and one of the outstanding eccentrics of his time. Two ideas emerge from his vast pile of unpublished and largely unfathomable manuscripts. He offered the age's most devastating account of the relationship between prostitution and the family: 'We devote some women recklessly to perdition to make a hothouse Heaven for the rest. ... One wears herself out in vainly trying to endure pleasures she is not strong enough to enjoy, while other women are perishing for lack of these very pleasures. ... Prostitution for man, restraint for women—they are two sides of the same thing and both are denials of love like luxury and asceticism.'

Hinton also wrote that the problem of prostitution could only be solved by the rehabilitation of sexuality, especially female sexuality. Men had to overcome selfishness and concentrate on their partner's pleasure. Hinton practised what he preached and once told his wife that 'Christ was the Saviour of Men; but I am the Saviour of Women, and I don't envy Him a bit'. He used the old language of service, altruism and the moral mission of women to describe and justify the radical new idea of sexual mutuality: 'I am looking for women to initiate a power that shall go to the root of man's confirmed habit of putting questions about himself before questions about others. ... Let women say and mothers teach, the needs of others must be absolutely enthroned.'[4] In quite a different context Ellice Hopkins used this idea as the driving force behind the White Cross Movement.

Ellice was a devotee though probably not a lover of Hinton's. Before his death in 1875 she promised to undertake the liberation of prostitutes. Mrs Hinton and Mrs Havelock Ellis pointed out that she hardly promoted his design. On their own terms, nevertheless, her efforts were remarkable. The approach was to recruit as many Christians as possible to 'Ladies' Associations for the Care of Friendless Girls' where they could undertake any one of a variety of measures to prevent prostitution or repair the fallen. In particular she helped to point rescue work in a new direction so that it came to focus on preventive work with the female poor.

Ellice developed the basic scheme in Brighton, grading all effort into three categories: preservative, preventive and reformatory. The moral, vocational and housing needs of respectable girls were already being provided for by the Girls' Friendly Society, the Church institution founded in 1874, and the YWCA. These should be expanded, she urged. The less respectable as well as young prostitutes should be recruited to new preventive training homes where they would be housed for up to nine months, fed well on a newly contrived cut of meat, silverside, and loaned servants' clothing against their wages to encourage responsibility; they would be visited after placement. The unruliest girls would be sent to certified industrial schools or the older penitentiaries. When they were under way, Ellice wrote that her Ladies' Association 'work up the rougher material into these other societies [GFS and YWCA] and as well take up emigration, workhouse wards, educational work, petitioning, etc. In fact they are a body of educated women banded together for protecting their own womanhood from degradation.'[5]

This was no threat to the social order. Yet the scheme was promoted with a radical rhetoric that was a revelation to church ladies. She savaged the double standard. She went so far as to suggest that since prostitutes were martyrs of purity, brothels should be put next to churches. The fallen were not without sin; but she told an audience, 'What I want you to do is to break down the artificial distinction between this and all other sins, and treat [the prostitute], and act towards her, and feel towards her, as a sister, even as you would treat the drunkard as a brother'.[6]

Before the white-slave revelations the gains were slow. The Metropolitan Association for Befriending Young Servants adopted her scheme in their work with workhouse girls in 1877. Two years later Mary Steer was inspired to open her Bridge of Hope Mission in the notorious Ratcliff Highway. By 1883 Ellice recorded, 'The progress our great woman's movement has made this year is almost startling'.[7] Within another two years there were Ladies' Associations in about eighty-five towns. Who were these new rescue workers, workhouse visitors, collectors of secondhand clothes and officers in a bewildering variety of training homes, shelters, free-employment registries and prison-gate missions?

The officers in at least eleven centres were local LNA leaders. In 1876 James Stansfeld had tried to revive the spirit of the new abolitionists in the days of the unsympathetic Disraeli regime by stimulating a rescue mission. Ultimately Ellice Hopkins reaped the advantage. Most of the Butlerites who moved into rescue work continued in the CD Acts agitation. But as Josephine feared, the critical edge was sometimes blunted. In Plymouth, where Daniel Cooper's Rescue Society had helped organise an underground railway in the early 1870s to spirit girls out of the district, Ellice Hopkins' visit in 1879 split the local LNA branch. Her new Ladies' Association was assisted by none other than the despised Inspector Annis, who informed them when a girl needed help.[8]

While Ellice was against regulation, she apparently was willing to work with the devil himself to gain her ends. She broadened the social-purity movement by bringing in people who were for regulation, but mostly by attracting those who had no strong feelings about it. Most of the workers were Church-of-England ladies of this description. She also left her Associations with an ecumenical complexion. Nonconformist leaders and their wives joined and worked under the presidency of local bishops or their wives or under a masthead topped by such celebrities as Mrs Gladstone, Archbishop Benson and Mrs Benson. The Manchester branch offers an interesting case study.[9] In 1882 Miss Hopkins addressed an influential meeting of the city's business and religious leaders called by Bishop Fraser and including Frank Crossley; the celebrated Alexander Maclaren, whose Congregational chapel Crossley attended in these years; and even Bishop Vaughan of Salford, Cardinal Manning's successor a decade later. The result was the formation of a Ladies' Association under Mrs Fraser's presidency, and within a year this well-endowed institution was running a training home, lodging house, free registry and clothing club. Crossley had been so inspired by Ellice's promotional address that he also initiated a vigilance society, which, with the support of the city's religious leaders, spent years fighting prostitution. Here and elsewhere influential and interdenominational purity institutions emerged in the wake of Ellice Hopkins' tour.

All along she had been trying to reach men by telling the ladies, 'Men will rise to any standard you set for them'. This commonplace symptom of the double standard, expressed typically in Ruskin's *Sesamie and Lillies*, was criticised by Josephine Butler as male hypocrisy. Ultimately Ellice decided that this indirect approach and rescue work were not the complete solution. In 1879 she told a conference of the Church Penitentiary Association that a kind of brotherhood for the protection of women and children was needed to give men 'a more aggressive form of purity, something higher and more vivifying than taking care of their own virtue, that manly, militant virtue which grows strong in fighting the battle of God for the weak and defenceless'. Here were Hinton's ideas emasculated, but the suggestion ultimately bore fruit.

We can trace the submission of her paper to the Lower House of Canterbury Convocation in 1879, her struggle to get the double standard discussed at Church Congress and her striking criticism of male sexual misconduct at the Derby Church Congress of 1882. This marked a revolution in sentiment since George Butler had been howled down ten years earlier in the same forum. At Derby a committee was formed to organise a central church society to promote purity; and in the following year at Lambeth Palace the Church of England Purity Society (CEPS) was established under the active presidency of Archbishop Benson.[10] Appropriately the founding motion was offered by Montagu Butler, George's brother, soon to be Master of Trinity College, Cambridge, and Chairman of the CEPS. But its founders agreed not to discuss state regulation: the secretary was a lieutenant colonel in the Royal Marine Artillery and the chief financial supporter was a rear admiral. With the White Cross League initiated in the same year and diocesan conferences all over the country discussing the sex question, Ellice predicted in her movement's journal at the beginning of 1884 that 'The corner has been turned'.

The function of the two chastity leagues, which merged in 1891, was to broadcast the good news that purity was possible and to help build defences against sexual incontinence. As early exponents of what may loosely be termed sex education, their activities will be considered in the next chapter. A brief look here at their beginnings gives some idea of the dimensions of social purity in the early 1880s.

The CEPS organised in diocesan branches and for a five-shilling subscription membership was open to men over the age of eighteen interested in promoting its objects: 'Purity amongst men, A chivalrous respect for womanhood, Preservation of the young from contamination, Rescue work, and a higher tone of public opinion'. While men unable to afford the subscription might share in the movement through membership of parochial and other clubs affiliated to the central society, the implication of the steep subscription was clear. Scott Holland later explained that the founders 'expected that the rich would take up the movement for Purity as the poor had taken up Temperance'. This expectation was not to be fulfilled and after a decade the CEPS admitted that 'its influence had been felt less by the wealthier than by the poorer classes'.[11]

Yet social purity compensated partially for its failure to impress its relevance on the rich by attracting a portion of the young elite and many of the Church's most influential and illustrious figures. By 1885 the Cambridge chapter of the CEPS had some five hundred members under the presidency of B. F. Westcott, who followed Lightfoot as both Regius Professor of Divinity and later Bishop of Durham; two years later about eight hundred were enrolled in the Oxford branch, from undergraduates to such celebrities as Scott Holland, Charles Gore and E. S. Talbot, Warden of Keble. These three were leaders of the Lux Mundi group and, with Westcott, of the Christian Social Union. Despite the opposition of Benjamin Jowett, the famous Master of Balliol, Josephine Butler paved the way at Oxford when she canvassed support in 1882, the same year that Dwight Moody ran a successful mission there. Talbot then asked her, 'But do you really think that the sin is equal in men and women?' She is reported to have converted him as well as Scott Holland to the cause. As vicar of Leeds, Talbot later helped clean up that city and while bishop successively of Rochester, Southwark and Winchester he was an active leader of the international movement against white slavery.[12]

Naturally Archbishop Benson, who completed the interesting triumvirate of lifelong friends that included Westcott and Lightfoot, was the key figure in spreading social purity in the Church. Benson spoke of purity in his 1883 enthronement sermon and never lost interest in the topic. It is reported that Benson first proposed to his wife, who was the sister of the philosopher Henry Sidgwick, when she was younger than Stead's victim, Eliza Armstrong. His Minnie seems to have been an alert young girl: 'Edward, I shan't look so little compared with you, shall I, when I'm twenty, and you're thirty-two, as I do now that I'm eleven and you're twenty-three'.[13]

While such idiosyncrasies might lie behind an interest in purity, the striking feature is that many of the Church dignitaries who led in social purity led also in the advocacy of social reform and the winning of the poor to Christianity. The Christian Social Union, whose 'sympathy and fair support' for social purity was secured by Scott Holland, is but the most outstanding of many examples.[14] Bishop Fraser, introduced above, was beloved by the Manchester working classes. Bishop Mandell Creighton of London, whom we shall encounter later as the founder of the Public Morality Council, was a progressive friend of socialists like the Webbs. Before devoting himself to the Public Morality Council, Bishop Winnington Ingram, Creighton's successor, headed Oxford House, the settlement house opened in Bethnal Green by Talbot's Keble College. Bishop How of Bedford, in effect bishop of the East End from 1879 to 1888, played a leading role in a whole cluster of purity institutions. To add one further dimension to the network of relationships in this hitherto unexplored movement, the wives of How, Creighton, Fraser and of many other figures amongst the bishops and lesser clergy presided over Ellice Hopkins' rescue committees or worked at some other aspect of purity.

The same dual advocacy of social reform and social purity characterised a number of leaders in other denominations, from Cardinal Manning to Hugh Price Hughes. Why did the issues coincide? Sexual abstinence was a personal strategy for improvement in the same way as temperance was. Each implied discipline, thrift and social mobility. Little wonder that Manning, Westcott, How and most of the nonconformist purity divines were also temperance advocates. Then too, after the white-slavery revelations, chastity for the rich took on the aspect of social restitution. As Bishop-designate Temple of London noted in 1885, 'Was it conceivable that any cruelty could be greater than that which the sensual passion of one class has inflicted on the other?'

While the CEPS aimed for the rich the White Cross directed its appeal to the masses and Ellice Hopkins left her stamp even more directly on this venture. In February 1883, two months before the CEPS was established, Bishop Lightfoot invited her to the mining village of Bishop Auckland in Durham.[15] Ellice had already been addressing large working-men's gatherings but this was to mark a new departure. Beforehand, Ellice and Lightfoot drew up a scheme for an association to be launched that evening. After her address the men would be read five obligations for membership in a White Cross Army. After five minutes of prayer, it would be hands up for purity pledge cards containing these rules:

1 To treat all women with respect, and endeavour to protect them from wrong and degradation.

2 To use every possible means to fulfil the command, 'keep THYSELF pure'.

3 To endeavour to put down all indecent language and coarse jests.

4 To maintain the law of purity as equally binding upon men and women.

5 To endeavour to spread these principles among my companions, and to try and help my younger brothers.

These were derived from the rules of a parochial rescue society founded a few months earlier in London's fashionable Eaton Square by one of those churchmen now awake to impurity, George Wilkinson, later Bishop of Truro. As an aid to sublimation, Ellice cast the pledge in the trappings of medieval chivalry, complete with St George and the dragon. After explaining how it was poor girls who usually fell victim to procuresses, she told her audience they were to be sent forth into the world 'Sir Galahads and King Arthurs by God's Grace, "made of a woman", in the image of the strong and tender manhood of Jesus Christ'. Hinton had finally ended up in King Arthur's court. This was a popular motif in Victorian literature. According to Tennyson's *Idylls of the King*:

> I knew
> Of no more subtle master under heaven
> Than is the maiden passion for a maid

Out of an audience of three hundred pitmen and clerks that first night 139 came forward for purity. The class argument and the evocation of helpless womanhood were a potent mixture. Now Ellice's progress left behind White Cross branches as well as Ladies' Associations. In Glasgow she addressed 3,000 men and initiated a major branch; in Edinburgh she conquered a shouting, crowing and whistling audience of medical students and left behind a university branch of some eight hundred members. In Dublin she mounted the platform in a state of near collapse, supported by the Archbishop. He later described how 'Her whole physical nature was trembling with fear . . . she came . . . to plead on behalf of her common womankind, and her tender, pathetic, and touching words went like winged arrows into the hearts of those who heard'. The aroused formed a Dublin White Cross Vigilance Society which soon fielded a midnight patrol of two-dozen young men who kept customers away from the city's brothels by accosting them in the dark with identifying lanterns.[16]

The White Cross Movement had little central direction and no church affiliation. Many of the 15,000 men who had taken the pledge by 1885 were nonconformists. While social purity made its first inroads amongst the Anglicans in these years, it was already evoking the full force of the nonconformist conscience. In February 1883, in preparation for the parliamentary assault on the CD Acts, the Quakers hosted a conference attended by virtually all the great chapel leaders of the day. With Ellice Hopkins barnstorming the country, it was not long before the nonconformists organised their own panel of purity lecturers. By 1883 Hugh Price Hughes was addressing large audiences on the straightforward theological topic of 'Immorality versus Christianity'. At the same time there began a public assault on sexual incontinence, unprecedented in its frankness and ferocity, in which medical arguments were introduced to support religious ones. The full dimensions of this thirty-year phenomenon are traced in the next chapter. But its origins lie in the climate of guilt and aggression that followed the Belgian white-slavery revelations.

Tens of thousands of men had been subjected to these purity lectures by the omnipresent Alfred Dyer and others when in 1884 George Gillet, Robert Morgan and Robert Scott launched the Gospel Purity Association. Morgan and Scott were co-editors of *The Christian*, telegraphic code 'Millenium', and old allies of Josephine Butler. This new group used a team of lecturers to distribute pledge cards identical to those of the White Cross Movement and to work up petitions for the Criminal Law Amendment Bill.

Amongst its speakers was Charles James, the 'Young Knight of purity', whose 'Fallen Men' is reported to have reduced an audience of Portsmouth sailors to tears; and James Wookey, whose powerful combination of class rhetoric along with the stock religious and medical arguments for purity, was heard by scores of thousands. His threat that 'God would make an inquisition for the blood of every poor girl who had perished in the streets' elicited a hundred and twenty signed pledges at the Birmingham YMCA. Wookey later became an alcoholic and went to dry out on Frederick Charrington's beautiful 'Osea Island', a teetotal resort and sanatorium off the Essex coast. But he played an energetic role in the campaign following Stead's 'Maiden Tribute' revelations of 1885 and the Gospel Purity Association alone held about three hundred and fifty meetings, many with audiences in the thousands, through 1885.[17]

Wookey apart, sexual vice was coming to rival intemperance for the attentions of churchmen, nonconformists and inner-city missionaries. In 1885 Bishop Temple of London said social purity would succeed temperance. While his prediction was not to be fully confirmed, there was considerable cooperation between the two movements and sometimes the issues were completely intertwined, as with the attack on the music halls, which promoted drink as well as prostitution and indecent entertainment, and with the campaigns against pub-based prostitution in Liverpool, Portsmouth and elsewhere.

Frederick Charrington, who played an important role in the events of 1885, was an inner-city missionary who joined purity with temperance. A description of his little puritan empire in the East End completes our survey of the purity network before 'The Maiden Tribute'. Born heir to the Charrington brewery fortune, he renounced everything after a religious conversion, took up residence in a sparsely furnished house in Stepney Lane which was known as 'The Monastery', and founded the Tower Hamlets Mission. Beginning in a tent in 1876, the mission was showered with gifts by the leading evangelical philanthropists of the day. By 1886 Charrington opened his Great Assembly Hall—with 5,000 seats the largest prayer hall in Europe. Understandably his primary opponent was drink and he derived great satisfaction from bringing in water for adult baptism in beer barrels. But by 1880 he began his first efforts for purity. The objects of his attention were the music halls, particularly the largest in the East End, Lusby's, which stood just a hundred yards from his mission and around the corner from Cleveland Street and its brothels.

Men like Charrington had long opposed the mixture of light-hearted entertainment and alcoholic refreshment in the halls. When he learned that Lusby's was being used by prostitutes for assignations it was too much to bear and so he began a five-year struggle with the proprietors. Failing to get their licence revoked, he took to distributing leaflets at the doors each night. For his trouble he and his helpers were repeatedly beaten, pelted with flour and excrement and finally legally restrained from describing the entertainment as obscene.[18] Foiled here, Charrington carried the battle of the music-halls to the West End and in his own neighbourhood closed scores of brothels. For militant missioners like him, sexual vice had become something to fight about; the equally militant Salvation Army was now beginning to deploy its formidable forces in the same struggle.

\* \* \*

In 1885 the frustrated builders of the new Jerusalem shattered public tranquillity with revelations of 'The Maiden Tribute of Modern Babylon'. It got them the Criminal Law Amendment Act and in the form they wanted; in other words it left room for private enforcement. Providentially, Stead's legal martyrdom after the passage of the Act enabled them to redouble their agitation and blanket the country with vigilance committees.

The events of early 1885 dramatically demonstrated to the reformers that officialdom was impervious to their designs. The London Committee for Suppressing the Traffic in British Girls, formed to expedite the Brussels investigations, came into possession of information which they thought would be 'the greatest blow that had ever been struck within living memory at corruption in high places'.[19] Certainly the scandal of Mrs Jeffries' string of high-class Chelsea brothels would be enough to get them the long-delayed legislation to protect girls. Their investigations turned up former servants who claimed that thirteen-year-old girls were raped in Mrs Jeffries' houses, which had been in business for twenty years across the road from a police station. It was rumoured that her clientele included the Prince of Wales and the King of Belgium. Not surprisingly, the Chelsea vestry backed off from touching the case. The London Committee found two ratepayers to prosecute and in April the case proceeded under the direction of the legal firm headed by William Shaen, a supporter of Josephine Butler and soon one of the driving forces behind the National Vigilance Association.

Before any evidence could be produced, the defence pulled off what must have been a pre-arranged coup. Mrs Jeffries pleaded guilty to keeping a brothel, had her £200 fine paid by a wealthy friend and drove off in a brougham supplied by an earl. Dyer wrote in his *Sentinel*, 'The inferences from the evidence ... point to a state of moral corruption, heartless cruelty and prostitution of authority almost sufficient ... to goad the industrial classes into revolution'. But it would take more than this travesty to galvanise the public. When James Wookey revealed Mrs Jeffries' clientele to an outraged Gospel Purity meeting a few days later, all he acomplished was to have *The Sentinel*, which covered the meeting, banned from W. H. Smith's. The protest about the cover-up fell as flat as the trial itself and the bill remained without momentum.

The latest instalment of the Criminal Law Amendment Bill had just passed the Lords with the age of consent lowered to fifteen, a development which compelled Ellice Hopkins to write to Lambeth Palace that the measure was 'completely crippled' and to enclose a collection of horrific newspaper cuttings describing some recent cases.[20] In Hull a procurer kept fifteen young prostitutes between the ages of twelve and fifteen in a so-called 'infant school' and the police could only free them by prosecuting him for selling intoxicating liquor without a licence. The Archbishop pressed Harcourt, the Home Secretary, to push at least the diluted measure through the Commons. Cardinal Manning had already informed him of dockland decoy houses where Irish and European girls were entrapped; one was run by a Frenchwoman locally known as 'the devil'. The 1884 measure had fallen victim to the Reform Bill's voracious appetite for parliamentary time and something similar happened again. With Gladstone's cabinet falling apart over Ireland, the subject was far from the Prime Minister's mind. On 22 May a thin House anxious to rise for Whitsun failed to proceed with it and James Stuart claimed the government had chosen a time when delay was assured.

The very next morning Benjamin Scott, City Chamberlain

and chairman of the London Committee, visited W. T. Stead in his offices at the *Pall Mall Gazette* to recruit him to assault public sensibilities and break the deadlock. Stead was a great power in the newspaper world and a pioneer in the kind of committed reporting and innovative layouts that Matthew Arnold disdainfully called 'the new journalism'. The son of a Congregationalist minister, he once said Cromwell had influenced him more than Christ. From the confines of the *Darlington Echo* in 1876 he had managed to seize the journalistic lead in the national agitation against the Turkish slaughter of the Bulgarians. At the time he had made the memorable statement that 'the honour of Bulgarian virgins is in the custody of the English voter'.[21] Scott knew he would do no less for English virgins.

Salvationist historians proudly assert that it was Bramwell Booth, son of General Booth, who recruited Stead. It hardly matters. The Salvation Army played a crucial role in the subsequent four-week investigation and in the national agitation following the publication of 'The Maiden Tribute'. The Army had eased into rescue work in 1883 against the General's wishes and its involvement with Stead was in the face of Booth's fears that his enterprise would be ruined. With Salvationists being assaulted and jailed all over the country he had good reason for prudence. When their first small rescue home was opened in Whitechapel, Catherine Booth, the General's wife, confronted juvenile prostitution first hand. Back in the 1860s she had abandoned midnight meetings because she noticed reformed whores were always replaced. Now the other reformers opened her eyes to the fact the bottomless well was replenished by trickery. Catherine and Bramwell overcame the General's reluctance to join Stead and the Army entered the fray with its usual enthusiasm.[22]

Stead had the blessing of Cardinal Manning as well as Archbishop Benson, though the latter gave him 'strenuous advice ...against his methods' when Stead revealed he would undertake a 'personation of vile character to obtain information'.[23] Frederick Charrington put him in touch with a former Mile End brothel-keeper who claimed he had courted country girls in the unlikely garb of a parson, brought them to town for the theatre, conveniently missed the last train and lured them to their downfall. This appeared in the first instalment of 'The Maiden Tribute.' But when Charrington's convert failed to deliver what Stead was really after—a young girl or two to enable him to write first hand they were available for a price—he made alternative arrangements through Bramwell Booth and Josephine Butler.[24]

In Winchester, where George Butler was now canon at the cathedral, Josephine had a small refuge where the Booths had sent one Rebecca Jarrett, a thirty-six-year-old regenerate prostitute who knew every facet of the trade. She was now recruited to purchase a virgin as close to her thirteenth birthday as possible on the clear understanding that the girl was destined for despoliation. Rebecca was less resourceful than everyone expected and she ended up taking Eliza Armstrong of Lisson Grove away from her mother for £5 on the apparent understanding that she was going into service. Eliza was taken to an underworld midwife who certified her *virgo intacta* for purposes of violation, as these things were arranged, and then to a low boarding house where Stead was lurking in grotesque make-up that made him appear like an old rake. He was enjoying himself and insisted on entering Eliza's bedroom to carry the charade as far as possible. Eliza was terrified and Stead retreated. After being subjected to another examination, this time so that a proper physician could certify her unharmed for their ultimate protection, Bramwell Booth sent the miserable girl off to the Salvation Army in France.

This was pathological playacting and, ironically, completely illegal. The purity reformers constantly made the point that most victims between the ages of thirteen and sixteen enjoyed no protection because they were already out on their own. It was illegal only to take a child from its parents or guardian without their consent. Later the Armstrongs were able to prove that Rebecca and Stead had done precisely the latter. William Shaen's legal advice had not saved them from a ridiculous blunder.

'The Maiden Tribute' began to unfold on 6 July and Stead's headings give some idea of why it was a sensation : 'The Violation of Virgins; Confessions of a Brothel Keeper; Strapping Girls Down; I Order Five Virgins; The International Slave Trade in Girls'. It was a prurient hash which centred on the disguised

Eliza Armstrong story. Some of the horrifying descriptions of child rape in fashionable brothels may well have reflected a shocking reality; but the accounts of international and local white slavery were exaggerated and the police had no trouble disproving his charges of complicity.[24a] There were useful disclosures about employment agencies and the recruiting of prostitutes in the needle trades; with characteristic hyperbole Stead revealed 'certain great drapery and millinery establishments' in which hundreds of thousands of girls were ruined yearly. This last abuse showed the 'responsibility of the dissolute rich for the ruin of the daughters of the poor'. Stead was a passionate radical and his enemies despised him for his class rhetoric as much as his salaciousness. The initial instalment declared 'the hour of democracy has struck' and warned that failure to act could mean revolution.[25]

By the third instalment mobs were rioting at the *PMG* offices in an attempt to obtain copies of the paper, inevitably banned at W. H. Smith's. The London dailies maintained a conspicuous silence broken only by the anti-puritanical Frank Harris's *Evening News*, which compared the series to 'a vile insect reared on the putrid garbage of the dunghill'. Hugh Price Hughes's *Methodist Times* intoned that Stead had 'done what we believe Jesus Christ Himself would have done in his place'.[26] With an election looming on the new universal household franchise the interim Tory government had to do something in response to the escalating class nature of the issue. Three days after the storm broke Richard Cross, the new Home Secretary, put the Criminal Law Amendment Bill through its second reading.

The parliamentary impasse was broken and the social-purity movement launched an agitation to get the bill it wanted, with the age of consent raised as high above fifteen years as possible and police powers altered to enable private enforcement of the brothel clauses. Ellice Hopkins had started about a score of vigilance committees but some had already failed. In 1883 a Central Vigilance Committee had emerged to fight prostitution in London. Now Stead urged the formation of 'vigilance committees in every town in the land'.[27] Archbishop Benson, the Bishop of London and even *The Times* ultimately spoke out for this approach to the enforcement of the new law. Stead predicted a national outcry that would compare with the one he had helped orchestrate over the Bulgarian atrocities. The agitation over the 'Belgravian atrocities', as the Social Democratic Federation nicely put it, was all the more remarkable because there was no Gladstone nor any other national political leader at the forefront. The London press boycott proved another obstacle, compensated for by one-and-a-half million reprints of 'The Maiden Tribute'.

The magnitude of the purity effort can perhaps be gauged from the fact that over four hundred meetings in the twelve months from July 1885 were addressed by one woman—Mrs Ormiston Chant, later to become an international celebrity when she helped lead the attack on the music halls. The new abolitionists put their institutions into top gear and there were those hundreds of Gospel Purity meetings. During two weeks that July the Salvation Army compiled a petition over two miles long with 393,000 signatures demanding that the age of consent be set at eighteen. There were similar stories from all over: a platform of notables drawn from Josephine Butler, Ellice Hopkins, General and Mrs Booth, James Stuart, James Wookey and local religious and political dignitaries; resolutions for raising the age of consent to eighteen or even twenty-one; an overflow crowd in Manchester Free Trade Hall, Sheffield Albert Hall, Leeds Town Hall and so on up and down the country.

Sometimes there were separate men's and women's meetings for intimate talk. Middle-class women predominated, though the poor came with babes in arms. 'Working men of the higher class' were evident and formed the majority of the six thousand who thronged Manchester Free Trade Hall to hear Wookey on 'The Massacre of the Innocents'. This harangue against the privileged who abused poor girls but whose own daughters were protected by footmen was one of the keynotes of the season. Wookey and others were able to point to one particularly flagrant piece of class legislation, which protected heiresses from seduction up to the age of twenty-one. When he gave this address at the Tower Hamlets Mission in July, the crowd of several thousand became ominously angry. Wookey and Charrington finally led them off to seize the possessions of three rescued prostitutes which were being detained by Victoria Park brothel-keepers.[28]

As social purity became a popular issue in radical circles,

especially through the north, the Social Democratic Federation also began seeing the possibilities. While *Justice*, its journal, insisted that only social revolution would eliminate prostitution, it speculated that the issues raised would advance class consciousness. By 18 July it was as caught up in the white-slave revelations as its readers:

> There can be no doubt . . . that the *exposé* of the crimes which are daily committed against children and young women, with impunity, in London has produced an unparalleled sensation among the workers. Men and women have recalled the constant disappearances of young and pretty girls of the working-classes in their immediate neighbourhood, throughout many parts of the metropolis and the hapless endeavours of the parents to trace them. The result is that a feeling of downright ferocity has been excited by the articles. . . . [29]

Two years earlier Josephine Butler had talked about the 'strange disappearances of so many girls at West Ham' who were spirited away to the Continent. It is hard to believe that Josephine credited these tales, though they were apparently circulating through the East End. But by 1885 they were endemic. *Justice* had nothing but contempt for the middle-class purity leaders, some of whom, like Samuel Morley, were important employers of cheap labour. However, SDF leaders including H. M. Hyndman, John Burns and H. H. Champion set up a platform to proselytise amongst the great crowds at the Hyde Park demonstration of 22 August that marked the culmination of the purity campaign and the launching of the National Vigilance Association (NVA).

Stead conceived of the NVA, wrote its statutes, made the obscure but capable William Coote its secretary and in the early days paid his salary. After canvassing support for a fresh institution to coordinate and promote the nation's vigilance work, one of the *PMG*'s sub-editors suggested a great rally to give it a popular start. Coote, then a compositor on *The Standard* and a minor official in the Working Men's League, caught Stead's attention when he was appointed grand marshal of the demonstration by Charrington's organising committee and proceeded to do most of the work. Coote's great display followed the day after a long and prestigious conference at St James's Hall to found the NVA. By this time a storm was raging around Stead. The true story of Eliza Armstrong was out and her mother was demanding her back from the Salvation Army. Some of Stead's supporters were backing away, feeling like Bishop Lightfoot that it was 'indeed sad that Mr Stead should spoil an especially good cause by such inconceivably bad taste and lack of judgment'.[30] General Booth was feeling vulnerable and the Salvation Army stayed away from Hyde Park. Yet the demonstration was the largest since the celebrated affair of the torn railings over the Reform Bill in 1866.

Estimates ranged up to 250,000, though the sponsors claimed half that many. While there was always controversy over the estimated size of Victorian crowds, this was certainly the most unusual spectacle of the period. With white roses for purity; with banners proclaiming 'Protection of Young Girls; Men, Protect the Girls of England; Women of London to the Struggle; War on Vice; Sir, Pity Us; Shame, Shame, Horror'; with tambourines, drums and fifes, ten columns set out for the park. They were made up largely of delegations from temperance societies, working-men's clubs, YMCAs and purity groups. There were wagonloads of young virgins in white flying the pathetic oriflamme, 'The Innocents, Will They Be Slaughtered?'. The six hundred-strong delegation from the LNA wore black. Then there was the hero, described by a bemused French observer 'perched on a wagon, proceeding as a conqueror' to shouts of 'Long live Stead'.

In the park the crowd gathered around a dozen platforms, each supporting a group of celebrated speakers, including Michael Davitt, the Irish socialist; Dr Barnardo; Henry Broadhurst, the trade-union leader; Dr Clifford, the Baptist divine; and our familiar nonconformist leaders and Gospel Purity orators. At 6.30 a bugle was sounded and the resolutions were simultaneously put expressing the shame of Londoners at vice, and pledging them to enforce the new law. According to our French witness, 'Then, suddenly, seized by a religious fit, the adepts, grouped around the orator or perched on the same vehicle, intoned a hymn or an anthem on national purity ... to the role of the tambourines, the beating of the drum and the tune of the fifes, everyone was shaking, gesticulating and seemed

suddenly taken up in a St Vitus dance'.[31] Hawkers had a field
day selling the pornographic magazine, *The Devil*. Coote had
his work cut out for him.

*        *        *

The Criminal Law Amendment Act was a symbolic and substantial triumph for feminists and puritans. They looked to the
events of the year as a turning point in the history of morals and
as an example of how women might cleanse society. Millicent
Fawcett, the suffragist leader whom Stead drew into the agitation, wrote to him, 'A gigantic step has been made through you
in the direction of purity and goodness'. On the day of the royal
assent, 14 August, Josephine Butler rose to a millenarian mood
at a rally : 'And now my dream has come true ! The storming
has begun, the walls are trembling and wherever they fall the full
Salvation will be proclaimed aloud to "the spirits now in prison"
and the earth will give up her dead.'[32] A lot more spirits would
be put in prison by this legislation. Considering the storm out-of-
doors, however, the new law was by no means as repressive as
it might have been. The purity party obtained a great deal,
though not everything it wanted to repress the despoilers of
females. As for the suppression of prostitution, most social-purity
leaders were satisfied that parliament was unwilling to provide
the police with the kinds of weapons against streetwalkers and
brothels that had been offered by Harcourt and the Liberals.

The age of consent was raised to sixteen. Since this is once
again an issue it is worth looking at the Home Secretary's reason
for throwing his weight behind that age. Cross stated that 'Below
that age very few marriages took place, and, they might, therefore, assume that girls under that age were looked upon as im-
mature, and as having not arrived at the age of puberty. These
were the girls they desired to protect in the bill'.[33] In 1884 there
had been 100 marriages recorded of girls between sixteen and
seventeen but only thirty-seven of girls between fourteen and
fifteen. James Stuart struggled with little support for the age
that social-purity leaders were to press on governments until the
1940s, eighteen. Those who felt sixteen was unrealistically high
provided offenders with a major loophole. It was made a defence
for the accused to prove he had 'reasonable cause to believe' a

girl was sixteen. It took thirty-seven years for feminists and purity workers to get this hated defence partly circumscribed. Benjamin Waugh of the new Society for the Prevention of Cruelty to Children obtained a crucial clause making the consent law fully operational: evidence of the young was made admissible even if they did not understand the nature of an oath. The clauses on procuring were thorough, with all women protected against being procured to become a common prostitute or to go into a foreign brothel or to have intercourse after being drugged. Some other modes of protection were denied those already prostitutes.

Despite this discrimination, prostitutes did not emerge as badly as they might have. The Tory government dropped the controversial clauses that would have enabled arrests for loitering or importuning. Reacting to opinion against street prostitution in 1883, the London police and magistrates had already launched a clean-up based on a stricter interpretation of the annoyance rule. This was the beginning of a cycle of repression and toleration in the capital that, in the absence of a new law, kept in phase with public opinion. After nearly a century of lobbying, an important summary procedure against brothel-keepers emerged and the purity party managed to get it extended to landlords who knowingly permitted their premises to be so used. These would be very important weapons for the vigilance committees.

Early in the morning of 6 August Henry Labouchere, the crusading editor of *Truth*, perfunctorily obtained his celebrated amendment outlawing on pain of two years' hard labour acts of gross indecency in private as well as public between males. His later attempts to get to the bottom of the notorious Cleveland Street scandal, involving homosexual brothels and the royal family, indicate a long-term interest in the subject, though it has been suggested that his intention in 1885 was to make homosexual assaults, rather than homosexual acts, criminal, or even to wreck the bill with extravagant amendments.[34] In any case, long before Oscar Wilde fell victim to this law, the NVA and the police were enforcing it to the full. Even more than prostitutes or child rapists, whom parliament voted against flogging, homosexuals were to suffer agony from the moral panic.

In the short run Stead happily went off to a six-month

martyrdom in Holloway prison. Following public protests, Lord Salisbury, the Prime Minister, used the royal prerogative to reduce his conditions of incarceration to those of a misdemeanant. He then had enough light to read his bible and Millicent Fawcett was able to send him her late husband's dressing-gown. In the December general election, Alfred Dyer went up to Derby to run against William Harcourt, resented for his record of delay at the Home Office. Dyer and Henry Varley, whom we shall meet as the pioneer of the religio-medical purity lecture, were stoned and beaten, though Dyer collected 1,251 votes. Taking the returns as a whole, 257 candidates pledged to the final repeal of the CD Acts were elected, compared to 169 in 1880.[35] This rough index shows that social purity was of some importance in the election. Its leaders even talked of forming a party. While this idea quickly passed, the heady victories of 1885 and 1886, when final repeal was accomplished, moved purity spokesmen to demand a higher standard of private behaviour from their political leaders. Soon when Sir Charles Dilke, the radical politician, and Charles Parnell, the Irish Nationalist leader, became implicated in divorce scandals, Stead helped hound the first from the Liberal Front benches while Hughes was instrumental in destroying the second.

The 1885 agitation left behind an important institutional legacy. In August General Booth announced an ambitious 'New National Scheme for the Deliverance of Unprotected Girls and the Rescue of the Fallen'. This project put the Salvation Army in the vanguard of rescue work and where it led, the Church Army followed. So-called preventive work burgeoned as well. In 1885 the Travellers' Aid Society began its railway station work under the auspices of the YWCA, an institution which had been helping provincial girls in London since it was founded to shelter nurses on the way to the Crimean War. It was apparently the dying Shaftesbury's last philanthropic act to throw his influence behind the founders of Travellers' Aid, who included Lady Frances Balfour, Arthur Balfour's sister and one of Millicent Fawcett's suffragist allies. Their promotional letter indicates how the old fears of the city and perhaps of independence were being vocalised and politicised by feminists and lady workers. It called for :

An agency in union with all [agencies for girls] to meet the country girl at the threshold of our wicked city and hand her over to one or other of the befriending societies—not allowing her to be entrapped within sight of a haven. We know girls are giddy and self-willed—we know they will come to London—we know they can be and easily are led by kind words—we know that deep plots are laid for their destruction—made by a 'flattering tongue'. God helping us they shall not be unwarned and unaided.[36]

With working men pleading for the protection of their sisters, chapelgoers thrashing themselves for the sins of their fathers and ladies up in arms over the double standard, Stead and Coote expected vigilance committees to spring up in every town. Stead's indictment for the abduction of Eliza Armstrong kept the promoters on the front pages. While Stead was out on bail in October he embarked on a two-thousand-mile tour with Coote, Hugh Price Hughes and Benjamin Waugh to raise a defence fund and establish NVA chapters. Stead was received as a conquering hero, with crowds in Manchester so large that Frank Crossley could not get near the Free Trade Hall. While the elation soon died down, the number of local committees paying their one guinea annual affiliation fee in 1888 was 300.[37] A number of these groups, as in Dublin and York where the archbishops were active, grew out of Ellice Hopkins' movement. There was a substantial influx of new abolitionists as their crusade wound down. More important than the ten LNA branch secretaries and many other notables who came over was the adherence of the resourceful South-West Counties Union and the Midlands Counties Union For Repeal. These became NVA regional centres.

Josephine Butler's name appears among the list of 127 persons on the first Council. She played no part in the NVA, however, and with the more libertarian of her entourage grew estranged as it inevitably became more repressive. In 1891 she wrote to a colleague, 'Coote is most *unsound* . . . [at least] Bunting . . . is *over* him in the Vigilance Association. . . . Coote loves coercion'.[38] Percy Bunting was chairman of the executive; grandson of the legendary preacher, Jabez Bunting, and editor of the *Contemporary Review*, he was one of the most powerful Method-

E

ists in the country. Before his death in 1911 he rarely disagreed with his secretary, whom Josephine had good cause to distrust. All that Coote's thirty-four years with the NVA had taught him was that the buying and selling of sex should be subject to criminal penalties. This was a single standard, but one of coercion.

On matters of art Josephine Butler and Coote had less dis-agreement. Josephine was opposed to all nudity as degrading and Coote held that the *tableaux vivants*, the popular music-hall poses struck by women in flesh tights, were 'the ideal form of indecency'. When the social-purity camp launched its attack on these, Bernard Shaw responded:

> Mr Coote is a person of real importance . . . backed by an association strong enough to enable him to bring his convic-tions to bear efficiently over our licensing authority. . . . [But he is] in artistic matters a most intensely stupid man and on sexual questions something of a monomaniac.[39]

This observation did not quite reach the pitch Shaw managed against Anthony Comstock over the censoring of *Mrs Warren's Profession*. Shaw gave us 'comstockery' rather than 'cootery'. In fact Coote did not manifest the uniform vindictiveness of his American contemporary. Unlike American social purity, where there was more of a functional division between the anti-vice societies and those for preventive work, the NVA did both. This probably softened Coote's attitudes.

He grew up near the Strand, close to where the NVA opened its offices. He once wrote a short and pathetic autobiographical account of the effect his father's death had on the family in 1845, when Coote was three.[40] They were literally forced to cross the tracks, to the poor side of the Strand, and Coote became a compositor instead of going to Trinity College, Dublin. At sixteen, after being handed a religious tract in the streets and persuaded to go home and pray, he had the kind of profound conversion experienced by so many of his colleagues in purity work. While his writings always betrayed his meagre education, there is no question about his ability. During his leadership of the international movement against white slavery in the new century he made a profound impression on heads of state on three continents and was decorated by Germany, France and Spain for his energetic efforts.

In the early days Coote had more to worry about than the opposition of Josephine Butler and Bernard Shaw. Money was always a problem, though the NVA was kept in the black through the largesse of evangelical philanthropists like Samuel Morley, Frank Crossley, J. P. Thomasson of Bolton, Francis Peek of London and the Corys of Cardiff. Many of the local committees collapsed or demonstrated incompetence. After the euphoria of the founding months there was a reluctance to get involved in the rather nasty day-to-day work. In 1893, when one of Coote's organising secretaries held up as a model Benjamin Waugh's Society, Mrs Sheldon Amos, an old Butlerite, replied, 'People who were anxious to be placed on Waugh's committee would probably shrink from becoming members of the NVA'.[41]

On the other hand, the central office despaired in 1889 when the Leamington branch was accused of getting up eight or nine false rape cases in an attempt to purify the town. Two years earlier the Shrewsbury branch was wrecked when it was revealed that a key clerical member had spent a large part of his time sending 'the most revoltingly obscene letters' to local servant girls.[42] Coote could never find enough competent secretaries to keep a large network running efficiently and from the 1880s on he was happy to consolidate.

As far as public reaction was concerned, W. A. Bewes, one of the eminent barristers on the legal committee, said that in the beginning 'nearly the whole world was suspicious of us'.[43] In 1887 mobs rioted in Cheltenham when the local branch closed brothels. At that time magistrates were sometimes hostile to private brothel prosecutions by chapters in Paddington and elsewhere. The greatest difficulty was the unpopularity of the new law on statutory rape. At first there was more than the usual judicial reluctance to enforce it and in 1887 Baron Huddleston was rebuked by the Lord Chief Justice for stating during one trial that most charges brought by girls between thirteen and sixteen were unfounded. On the other hand, as part of the denial of child sexuality some judges as late as 1893 were punishing the rape of an adult more severely than the rape of a child 'because the consequences to the victim are much more serious and permanent'.[44]

The NVA overcame all these obstacles and became a force to be reckoned with. In conjunction with the whole purity lobby, it exerted an immense influence over questions relating to sexual vice and sex crimes, as we shall see. In the early days much of the central office's energies were taken up with prosecutions, some of which led to legal precedents, as in 1892 when seduction under the false pretence of marriage resulted in eighteen months' hard labour for a Cardiff man who was already married. The legal sub-committee in London handled about two hundred cases annually against rapists, homosexuals, sellers of obscene wares and brothel-keepers, though the latter were usually left to the local committees. Wyndham Bewes claimed the success rate was higher than that of the Director of Public Prosecutions, who was free to undertake cases if he deemed them important enough. While this official never did as much as the NVA wished, the vigilantes were soon on close terms with other public authorities of all kinds.

A busy two-way referral system developed in which NVA branches all over the country sent police forces information about brothels, obscene books or rape cases, and public officials referred cases back: in 1887 the Shoreditch Guardians referred the case of a man who had assaulted his step-daughter; in 1906 and 1910 the Metropolitan, Hull and Southampton police referred cases of procuring, and of selling obscene cards. The division of labour was based partly on local conditions. In Hull it was easier for a private group to get a conviction. With rape cases there were other factors involved. By the 1890s the police were dealing effectively with assaults against young girls, but the NVA report for 1896 explained that in many instances it was useful for a private group to take the first steps, and sometimes it was easier for such a group to deal with victims and hunt up evidence.

From the early days Millicent Fawcett's preventive sub-committee was very busy. In 1885 she wrote to Stead that she had not been able to speak in public on such issues for fear of bursting into tears. Now she threw herself into the work of protecting servant girls, stage children and other vulnerable females. On one occasion in 1887, after a man repeatedly tried to solicit the attention of a servant girl on her errands, Coote and Mrs Fawcett set a trap. A rendezvous was arranged at the gates of the British Museum and when the man repeated his advances, the vigilantes sprang and pinned a sign on his back : 'Dr W. Muschamp of the Army and Navy Club. This scoundrel has been caught in the act of attempting to abduct an innocent girl'.[45] While Mrs Fawcett remained a moderate suffragist, the events of 1885 had made her a social-purity militant.

As for the unwieldy structure of the NVA, the first step was to consolidate and impose more supervision. The two former new-abolitionist centres in Birmingham and Bristol served as prototype vigilance centres to which local branches were encouraged to affiliate. Others followed in Cardiff, Sunderland and Manchester. Quite early in most of these regions a partnership was struck with local officials. The Birmingham centre, autonomous until 1894, was supported by George Cadbury and about a dozen justices and councillors, including the mayor and the chairman of the watch committee. Frank Crossley bequeathed his vigilance committee to the NVA and it helped the Manchester police keep the city relatively pure up to 1914. The Cardiff centre attracted the support of some of the leading figures of the region, including Mabon, the well-known miners' leader, the Marquess of Aberdare and Lord Bute. In 1896 Donald Maclean, later an important nonconformist spokesman and a member of the 1931 National Government, told Coote that 'public opinion in South Wales and notably the Rhondda Valley had entirely changed for the better with regard to the whole moral question and that this was due entirely to the work done by our South Wales Branch'.[46]

Up to 1914 and even through the interwar years, the social-purity movement made its influence felt. It proceeded along a number of more or less distinct fronts : for the diffusion of information about chastity and the rescue and protection of females; against prostitution and commercialised vice as well as sex expression in literature, art, entertainment and advertising. The following chapters trace the fortunes of its war against sex.

# PART THREE

# AFTER 'THE MAIDEN TRIBUTE':
# SOCIAL PURITY IN ACTION

# 6

# Education for Chastity

THE late-Victorian and Edwardian years are generally recognised as the germination period for 'the new sexuality'. The work of pioneers like Ivan Bloch, Magnus Hirshfeld and Albert Moll in Germany, Charles Féré in France and Havelock Ellis in England as well as the development of Freudian psychoanalysis created a new anthropological, medical and psychological basis for a liberalised if not revolutionary sex ethic. The frontiers of sex expression in literature were pushed back by the work of Oscar Wilde, Zola and many others. In terms of actual behaviour, the falling birth rate indicates how birth-control was spreading amongst the middle classes anxious to defend their standards of living.

In the midst of these developments the NVA and the police suppressed the works of Bloch, Havelock Ellis and Féré. Zola's old and sick publisher was sent to jail and died soon after his release, a martyr like Wilde to the new sexuality. By the first decade of the century the average age of first marriage reached twenty-six, the highest in English history, and the illegitimacy rate was down to a very low four per cent. These facts, combined with the likelihood that prostitution was past its peak and the belief that only a very small minority of the working classes used contraceptives, inevitably lead to the question : was sexual restraint spreading down through society?

Dr Abraham Flexner, the American investigator who undertook a pre-war survey of *Prostitution in Europe*, reported that while the demand for prostitutes was universal amongst continental males, in England 'there is a very strong presumption that correct living is in certain strata of society distinctly more probable than on the Continent. Organisations like the White Cross Societies and the Alliance of Honour testify to the existence of sound sentiment to promote sound practices'.[1] Flexner concluded with the cautionary note that 'as to the extent to which continence prevails I have been unable to form a conception'.

This must remain an open question. Nevertheless, 'education for chastity', as it was called after the First World War by the Bishop of Birmingham, president of the National Council of Public Morals, far exceeded the institutional limits of the purity leagues. The torrent of anti-sexual lectures, tracts, books, lantern shows and films emanating from these societies reached millions of adolescents and young adults from the 1880s to the interwar years.

Naturally there were other sources of sex information for adults. Married couples could easily obtain birth-control tracts. After the Leeds Vigilance Association managed to get Dr H. A. Allbutt struck off the medical register for publishing his *Wife's Handbook* in 1886 at a cheap price, the book went to 450,000 copies before the war. There were also medical treatises on sex for popular consumption, though as the nineteenth century wore on they were likely to become more vague in anatomical and functional detail. For example, Dr R. T. Trall's *Sexual Physiology*, which Marie Stopes called the best practical guide to birth control and sexual relations produced in the century, first appeared in 1866 with explicit details and illustrations. After 1884, however, it was emasculated by its publishers, no doubt in deference to the purity crusade. Modern marriage manuals were a post-war phenomenon. There was no English equivalent, for example, to A. Debay's *Hygiène et Physiologie du Mariage*, which instructed husbands in the various ways they could satisfy their wives. It was in its hundred-and-seventy-third edition in 1888; anything similar in England would have been suppressed by the NVA.

The purity leagues were concerned most with getting their message across to the young and their efforts comprise the early history of formal sex education. Virtually no other formal information was being disseminated for the young. There was of course what Thackeray in *Pendennis* described as 'the theory of life as orally learnt'. There was also the common-sense resistance to the hoary myths about masturbation and fornication, though the young are hardly strong on common sense in sexual matters. As the pioneers of psychology pointed out in criticism of the

mainstream of sex education, frightening young people could
lead to phobias and neuroses. While the influence of social purity
on sexual behaviour in general is difficult to determine, its
instructional efforts certainly kept the campaign against masturbation going for another two generations and increased the
burden of anxiety on the young.

Education for chastity was entirely negative, reflecting the
belief that sex was a nasty appetite to be curbed by faith, cold
water and lessons in good citizenship. Yet in the context of
Victorian reticence on these matters, even warnings about sex
could appear dangerous. Thackeray explained that with
Pendennis's secret knowledge 'the shades of the prison house are
closing very fast round him'. Archbishop Benson's statement at
the CEPS inaugural that 'This work should be commenced not
only in what we call childhood, but in the nursery', was revolutionary. By 1889 when the self-styled 'moral sanitation' effort
was well under way, *Truth* complained that the flood of purity
literature was more dangerous to youth than pornography. Social
purity had to fight on two fronts, against sex and also against
what Edward Lyttleton, Headmaster of Eton and pioneer in the
field, referred to as the belief that 'the human mind has a fatal
power of turning [the instruction] into poison'.[2]

Concentration on the young was based on a number of factors.
While little could be done with the habitual fornicator, adolescents taught self-control would not resort to prostitutes later in
life. This was the argument used by Clement Dukes, the physician
at Rugby, in his influential 1883 attack on masturbation, *The
Preservation of Health as it is Affected By Personal Habits*. At
the forefront of the movement, disturbed adults like Dyer and
Varley projected their own sexuality on to the young. Like the
American evangelical clergymen who wrote 'advice to youth'
books earlier in the century, these preachers experienced passionate adolescent conversions in others as well as in themselves and
understood the special susceptibilities of the young to warnings
against sex coupled with the promise of the gospels.[3]

The late-century attempts to control young people sexually
were part of a broader concern with ordering their lives. By
1900 the school-leaving age was raised to fourteen and adolescents were being scrutinised by experts and organised by religious
and voluntary workers. Stanley Hall, the eminent American

psychologist, wrote in his *Adolescence* of 1904 that this stage was a time of 'new birth'; Augustine Birrell, Liberal education minister, referred to it as 'the unguarded years of life'. To protect, guide and socialise the adolescent, a variety of new leisure-time institutions appeared and many included education for chastity in their routines.

When social purity began its campaign against masturbation in the 1880s, medical opinion was still on its side. Experts held that self-abuse was fraught with terrible consequences, though the emphasis by then was on the mental rather than the physical effects. The great departure on this subject can be traced back to the early eighteenth century.[4] In about 1716 an anonymous quack pamphlet, *Onania: Or The Heinous Sin of Self-Pollution*, asserted that the costs included a variety of physical maladies as well as madness. The symptoms could be relieved by the author's secret remedy at half-a-sovereign a box. *Onania* fell on fertile ground and historians have suggested a variety of causes for its success, including the fear of venereal disease and the attempt to root out child abuse by desexualising the child. By mid-century Tissot, a Swiss physician, gave anti-masturbatory ideas respectability; he wrote that self-abuse was 'an act of suicide'. Soon Voltaire and even Kant were making contributions to the subject.

Throughout the nineteenth century quacks had a field day with 'masturbatory disease' and allied complaints like impotence and spermatorrhea, the main symptom of which was wet dreams. There was electrical treatment for weak erections and a variety of nostrums for masturbation and other complaints. Early in the century Samuel Solomon built himself a great mansion near Liverpool, Gilead House, with the proceeds of his Cordial Balm of Gilead, recommended for 'bad menses . . . child-bearing, turn of life, preventing or bringing on abortions, consumption, venereal disease and masturbation'.[5] As the pretensions of the medical profession increased, doctors expressed considerable regret that quacks had so much influence over venereal matters. By mid-century the physicians joined the quacks in designing douches to cool the genitals and devices to restrain them like the spiked penile ring; they then took the ultimate step to clitoro-dectomies and circumcisions as treatment for masturbation.

The departure of the 1880s was not novel. Its timing is what made it so important. Social purity began to permeate the country with the old ideas just before expert opinion was becoming available to debunk them. In 1898 Havelock Ellis reported, 'Recent authorities are almost unanimous in rejecting masturbation as the cause of insanity'.[6] Some of the new experts continued to believe that the neuroses were possible consequences and even the young Freud held this idea for a short time. But the horrid old myths about insanity and death were perpetuated by the proponents of education for chastity until the 1920s. They retarded the acceptance of the new ideas by British physicians and they were responsible for the time lag between advanced opinion and popular belief.

While girls were not ignored, the restraining effort was largely directed at males. Especially before 1900, social-purity experts promoted the common though far from unanimous view that females were sexually anaesthetised or at least passive. The most complete catalogue of purity tracts is the approved list of hundreds of titles offered for sale by the Moral Reform Union.[7] This was a small middle-class ginger group formed by some of the new abolitionists in 1882. Its 1896 list of publications from all purity sources shows just a handful of titles for girls, mostly warnings about seduction. There is little concern with active sexuality or masturbation, the obsessive target of the purity reformers. During the long history of anti-masturbatory ideas in England clitorodectomies had only lasted for a few years. The English did not show the same sustained interest in female masturbation as the Americans, who were still mutilating girls early in the twentieth century, or the French, whose belief that girls masturbated as much as boys was a concomitant of their greater willingness to ascribe to women enjoyment of sex.[8] The struggle against the double standard therefore reinforced the myth of the desexualised female and added to the anxieties of young males.

While purity information was distributed to all classes and even left its mark on public-school traditions, its main impact was on the lower middle classes and the working classes. From the 1880s on there was a sustained attempt by reformers to bring the benefits of sexual respectability to the poor. In *Damaged Pearls*, a work that sold 50,000 copies in a year, Ellice Hopkins wrote that the White Cross 'is essentially a working man's movement'. We have seen that the CEPS worked out that way in practice. Membership apart, Ellice Hopkins carried on a vigorous educational campaign aimed at the poor. She addressed thousands of working mothers through the north on child-rearing and instructed her genteel ladies, young and old, in how to make the poor more respectable.[9]

Her message to poor mothers included advice on how to overcome the moral dangers of overcrowding. Sleeping accommodation could be divided up by hanging a curtain between beds, using hammocks or making beds from chairs. Washing and bathing could be organised so that brothers and sisters never saw each other naked. Boys should never be allowed to wash their little sisters and children should be instructed not to urinate in the streets. Mothers were told about the Girls' Friendly Society, and the constructive activities available for their sons.

The Christian ladies of Ellice's Associations and those who read her books were instructed, in country districts, to 'keep a watchful eye on the hayfields at meal-times', to check on sleeping arrangements in their parishes and press landlords to improve accommodation. Urban ladies could promote factory girls' clubs and after 1885 those everywhere could initiate Mothers' Unions. Members of these were obliged to pray once a day for their children and more practically, to keep brothers and sisters apart at night; to avoid bad language in the presence of their children and promise neither to let their daughters stay out late nor to send them out to bring back beer from the pub. Ellice even spoke guardedly at Newnham College, Cambridge, and at high schools around the country on preventive work through clubs for shop and factory girls.

The importance of this advice to the poor and their superiors is difficult to gauge. The strict timetables drawn up by Edwardian mothers for segregated washing and their insistence that children keep their bodies covered may well have been an instinctive and long practised way of reducing the danger of incest amongst adolescent children.[10] However, it is very likely that the incidence of incest was lower in 1908, when the NVA finally obtained its bill on the subject, than a quarter of a century earlier. Social purity contributed to the improvement. Mothers' Unions proliferated in this period and by the 1890s 'Snowdrop Bands' spread from Sheffield through the north. These were for working girls who were willing to listen to purity lectures and pledge themselves to 'discourage all wrong conversation, light and immodest conduct and the reading of foolish and bad books'.[11] Social-purity workers were doing their best to popularise chastity. White Cross and CEPS literature included tracts for all social groups, including one aptly-named work for agricultural labourers called *Smut in the Wheat*. Much of this literature found its way into the boarding schools and the new leisure-time organisations for youths and adults, as might be expected. To reinforce its effect, purity reformers latched on to a much more dramatic means of disseminating information, the public lecture.

The new genre of the religio-medical purity lecture would barely have been possible before the 1880s. Earlier the YMCA had occasionally scheduled talks on what it called 'the fascinating sin of impurity'. But in the 1860s when Dr Brock, the eminent Baptist divine, had tried to talk on 'the Seventh Commandment', he was boycotted at Exeter Hall, the home of evangelicalism, and cancelled elsewhere. The real pioneer was Henry Varley, who fittingly started out as a butcher's assistant on Tottenham Court Road.[12] Another adolescent convert of Baptist Noel's, Varley went on to become a minister at the 1,800 seat West London Tabernacle and editor of *Christian Commonwealth*. He first tried his lectures in the mid-1870s, soon after the Moody and Sankey revivals. The time was not right and he gave them up. When he started again in 1882 young men thronged to hear him; within three years his *Lecture to Men Only* is alleged to have been heard by audiences totalling a quarter of a million, while the pamphlet sold 90,000 copies. Varley was the first of many in the field. James Wookey was soon on tour with *Human Wrecks*, as was Dyer with his *Plain Words For Young Men on Avoided Subjects* and *Safeguards Against Immorality*, the sales of which were each up near 150,000 in the 1890s.

These lectures represent purity propaganda at its most tortured. F. B. Meyer, the influential Baptist who later became president of the Free Church Council, admitted that Varley 'may have been carried to an excessive strength of statement'. Yet Meyer himself, in addition to leading the attack on prostitution in south London, was a blunt purity lecturer up to 1914. One witness at an address he gave in Nottingham indicates that even Meyer, 'as a grey-haired, kindly-faced old man', did not mince words:

> His method was dramatic. His audience, more than a thousand men and youths, were on their knees with bowed heads and averted eyes for the whole half-hour of his address. His topics were brutally intimate; his warnings and appeals deliberately crude to the point almost of coarseness.[13]

While these lectures provided the setting for a particularly frightening rhetoric their substance was typical of the early effort at moral sanitation. Fornication was attacked somewhat defensively, with the testimony of those doctors who held that continence was not harmful. Dyer added a nauseating description of the ravages of syphilis to show that divine punishment caught up with the sinner in this world or the next. Masturbation was revealed as the cause of idiocy, consumption and just about every other imaginable affliction. Safeguards against the varieties of sexual incontinence included things like avoiding music halls and theatres, cold water for drinking and bathing and plenty of faith and prayer. Purity workers expected that with some advice believers would be able to keep their bodies in subjection. Only rarely did they recommend circumcision to parents of masturbators.

The self-made Varley provided a colourful version of that Victorian notion that has been called the 'spermatic economy'. Retention of the seed created a fund of personal energy that could be sublimated and might thus result in upward mobility: 'The vigour . . . of the nervous system is mainly dependent on the seed [also] the strength of the brain, the richness of the blood, the brilliance of the eye, the vigour of the mind, the hardness of the muscle and the firmness of the flesh'.

Varley offered the same message in his *Christian Commonwealth*. In a piece on 'The Serfdom of Clerkship' he warned against early marriages: 'Then the misery commences.. . . . Let a clerk be a total abstainer; let him keep his body healthy and his mind clear by physical exercise; let him cultivate self-control, be ever ready to learn. . . .'[14] In his lectures Dyer repeated advice on how to divide off rooms by erecting thin-wood partitions covered with wallpaper. After all, he did just this at Paternoster Row. Sometimes members of the audience were described as un-

1. Eighteenth-century white slavery: Hogarth, 'A Harlot's Progress',
Plate 1, 1732.

2. 'The Tar's Triumph, or Bawdy House Battery', showing the destruction of a
brothel in the Strand, 1749.

3, 4. Prostitutes redeeming themselves in the washing and ironing rooms of the Albion Hill Home, Brighton, in the 1870s.

5. Ellice Hopkins

6. Josephine Butler

7. Alfred Dyer

8. William A. Coote

MRS. PROWLINA PRY.—"I HOPE I DON'T INTRUDE!"

THOUSANDS OF FELLOW-CREATURES FLUNG FROM WORK
  AT THE MERE PEN-STROKE OF A HASTY CENSOR!—
AN UNCONSIDERED TRIFLE ZEAL MAY SHIRK!
  BUT SENSE MAY NOT, NOR JUSTICE! THEY ARE DENSER

THAN PUNCH IMAGINES, OUR NEW BUMBLE-BAND,
  IF MISTRESS PRY'S DECISION THEY ABIDE BY;
BUT SHOULD THEY FAIL US, PUNCH THROUGHOUT THE LAND
  WILL WAKE THE PEOPLE PRUDES AND PRIGS ARE TRIED BY!

9. Mrs Chant portrayed as 'Mrs Prowlina Pry' by *Punch* during the 1894
campaign against the music halls.

11. The image of white slavery in Germany. The trafficker as 'Asiatic peddler' in film of 1926.

10. The image of white slavery in France. Theophile Steinlen poster for popular serial of 1895.

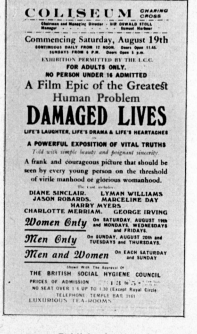

12, 13, 14. Publicity for the 1934 film on venereal disease.

15. The Seldons, victims of the 1907 crackdown on living statuary.

16. The popular 'La Milo', another victim.

17. The music halls retaliate: 'The Vigilance Committee', at the Duke of York's Theatre, 1895.

19. Suffragists and white slavery, 1912.

18. The controversial Zaeo poster of 1890.

washed. The ambiance of nonworking-class listeners was caught by the author 'One who has had it', in his 1903 book on nonconformity: they 'frequent the bethels on Sunday; and spend their week-days selling drapery in dark stores. . . .'[15] When we reach our discussion of pre-war educational efforts, it will be seen that purity lectures were still in vogue in 1914. They were promoted by purity leagues and local vigilance societies and countless numbers were delivered to temperance clubs, bible classes and youth groups. In the meantime, Britain's future leaders were not being ignored.

\* \* \*

The war on schoolboy masturbation was another development evoked by the events of the early 1880s. Edward Lyttleton was the figure who worked longest to cleanse the schools. When the struggle began he was a young assistant master at Wellington, on his way to the headmastership at Haileybury in 1890 and his beloved Eton in 1905. Lyttleton was one of twelve children of the Fourth Earl of Lytton and this great Edwardian establishment family made a key contribution to purity work. Three of his brothers held office in various purity institutions while a sister was married to Bishop Talbot. Edward's close younger brother Alfred, later a member of Balfour's Tory cabinet, traded on his legendary cricketing prowess, which W. G. Grace said was as smooth as champagne, to visit Oxford a few years after graduation and help launch a White Cross branch.

Edward described his and Alfred's period at Eton in the early 1870s as 'the closing years of the barbaric epoch of public school life'.[16] It was true of the schools generally that masters exerted little 'pastoral care' over their charges, considered drinking the main vice and left purity to chance. Lyttleton considered the expulsion of fourteen boys from Eton in 1875 for wild behaviour a turning point in school discipline. Little attention was given to purity until a little later. The pioneer in this field was the great Edward Thring, who had taken over Uppingham in 1853 and built it into one of England's most famous and athletic schools. Thring's diaries reveal an obsession with masturbation and in 1879 he began an inquisition at Uppingham. First he took to issuing solemn warnings to the school at confirmation time—warnings which were ignored at the risk of being hunted down and expelled. Thring put as much energy into this as he did into his games, recording how he was 'probing each time to the very end every bit of evidence I got, and following every clue'. After a series of expulsions the school solemnly pledged to behave itself and Thring recorded the 'result' with great satisfaction.[17]

By 1884, when the Church Congress actually invited Thring to give an address on 'The Best Means of Raising the Standard of Public Morality', anti-masturbation fever was sweeping the schools. In the previous year the physician at Rugby had published his claim that ninety to ninety-five per cent of boys at boarding schools engaged in the solitary vice. This revelation won him the Howard Medal for a prize essay submitted to the London Statistical Society. Actually it merely confirmed what old Dr Pusey had claimed after fifty years of employing a confessional system with his Oxford undergraduates. But Pusey had been dismissed as a crank because, as Edward Lyttleton explained, 'The subject had taken such a hold on him it had "coloured his atmosphere" '.[18] Clement Dukes, the prize-winning statistician, also confirmed that expulsion was the normal punishment in 1883. The CEPS was alarmed enough to form at that time a prestigious schoolmasters' committee, chaired by Montagu Butler, then headmaster of Harrow. Soon it was investigating how far the evil was 'connected with or prevented by athletics, bathing, lounging, tuckshops, sleeping accommodations, walks in the country, exeats, books, unexpurgated editions, etc.'.[19]

While the witch-hunt soon simmered down, it had long-term implications. The special CEPS committee dissolved in 1887, but not before it had arranged for headmasters to write to parents about their duty to alert their children to the dangers of boarding-school life, and telling them there was a selection of purity literature available to help. The masters agreed that their own warnings could do little if children left home without parental guidance. By the mid-1880s there were a number of guides available for parents willing to break the taboo on speaking about sex. To put this prohibition in perspective, it was considered very unusual that both Thring's and the Lytteltons' fathers had sent their boys letters of warning about sexual sin. Lord Lytton seems to have addressed the same message to each of his six sons, beginning 'I write rather than speak, because from the nature of the subject you might be embarrassed by being spoken to about it'.[20]

Now there was Elizabeth Blackwell's *Counsel to Parents*; the Social Purity Alliance offered the popular *Schoolboy Morality*, whose author told mothers to warn their sons that 'boys who indulge in these wrong acts invariably become weak and sickly, and unfit for playing games, that they often die young or go mad or become idiotic'. In 1882 Ellice Hopkins published *On the Early Training of Girls and Boys*, a general manual whose overblown religious rhetoric obscures her radical suggestion that mothers should explain the facts of life when children became curious or before they left home. She followed this with *The Power of Womanhood* in 1899, whose goal was the young man who would 'never foul his manhood in the sty of the beast'. The secret was to instil wonder by couching the facts of life in the natural context and to instil reverence for women and mothers. Ellice's last book was banned by the puritanical circulating libraries because of some very frank information on infantile masturbation.

Edward Lyttleton's three guides for parents written between 1883 and 1900 emerge as some of the saner contributions to a body of literature insipid at best and harmful at worst.[21] At Cambridge Lyttleton had come under the moral influence of James Stuart, who had been elected to the university's first Professorship of Applied Mechanics in 1875; as with Ellice Hopkins, Lyttleton's goal was to mobilise a boy's 'religious reverence and his love for his mother'. At least he avoided excesses. When their sons were eight or nine mothers could venture to explain that God planted a seed in women; in some cases it might be advisable to go on and explain the role of the father. After puberty he should take over and warn his son 'to preserve his treasure inviolate'. Fear should never be used to curb vice. Havelock Ellis, who shared the pre-Freudian notion that sexuality was dormant in children, called Lyttleton's books 'excellent', high praise from one who felt most social-purity advocates were cranks. Ellis even published an account of an unnamed lady purity leader who 'discovered, through reading some pamphlet against solitary vice, that she had herself been practising masturbation for years without knowing it'.[22]

There was an even larger selection of tracts available for direct distribution to children about to go off to school. One White Cross pamphlet, *Letters to A Son*, was so graphic about mutual masturbation that the CEPS refused to distribute it. In any case, Lyttleton and others soon concluded they would have to fill the gap because parents would not rise to the task. The school warning became institutionalised. Rev. Welldon, the purity advocate who was headmaster at Dulwich and Harrow, had staff take each boy aside individually. For years Lyttleton spoke of self-control to young men at Eton. In the 1880s J. M. Wilson of Clifton College sermonised on purity and proselytised amongst his fellow headmasters. Soon these warnings became perfunctory and an embarrassment to staff and students alike, but they remained part of school tradition. The Headmasters' Conference was now awake to the problem of vice and in the years before 1914 it formed an important constituency in the anti-obscenity lobby.

* * *

While the White Cross League and the CEPS were making their voices heard, they ran into organisational problems by the late 1880s. Since permeating other institutions was the goal from the start, however, there was no slowdown in output. Ellice Hopkins had anticipated 'a certain amount of difficulty in keeping [the White Cross] going as an independent organisation from the nature of the questions involved which do not admit of outside treatment possible in the temperance question, the anecdotes, the laughter, the statistics, the songs, etc.'. She advocated a policy of permeating existing religious institutions with 'inner White Cross bands'. Lightfoot commented that 'England in 1886 was dotted over with associations, guilds, brotherhoods and the like, enrolled under the White Cross banner'.[23]

Before the two founders departed the scene they tried to entice the YMCA to foster the movement. George Williams, its founder, was very keen about making it 'the very centre for coping with the monster of impurity'. However, while the YMCAs of Scotland, Germany and America officially promoted the White Cross the English central office backed off from a formal tie.[24] In 1891 the White Cross was forced to amalgamate with the CEPS on terms arranged by Archbishop Benson; after

that it maintained a nominal existence for work with nonconformists until Bishop How, its last president and a leading temperance reformer, wound it up in the mid-1890s. The CEPS
took its name.

Before the takeover Benson was informed that 'The White
Cross League seems to have progressed rousing enthusiasm without organisation. The [CEPS] to have moved more slowly
organising without rousing enthusiasm'. This is a fair estimate
of the churchmen's conservatism. The Lambeth Conferences of
1888 and 1897 might resolve that everyone should 'rally around'
the 'standard of high and pure morality'; yet a church committee
on purity chaired by Bishop How typically recommended in
1890 that 'social purity must be carried on by separate meetings
of the sexes and with the greatest care and circumspection. . . .
There is no room for that exciting advocacy by which movements can be maintained'.[25]

At its peak in the 1890s, the White Cross Society, as the
CEPS called itself from then on, had nineteen diocesan
branches. At the beginning of the decade the central office had
also affiliated directly 120 parochial associations that had
appeared in parts of the country without diocesan branches, and
enrolled 1,150 central subscribers, mostly clergy and churchmen of means. The Manchester branch was a model of activity.
This so-called St George's Association, with its affiliated
societies and full calendar of lectures, was still considered 'a
great success' on the eve of the First World War. The overall
effort, however, did not rival that of the Church of England
Temperance Society, with branches in all thirty-four dioceses and
a following in the hundreds of thousands.

From the start Benson also advocated permeation, especially
of the temperance movement. This made good sense, as it was
easier to promote sexual control if it was related to other modes
of self-mastery. Under the secretaryship of George Butler, the
Winchester branch, which again recruited the popular St George
for its title, pursued the objectives of 'temperance, soberness and
chastity'. This was suggested in the central office's guidebook
and the pattern was repeated elsewhere. There was always
cooperation between social purity and temperance, with a certain sharing of personnel and even local joint missions. But there
were limits to the facilities temperance societies would offer.

When the Church of England Temperance Society was asked to use its own branches to promote purity meetings, it refused, probably on the grounds that blatantly combining the two issues would slow down the anti-drink crusade. The formation of an active social-purity department in the British Women's Temperance Association led to a schism in that group in 1893, when those critical of the 'do everything policy' split off to form the Women's Total Abstinence Union.[26]

While social purity failed to permeate the YMCA or the temperance movement, it found innumerable outlets for its message. The White Cross Society was down to three diocesan branches by 1909; but its actual propaganda work had never been greater and the central office could not keep up with requests for speakers and publications. By then the distribution of tracts measured in the millions. There was something for every contingency and audience. One title alone, *True Manliness*, had sold over one million copies. This was an insufferable call to chivalry by Ellice Hopkins as updated by Bishop Lightfoot. Many titles had been translated into Welsh, others into German; there was demand from India, where an Army Purity Association had been affiliated, and from South Africa, where Sir Robert Baden-Powell ordered a consignment of Blanco Books, a special compendium, to keep the constabulary chaste.

But the main demand for sex information was from home and the White Cross could not meet it totally. In 1901 it pressed a chapter on the dangers of masturbation by the American, Lyman Sperry, into service as *The Curse of Boyhood*. Three years later Sylvanus Stall's thoroughly reprehensible *What A Young Boy Ought to Know* was brought to England. By then the call for 'enlightenment' was evoking independent new ventures. In Edinburgh a Congregationalist minister named E. B. Kirk began a 'Kirk Sex Series' and a run of 'Papers on Health' whose circulation was well over 100,000 by 1905. The Sex Series was as retrogressive as anything that could be found; but the *Talk With Girls About Themselves* had a special attraction for parents. Pages 47A and 47B provided alternative explanations of the facts of life, one explicit and the other incomprehensible. One or the other was to be clipped out along the perforation.

Much of this and similar information found its way into the new 'institutional church'. From about 1880 the nonconformists developed this concept of church as social centre to attract people of every age and class. The Church of England copied it. One of the earliest and most successful ventures for adults was the National Brotherhood Movement, which emerged in the 1870s when an enterprising young Congregationalist, unable to gain entry to a crowded Moody and Sankey revival meeting, went along to a bible class and found it dreary and deserted. He began what was first known as the Pleasant Sunday Association, whose design captured some of the revivalist excitement and music on a weekly basis. By 1906 the movement had a predominantly working-class membership of a quarter of a million under the presidency of F. B. Meyer and it was on intimate terms with the social-purity cause. Its 1,200 branches were regular stops for purity lecturers and when the NVA initiated a national promotional campaign in 1902 it used the Pleasant Sunday Association as a base in many towns. While there was never quite the same identity of interests with the Anglican societies for adults, after 1900 the Church of England Men's Society, with nearly 100,000 members, worked to further White Cross chapters and it too formed part of the anti-obscenity lobby.

There was a bewildering number of church and chapel-related societies for the young. As for the national institutions, the oldest was the Church of England Young Men's Society, dating from 1843. Along with debating, singing, football and a variety of other activities, its winter calendar for 1887 typically shows White Cross meetings. It was the same story with the Young Men's Friendly Society, with 35,000 members in the 1890s, the largest church society of its kind. Its organising secretary made sure that purity lectures were part of the programme of self-improvement and recreation, stating in 1894 that purity was 'the most important subject upon which advice needs to be given'.[27]

In the quest to organise adolescents and direct their idealism, the Boy's League of Honour exalted fair play, courage and chivalry with drill and uniforms. The Church Lads' Brigade copied it and the Boys' and Girls' Life Brigades taught life-saving. These institutions used purity literature in a modest way; the Alliance of Honour, with a panel of eight medical men supervising its substantial literature, supplied the Boys' Life Brigade with materials intended to create opportunities for discussions about sex. It was Sir Robert Baden-Powell who tackled sex instruction directly rather than relying on the general influences generated by the Boy Scout movement. The hero of Mafeking saw to it that the scouts were put through a course of warnings from the time they entered the movement at the age of eight. By eleven they were ready to learn that semen had to be hoarded. At the age of seventeen his rovers were given *Rovering To Success*, a guidebook whose chapter on 'Woman' instructed them that the 'rutting season' could be negotiated without loss of semen if they bathed their 'racial organ' in cold water daily. By a tortuous but inevitable logic filthy talk led to venereal disease.

Baden-Powell originally added this section to the handbook after a visit from Dr A. T. Schofield, a Harley Street consultant and one of the many physicians active in purity education. Soon after the scouts were begun, Schofield wrote, 'I saw that if one could only link the cause of purity onto this great movement, there would be a blow struck for the manhood of England that had never been struck yet.'[28] Baden-Powell also put Schofield to work lecturing to scoutmasters and then he sat down with his sister Agnes to add a section to *The Handbook For Girl Guides* explaining how 'secret bad habits' led to hysteria and lunacy. This explicit admission that female sexuality was alive shows that purity work was now being carried on amidst the gradual disintegration of Victorian sexual ideas. Yet *Rovering to Success* alone was distributed to 200,000 scouts in its revised form over the years, making it one of the most enduring bearers of the purity message.

*     *     *

In Baden-Powell's imperialist version of sex instruction the spermatic economy is recruited for king and country. There is a mixture here of old and new, epitomised in the solemn advice to keep the racial organ cool. This mirrors the main developments in the social-purity camp after about 1900. The catalogue of horrors attributed to sexual vice was lengthened to include the declining birth rate and alleged increases in venereal disease and degeneration of the racial stock. The focus of social purity was partly altered in a way analogous to the contemporaneous shift from 'internal' social Darwinism, the doctrine relating to competition between individuals, to 'external' social Darwinism, which emphasised the struggle between nations. Social-purity platforms became broad enough to support leading eugenicists like Caleb Saleeby, who believed that most prostitutes and unwed mothers were feeble-minded and ought to be kept from procreating; such advocates of national efficiency as Beatrice Webb and the leading medical experts on venereal disease. However, social purity remained firmly anchored in church and chapel and firmly wedded to old repressive sexual attitudes. An alliance of Christian leaders, social engineers and imperialists made sense and was grounded in a common interest in social reconstruction. Hugh Price Hughes was an ardent imperialist and after his death in 1902 many of his fellow divines carried on the tradition. Bishop Creighton of London and Mrs Louise Creighton were also very interested in national efficiency as well as purity.

In the years preceding the war these concerns about national efficiency and the social implications of vice were international in scope. Across Europe and North America new laws for the protection of women and against obscene wares and commercialised vice testify to the connection made between purity and preparedness and to fears generated by the social dislocations as well as the new artistic and personal standards of the period. Writing of sex education, one response to these anxieties, Havelock Ellis noted in 1912 that 'during the past ten years more has been done to influence popular feeling ... than during the whole of the preceding century'.[29] In Britain this advance was due partly to the rejuvenation provided for the whole social-purity movement by a timely series of revivalist missions. These revivals launched by the Free Church Council in 1901, form the fourth and last cluster of awakenings that were significant for anti-vice crusading. The Free Church Council, the powerful voice of the federated nonconformists, succeeded in its primary goal of attracting new communicants; a look at the planning sub-committee for the great simultaneous mission of 1901 indicates that purity would have been of direct concern. It included Meyer, Hughes, Bunting and Sir Joseph Compton Rickett, MP, the main financial supporter of both the NVA and the new Public Morality Council.

Henry Varley was back from a long stay in Australia and

took part in the missions. The main effort was borne by three electrifying evangelists, Gipsey Smith, W. R. Lane and Tolfree Parr. The usual plan was to speak on intemperance on Saturday nights and on impurity on Sunday afternoons. From what we know about the way many parents organised their weekends at the time, packing their children off to Sunday school to have privacy for lovemaking, this showed impeccable logic. Tolfree Parr's comment during the 1902 season was repeated over and over again: 'Undoubtedly the most impressive services of the Missions have been the services for men only.'[30]

At this time Coote was anxious to launch a national campaign to achieve certain limited goals; the setting up of NVA regional centres, the tidying up of the Criminal Law Amendment Act and the passage of the long-delayed incest bill. He was encouraged not only by the missions but by the appearance on the scene of the young Rev. James Marchant. In 1901 Marchant had arrived at the Presbyterian church at Chatham and decided to purify the 'sea of iniquity' in this garrison town. He went to Coote for advice and there ensued a local clean-up which achieved such notoriety that even King Edward sent his good wishes. Coote then engaged the tireless Marchant 'to take Drawing Room and Public Meetings every day in the week and to thoroughly raise the country on the subject of social purity'.[31] Some of his meetings were held jointly with the free-church missioners.

Marchant's campaign was a triumph. A comment by Ellice Hopkins in 1904, the year of her death, indicates how Marchant went beyond the revival:

> He has gone straight to the organs of our civil life. He has appealed all over the country to the municipalities, he has held meetings in Mayoral parlours and council chambers, addressed himself to poor law guardians, as well as to all leaders in the movement towards a purer and truer life. To me most of this was impossible. But there has come a great change. These public bodies are becoming more and more the organs of a higher morality in civic life.[32]

Marchant established new vigilance committees. He himself addressed nearly 400,000 people and most heard his 'Men and

Morals', an uncompromising condemnation of sexual incontinence.

In this promising climate there were new efforts to expand
education for chastity. The London Diocesan Council for Penitentiary, Rescue and Preventive Work, which coordinated
church rescue homes, had formed a men's committee in 1900
and within a few years its purity lecturers were addressing
audiences of four and five thousand. Some of them were captive,
including Baden-Powell scouts and young clerks trooped over
from city business houses where they still lived in.[33]

There was nothing coercive about the Alliance of Honour.
Very similar to the original White Cross, by 1914 it had enrolled
42,000 young men, mostly clerks, shop assistants and artisans
but also Cambridge students and boys between the ages of fifteen
and eighteen. The Alliance began simply in 1901 when two
Sunday-school teachers launched a devotional society for a group
of friends. They attended a purity lecture by Dr Harry Guinness,
a physician and missionary, and persuaded him to become president of an ambitious new league. John Scott Lidgett, called the
greatest Methodist since Wesley, provides in his comments to a
rally in 1913 some idea of how these leagues tried to turn
repression into sublimation: 'Purity is not merely an outward
and negative thing. . . . It is a great positive enthusiasm'. Many
young men seemed to agree. If any doubt remains about the
attractions of social purity before the war, the influence of its
leaders and the severe nature of its message, there is an account
of the 1910 lecture given by Sir Robert Anderson, a former head
of Scotland Yard CID, to 4,400 Alliance men in the Great
Assembly Hall, Mile End Road. After the Silver Band of the
Salvation Army had finished its selections, Anderson, who had
written seventeen books on religion, told

> a harrowing story of an Eton boy, son of a colonel in the
> army, a brilliant lad, always head of his class . . . who had
> been reduced to drivelling imbecility as the result of secret
> sin, induced by the sight of an obscene photograph exhibited
> by a scoundrel whom he met in a railway train. I had the
> satisfaction of hunting the villain down and of procuring him
> a long sentence of penal servitude.[34]

While such familiar scenes continued, the issue of race

regeneration became an important motive for those who wished to spread sex information. The 1899 Brussels international medical conference on venereal disease provided a major impetus. While the eminent physicians present were expected to continue their support of state regulation, they partly deferred to the growing evidence against it and passed no resolution at all on the subject. Leading former regulationists like Professors Fournier of Paris and Blaschko of Berlin went away with the conviction that moral methods would have to be substituted for sanitary ones. They formed an International Society for Sanitary and Moral Prophylaxis and by 1905 committees on the Continent and in the United States were involved in furthering the theory and practice of sex instruction.

Everywhere women shared the new interest in using moral instruction to prevent social contagion. Back in 1690 the Tower Hamlets Society for the Reformation of Manners had called attention to husbands catching a 'venomous Plague' from prostitutes and communicating it to their 'Honest and Innocent' wives. This now became a haunting fear, expressed most dramatically in Eugene Brieux's widely produced *Damaged Goods*, a 1901 play about how congenital syphilis destroys a middle-class French family. The women's movement was quick to articulate the danger and suggest education. In the United States after Dr Prince Morrow of the Moral Prophylaxis Movement published *Social Diseases and Marriage* in 1903, it was taken up by the suffragists. In Britain there were a series of titles on the contagion, from Dr Louisa Martindale's *Underneath The Surface*, commissioned in 1908 by the National Union of Women's Suffrage Societies; to Christabel Pankhurst's *enragé The Great Scourge and How to End It* of 1913, with its famous formula of votes for women and chastity for men; to Louise Creighton's moderate reply of the following year, *The Social Disease and How to Fight It*, which held that purity was harder for men and called for an educational campaign.

The National Council of Public Morals provided a forum for public figures concerned with the various aspects of national degeneration. After James Marchant left the employ of the NVA in 1904 he became secretary to this alliance of purity leaders, eugenicists and experts on VD. The National Council carried on an ambitious public campaign in 1908 and finally adopted its definitive title three years later, when its aims became 'the regeneration of the race-spiritual, moral and physical'. Social purity had indeed broadened its base; when the National Council issued a widely publicised 'Manifesto on Public Morals' in 1911, the sixty-six signatories ranged from Christian leaders and medical dignitaries to Caleb Saleeby, Beatrice Webb, Ramsay MacDonald and the speaker of the House of Commons.

The Manifesto expressed a mixture of the old and new fears and the contents betray the fact that it was issued while a controversial Royal Commission on Divorce was in the midst of its deliberations. After voicing 'alarm at the low and degrading views of the racial instinct which are becoming widely circulated', at the low birth rate and alleged proliferation of the feeble minded, and the corrupting influence of pernicious literature, it went on to insist that the young 'should be taught to entertain high conceptions of marriage, as involving duties to the future of the nation and the race. The great truth must be enforced that the racial instinct, as this term declares, exists not primarily for individual satisfaction, but for the wholesome perpetuation of the human family'.[35]

In practice this meant another influential voice in the formidable anti-obscenity lobby and investigation into sex instruction. But while the members of the National Council's impressive subcommittees on this subject all agreed on what such instruction was for, to preserve chastity and the family, they could not agree on how far it should go or whether it should be introduced in the schools. Ignoring Freud's work, some eminent physicians still saw the process as one of issuing warnings without prematurely awakening the dormant sexual instincts of children. The British were still too reticent to try experiments in sex education in state schools, even though national power was believed to be at risk. Such pilot projects were being carried on in Germany and the United States but they were not conducted in Britain until after the First World War.

The National Council issued a few adventurous titles in its 'New Tracts for the Time Series'. The first, Havelock Ellis's *Tasks of Social Hygiene*, advocated birth control and alarmed the White Cross. *Problems of Sex*, by J. Arthur Thomson and Patrick Geddes, two eminent Scottish biologists, recommended the use of nature study to teach the facts of life. This later became a popular approach. Their chapter on married life admitted sex could be enjoyable for both parties but added the admonition that 'the married state gives opportunities for uncontrolled self-indulgence' and could lead to 'monogamous prostitution'. As their Manifesto suggests, the National Council's lapses from Victorian morality were few. Its 'Confidential Talk Series' for the masses assembled some of the worst rubbish available by Dr Schofield, Lyman Sperry and even by Dr Mary Wood-Allen, the superintendent of the social-purity department of the American Women's Christian Temperance Union. Her *Ideal Married Life* proposed as little married life as possible.

\* \* \*

It is generally accepted that the war speeded the decline of Victorian attitudes to sex. With the unusual intensity of personal experience, the undermining of old religious standards by the carnage, the dislocation of family life and the distribution of condoms to the forces it could hardly have been otherwise. Contemporaries talked of 'khaki fever', as they were to point to allegedly uncontrollable 'goodtime girls' in the next war; one scholarly account between the wars spoke rather recklessly of 'war nymphomania'. Social purity tried to stem the tide. A variety of women's organisations initiated police patrols to keep watch for loose behaviour in open spaces and near military and munitions installations. Coote helped the first such group, an *ad hoc* task force of the National Union of Women Workers under Mrs Creighton, establish links with the authorities and then organised their training for street work.[36]

The war modified the sexual ideas of the purity leagues, though it hardly emancipated them or put them out of business. In 1923 the White Cross spoke of the 'vast growth of market for purity literature during the past ten years'. Between the wars the Alliance of Honour enrolled over 100,000 young men in branches in YMCAs, churches and clubs, and continued to attract public figures like Margaret Bondfield, the Labour pioneer, and Thomas Inskip, the Tory attorney general.[37]

Yet psychoanalytic ideas about sexuality belatedly registered on most responsible agencies concerned with young people. In 1921 the White Cross appointed a subcommittee to revise its literature and invited Dr Ernest Jones, author of the great Freud biography, to contribute his expertise. There was a fascinating confrontation between his hosts who criticised his 'vague' knowledge of Christian ethics, and Dr Jones, who described how the worst psychiatric problems he had seen resulted from the 'intolerable burden at present heaped on the auto-erotic by clergy, doctors and schoolmasters alike'. Jones won his point and the White Cross withdrew such enduring classics as *The Perils of Impurity* and issued other titles which instructed parents that 'understanding, warmth and affection were the best response to masturbation'. By the early 1930s Alliance publications were informing parents and schoolmasters that 'the fabric of the old purity literature ... rested to a large extent upon a rotten foundation'. If masturbation was so destructive, one author reasoned, how could Britain have won the war?[38] While other sources like the popular *Mothercraft Manual* perpetuated the old ideas, the main source of supply was turned off. In 1932 the White Cross published *The Threshold of Marriage*, a Christian manual which ultimately went to well over half-a-million copies and gave instructions on simultaneous orgasm. Ellice Hopkins' brainchild had finally done justice to James Hinton.

In the interim the cost of social-purity information in terms of human anxiety was tremendous. To cite one example, the author William Kent recorded that in about 1903, when he was nearly twenty, his father had given him one of Henry Varley's tracts: 'You felt you were past praying for when you started to read it. So ignorant was I that I had no knowledge whatever of the biological significance of my impulses. . . .' He began wondering if life was worth living.[39] The White Cross, Alliance of Honour, Meyer, Varley, Baden-Powell and others all mention the heavy burden of their private correspondence with young men. They were in direct descent from the quacks, except that they took no money.

While the campaign against masturbation was being undermined, however, social purity found a useful alternative during the war. In terms of the history of formal sex education, 1914–18 was no turning point in the emancipation of the public, who were systematically terrified for years, from 1916 on, with the most horrific images of venereal disease. The incidence of VD and the horrors of mercury treatment had made syphilophobia a well-known phenomenon in the nineteenth century. Moralists did their best to reinforce it and French fathers sometimes took their sons through the local VD ward to complete their moral education. Early in the new century, as we have seen, there was intensified interest in the contagion. As with masturbation, the purity reformers merely promoted anxiety about VD when it would otherwise have died down.

The anti-VD campaign grew out of the Royal Commission on Venereal Diseases, established in 1913. Medical experts had taken advantage of Paul Erlich's dramatic announcement to the International Congress of Medicine in London in 1912 that he had developed salvarsan, a drug against syphilis, to win the important enquiry. Its composition was not auspicious for radical policy departures, as the thirteen members included a host of purity regulars including John Scott Lidgett, old Canon Horsley and Mrs Creighton.

By the time the Royal Commission issued its final report in 1916, two years of war had focused its attention on the rising incidence of VD and also on altering mores at home. Its recommendations, quickly implemented by the government, called for a revolution in the *laissez-faire* policy that had persisted toward sufferers since Josephine Butler's thorough victory in 1886. The state should distribute free salvarsan to doctors and open laboratories to expedite diagnosis while local authorities should set up free clinics to provide treatment. On the other hand the Commission refused to tackle the sensitive issue of prophylaxis. Now and during the intense post-war debate on this subject medical arguments were put forward against the prophylactic advantages of the sheath and immediate post-coital disinfection when carried out by untrained or careless individuals. Yet Dr Mary Scharlieb, a well-known gynaecologist who believed condoms were 'actively injurious' to men and women, admitted that nonmedical factors prevailed when she said of the Royal Commission on which she sat, 'It was thought that the offer to make unchastity safe was a blow to the country's morals.'[40]

British reluctance to introduce prophylaxis even extended, uniquely among the belligerents, to the armed forces. The British Expeditionary Force went abroad in 1914 armed only with a warning on continence from Lord Kitchener, an old friend of the White Cross. Tents for disinfection were introduced belatedly in 1916. The refusal to divorce immorality from its physical consequences on the home front was only slightly less notable. Britain was rife with scare stories about the undermining of the war effort by diseased prostitutes. One series in the *Weekly Dispatch* on 'The Grave Sex Plague' claimed on 2 July 1917 that two women from Waterloo Road 'recently went to a seaside town and practically polluted a whole regiment'. While emergency regulations were passed to facilitate the expulsion of prostitutes from near military camps and the jailing of women who solicited or engaged in sexual intercourse while suffering from VD, the experts knew that 'amateurs' and not professionals were responsible for the increasing rate of infection. The army concluded that only twenty-eight per cent of its diseased personnel had been infected by prostitutes.[41]

Rather than encourage this 'khaki fever', the authorities refused to make preventive measures readily available on the home front. In fact, by banning treatment by nonmedical personnel, the VD Act of 1917 made chemists very reluctant to promote the scientifically preferred items for immediate post-coital application, calomel and potassium permanganate. Morality won over efficiency. Naturally the alternative to prophylaxis was education for chastity. As the Royal Commission concluded, '... the importance of wisely conceived educational measures can hardly be exaggerated.... The fact that we recommend that free treatment should be provided for all sufferers makes it ... all the more necessary that the young should be taught to lead a chaste life as the only certain way to avoid infection.'[42]

The government's VD regulations of 1916 encouraged local authorities to enlighten the public about the contagion. This set the stage for the greatest effort to date in sex education. Though it used the most repulsive scare tactics, it did at least break down the taboo on talking about VD, encourage attendance at the new public treatment centres and bring real advances in the teaching of human biology in schools. All this was accomplished by the National Council for Combating Venereal Disease (NCCVD), established in 1916 by the Royal Commission's chairman, Lord Sydenham of Combe, the former army officer and high imperial official. Its semi-official status was reflected in substantial annual grants from central and local government and in Ministry of Health vetting of its copious propaganda. In 1924 it became the British Social Hygiene Council, with its

F

objects broadened to the familiar ones of strengthening the family, promoting an equal standard of sexual conduct and improving the race by educational and social measures.

Coote and many of the other pioneers flocked to the new Council during the war as social purity rallied to the flag. Lady activists lectured munitions workers on the pitfalls of sex, but in the massive instructional campaign it was E. B. Turner who led the way with a superhuman effort. A former student of Thring's at Uppingham and a power in medical politics, he had lectured to a million men by 1920. Describing his wartime appeal to soldiers, he said, 'Whenever I spoke to them I always appealed to their patriotism and put it up to them how much better they would be employed pumping lead into the Hun rather than lying in hospital and having "606" [salvarsan] pumped into them'.[43]

While the NCCVD had to surrender this appeal in peace-time, it was soon exploiting a new propaganda vehicle with almost unlimited potential. This was the VD horror film, the natural sequel to the religio-medical lecture. Not all purity leaders were keen on the cinema; the darkness was threatening and Edward Lyttelton told an enquiry by the National Council of Public Morals on the subject in 1917 that 'a large number of people come out of the cinema shows in a state of coma'. But the VD horror film prevailed and Lord Sydenham's forces soon considered cinema 'the most attractive form of propaganda'.[44]

The wartime prototype was *End of the Road*, with its topical sequences about the dangers of contracting VD from a soldier's kiss and the good works of the women's voluntary patrols that scoured the outdoors for loose behaviour. One of the points of this cautionary tale, incidentally, was to promote sex education. After five-year-old Mary finds a bird's nest and her mother tells her about, the birds and bees, she goes on to marry the hero. Once little Vera is lied to in similar circumstances there is only disease and disaster. Titles of other early films in this genre are self-explanatory: *Whatsoever a Man Soweth; Waste; The Flaw; The Girl Who Doesn't Know.*

Between the wars local authorities waived the strict prohibition on sexual realism to permit VD films and the equally popular white-slave titles. Cinemotor lorries plied the country showing them to youth groups, mothers' meetings, factory work forces and audiences collected from among the idle unemployed. New features were produced or imported from North America and the British Social Hygiene Council obtained special permission for public and private screenings. In 1919 there was *Damaged Goods*, an updated version of the pre-war play; this was followed in the 1930s by yet another version updated by Upton Sinclair, *Marriage Forbidden*; in 1934 it was reported that *Damaged Lives*, a melodrama on the same theme with Jason Robards, had played to four million people in 327 towns. The scare tactics were evolving into entertainment, though sometimes the effect could be disastrous. One expert told a parliamentary enquiry in 1920:

> I think it does not prevent a man from occasionally exposing himself to risk. He may go to a film lecture like *The End of the Road*, which is a terrible film, which suggests that every man who indulges in irregular sexual intercourse will get venereal disease, will commit suicide, or get covered with sores, or end in a madhouse.... The impression will not remain and it will not have a permanent deterrent effect.... [yet] We are very much against it because it terrifies people. I myself know of several suicides which have occurred because the poor people had seen the film and thought that there was nothing but the madhouse lying before them.[45]

The witness was Dr H. W. Bagley, president of the rival Society for the Prevention of Venereal Disease. It fought a losing battle trying to commit the government to what was seen as the alternative, removing the legal obstacles to the retailing of officially approved disinfectants. When Dr Bagley led an influential deputation to the Minister of Health in 1923, after the expert Trevethin Committee had virtually recommended just this, Neville Chamberlain, who had been president of the Birmingham NCCVD, was unsympathetic. He explained that if the issue reached the Cabinet, which had rejected prophylaxis two years earlier, it would hardly now be considered solely on the medical arguments.[46]

Except for the free clinics, the only novel departures sanctioned by the government were the so-called early ablution centres opened in 1920 by the Manchester City Council in two cubicles of two men's public conveniences. Certainly this was one of the most curious experiments in the history of public health. The idea was that there ought to be a place of last resort where those engaging in intercourse could rush for an assisted wash. This amounted to the adoption for fornicators of the harsh principle that informed the Victorian poor law, 'less eligibility', or minimal relief in a public institution. Yet for most social-purity advocates these inconvenient installations were a terrible danger, opening the door to a future in which 'moral degenera-tion and sex excesses would rot the very foundation of society.' While the NCCVD supported the early ablution centres, they were opposed by feminists like Alison Neilans, secretary of the Association for Moral and Social Hygiene, as Josephine Butler's followers were now called, and by the influential Manchester branches of the White Cross and the Vigilance Society. Public opinion forced the removal of advertisements for them, and of posted instructions lest the customers learn to undertake disinfec-tion themselves, and finally closed them up in 1922. By then nearly 18,000 men had visited the cubicles, the great majority in the early hours of the morning just after contact.[47]

With preventive measures limited by legal, moral and finan-cial considerations, official policy fell back on education to keep people pure or to get them to the clinics. Did the ongoing social hygiene campaign have any influence? The comments of Dr Bagley apart, medical officers of health sometimes reported that VD clinics were busiest after local authorities invited in the Social Hygiene Council with its films. Officials in the Ministry of Health were convinced that by pushing people to get treatment, such propaganda was a contributory factor in the steady postwar decline in the rates of infection.[48]

Fighting the contagion was but one of the objects of the new semi-official sex educators. In fact as VD declined the Social Hygiene Council's sense of mission became more urgent. The secretary, Mrs Sybil Neville Rolfe, whom Dr Mary Scharlieb called 'the very spring' of its action and who was still helping the Public Morality Council weed out books for prosecution in the 1950s, explained in 1931 that the great danger of the day was sexual freedom among the young: 'The problem before us is to see that the laxities of today, which are those of the transi-tion period between the relaxation of control and restriction and the remaking of new institutions do not become revolutionary'.[49] As mores changed social purity promoted its last demon, the old social contagion. By now, however, there was much constructive activity befitting the new age. With the help of such figures as Julian Huxley, Bronislaw Malinowski and J. Arthur Thompson, the Social Hygiene Council made real progress with sex education between the wars. Their strategy was to stimulate the teaching of biology in the elementary schools to prepare the way for the teaching of the facts of life; that step would be undertaken in special courses for school leavers or in secondary school hygiene. Some indication of the Council's prodigious activity is given by the cumulative figures to 1931 : 24,000 meetings attended by five million people, excluding soldiers; 3,000 conferences and seven hundred courses of lectures for parents, youth leaders and teachers on the art of teaching about sex.[50]

At the same time the White Cross lectured on sex at the theological colleges, an altogether necessary task, considering that after one talk to some five hundred clergy on venereal disease, a confused group came forward to Sir Malcolm Morris, the eminent physician, and confessed they thought sexual inter-course was venereal disease. Lecturers from the Social Hygiene Council and the Alliance of Honour were invited into state schools. Trained speakers used films for children under fourteen like *The Gift of Life*, which traced reproduction from the amoeba to the rabbit. Older groups could look at *Youth and Life*, one version with male sex organs and some mild warnings about masturbation, the other with female organs and warnings against premarital sex. The organs met in an optional last reel which was occasionally shown to adventurous YMCA audiences.

In 1943 the Board of Education complained again of the weakening of sexual restraints in its survey of sex education that preceded the 1944 Education Act's delegation of responsibility to the local education authorities. At the time about one-third of the secondary schools in England had already made some provision, many through specialist lecturers.[51] For better or for worse, the social-purity forces had monopolised sex education since its beginnings in the 1880s and their negative approach was not to disappear overnight.

# 7

# Social Purity and Prostitution

THE social-purity crusade of the 1880s produced the first sustained attempts to repress prostitution since the forays of the Societies for the Reformation of Manners. The cluster of municipal clean-ups in the thirty or so years before the First World War show that a hard line was replacing the earlier policy of legal compromise. Between 1875 and 1885, when summary jurisdiction over brothels was obtained, an annual average of only eight-six brothels were prosecuted in England and Wales. This amounted to the toleration of well-run bawdy houses. Between 1885 and 1914 the annual average jumped to over 1,200.[1] Through the major provincial cities and the metropolis there were also unprecedented drives to liberate the streets from prostitutes.

The changeover to repression was gradual. Prostitutes were still too much a part of the scene to be hounded off the streets everywhere. Havelock Ellis pointed out before the war that 'English love of freedom and English love of God combine to protect the prostitute'.[2] In other words, religious sensibilities had defeated state regulation and if the police overstepped the mark magistrates would set them free or the public would raise one of its periodic clamours. Yet even as Havelock Ellis wrote, the London borough councils, police and magistrates were cracking down hard. After parliament withdrew its sanction for the double standard by repealing the CD Acts and passing the Criminal Law Amendment Act, it became more difficult for public authorities to permit brazen soliciting and known brothels.

Did repression diminish prostitution? Coote, who was introduced as a virtually unrivalled expert when he testified at the Royal Commission on the Duties of the Police in 1907, claimed that compared to the way it was in his youth, London 'is an open-air cathedral'. There was similar and equally dramatic evidence from a series of rescue workers. Coote estimated there were 8,000 prostitutes then in London, a figure that would put the trade well beyond its Victorian peak. Such estimates are always suspect and an accurate assessment was particularly difficult at the time because repression was hastening the decline of the brothel and scattering prostitutes into flats. The heavy hand once again changed the venue of the whore. It seems likely, however, that the clean-ups diminished prostitution by hurting recruitment. While fleabitten professionals might be impervious to repeated convictions, the increase in arrests of streetwalkers and brothel-keepers created an outcast group which made prostitution an unattractive option for working-class girls.

Ellice Hopkins's Act for the committal of brothel children to industrial schools reinforced this development. It became risky for poor landlords with children to rent rooms to prostitutes in their homes; and it was made more difficult for mothers to pass on their mystery to their daughters. In 1918 a Home Office official told a parliamentary enquiry, 'One of the things we have seen in the last twenty or thirty years is the decay of the professional prostitute as a profession'.[3] While new vocational and educational opportunities for women played an important part in this process, as did altering mores and the likely increase in non-commercial sex, this official expert was convinced that repression was of central importance.

Social-purity leaders were divided on the wisdom and justice of repression. When the campaign to deny the cosy music-hall promenades to prostitutes was at its height in 1894, Josephine Butler wrote, 'I continue to protest that I do not believe that any real reform will ever be reached by outward repression. . . . The principle of the Federation has always been to *let individuals alone*, not to pursue them by any outward punishments, not to drive them *out of any place*, so long as they behave decently— but to attack *organised prostitution* . . . a third party. . . .'[4] While the vigilantes relentlessly pursued third parties like procurers and bullies, well before 1894 all but Josephine's radical band in the LNA were deeply involved in harassing the prostitutes themselves.

The justification was formally put forth by Alfred Dyer in a pamphlet of 1884 extolling the virtues of 'the repressive system'

in Glasgow. Vice was as open and raw on the Clyde as anywhere in mid-Victorian Britain. Whores were said to sit semi-
nude in their windows and parade through the streets in troops.
What made the permanent police crackdown that began in 1870
popular with the social-purity movement was that it was based
on a spiritual awakening amongst the leading people in the city.
An elevated public opinion justified the unleashing of the police.
Furthermore, whenever possible, displaced and arrested prostitutes were given the offer of the busy Glasgow Magdalen Home.
None need go hungry or remain in jail. The so-called 'repressive
system' became very popular with the new abolitionists and even
Josephine had some good words for it.[5] After 1885 vigilance
committees always justified their aggressive policies by pointing
to the omnipresent penitentiaries and asylums, while officials in
purity-minded cities like Manchester, Liverpool, Sheffield and
Leeds tried to make it easy for prostitutes to enter the homes. In
1887 the NVA stated, 'It is one of the principles of our work
that we never attempt to close such houses without previously
offering the occupants an opportunity of leading a better life'. At
that time Coote reported that 'in many parts of the East End
ladies were allowed to enter bad houses, and allowed to take
away repentant girls, their mission and good intentions being
recognised and respected'.[6]

Did the formula of repression with rescue operate in practice
to soften the blow for prostitutes? Ellice Hopkins had drawn
hundreds of ladies on to her committees while she and Josephine
Butler had laboured to alter the punitive tone of the homes.
However, the old hands were uneasy about the influx and the
changes. One penitentiary chaplain complained that 'the sudden
great interest' was creating as many problems as it was solving;
Arthur Maddison, head of the Female Mission to the Fallen since
the 1850s, held 'There is a certain class of masculine women who
object to a woman who has lost her virtue being spoken of as
fallen; but the latter expression has at least the advantage of
veracity'.[7]

In fact, while women workers came to dominate numerically,
they never managed to impart to the endeavour the radical
impulse of a Josephine Butler or even an Ellice Hopkins. That
impulse was largely submerged by the old system and the rehabilitation of the fallen remained, with some notable exceptions,

what Ellice had excoriated as an uninviting regime of 'bread, dripping and prayer'. When the NVA tested the new policy in 1888 by closing twenty-two brothels in the garrison of Aldershot, the inauspicious result was that four hundred whores paraded the streets in protest and only a handful availed themselves of the offer of a new life, including one who could hardly walk.[8]

Rescue work kept attracting new devotees well after the furore of 1885. Coote despaired in 1892 that one of the tendencies weakening NVA branches, like the one in Ipswich, was that 'They immediately started a rescue home' and squandered subscriptions keeping it going.[9] There was competition between denominations. The Salvation Army was first off the mark in 1885 with its bold scheme to bring comfort and the gospel to the female residuum. In the beginning it was none too easy to find landlords willing to let properties earmarked for prostitutes and drunkards and then General Booth was disappointed when his grandiose plan to populate rural and overseas colonies with the redeemed did not materialise. Yet by 1912 over 50,000 girls and women had passed through its forty homes. Where the Salvation Army pioneered the Church Army, formed by the Anglicans when they failed to reach an understanding with the independent General, was sure to follow. By the eve of the war it was running a dozen rescue and preventive homes. Hugh Price Hughes told the annual Wesleyan conference in 1887 that 'The Salvation Army was far in advance of them'; his new West London Mission soon began its own rescue department, as did the Quakers and a bit later a number of the local Free Church Councils.[10]

By 1900 there were over three hundred homes and refuges in Britain caring for about six thousand women annually. Outside workers visited workhouse wards and helped discharged prisoners. The Manchester Friendless Girls' Association arranged with magistrates to let them take charge of first offenders where possible and soon this police-court mission work spread to Cardiff, London and elsewhere. Helping prostitutes and the endangered was an intrinsic part of social work. On the calculation that each home required matrons over laundry, needle, and housework to support the superintendent, the full complement of internal workers alone was 1,200. The Salvation and Church Armies had their own training homes for rescue workers and another was opened in 1901 by the London Diocesan Council for Penitentiary, Rescue and Preventive Work. Gentlewomen served on committees and usually filled the superintendents' posts. Many of the inside jobs were salaried and in 1889 there was a complaint that they were being taken by middle-class women not clever enough to become governesses. The trend, however, was to recruit inside staff from the working classes; the Salvation and Church Armies let poorer women run some of their homes, with the best results obtained. It is interesting to discover that it was as difficult to fill the post of laundry matron as it was to find girls to work under them.[11]

The practice of seeking out the fallen reached a peak at the end of the century. The Salvation Army fielded midnight patrols whose efforts in identifying young prostitutes were sometimes assisted by the police and the reclaimed, who had an instinct for this sort of work. At first Booth held back because of the lack of accommodation. Then in 1894 during the anti-music-hall campaign he launched a series of spectacular midnight marches through the West End. Undaunted by verbal and physical abuse, the band struck up 'Home Sweet Home' as the procession crossed Piccadilly Circus and the lasses distributed hundreds of invitations to dinner at the Oxford Street hall. Sister Mildred and her helpers in the West London Mission preferred to approach the fallen with sweet williams and wallflowers, as did the Church Army sisters. These well-intentioned ladies exhausted every possibility, going into the strawberry fields at harvest time to rescue the immoral and to the seaside on summer mornings in search of prostitutes asleep under boats.[12]

All this, along with the continuing efforts of the Midnight Meeting Movement, failed to keep the homes full. In 1900 it was estimated they could have handled another 1,200 inmates. As long as their mission remained religious conversion, it was difficult to create an appealing environment. While the failure to consider prostitution in a modern psychological and sociological context simply marks the workers as part of their time, some were drawn to the work because they enjoyed punishing the fallen. In 1896 the Bishop of London appointed a committee to visit the diocesan homes and some of the reports provide an appalling commentary on what purported to be Christian charity on the eve of the twentieth century.[13] At the Church

Penitentiary Association's Highgate Penitentiary, the country's largest, the inmates were sweated in the laundry, fed mainly bread and butter, flogged and subjected to 'black hole' punishments in the coal cellar. Exercise had been ruled out because an earlier chaplain believed it stirred up the passions. There was little to choose between Highgate and Holloway. Maddison claimed that some asylums kept consumptive girls in the laundry until they were too sick to work and then put them out of the house. This is an indication of the financial strain the movement was suffering. The laundry vans providing a cut-rate service to large hotels and institutions had to be kept going at all costs. In 1894 the Church Penitentiary Association, with eighty-seven homes and refuges, reported it was nearly bankrupt. This made it difficult to turn down unsuitable applicants or consistently to segregate professional prostitutes from so-called preventive cases.

But there was positive achievement as well. Like many of the older evangelical homes, those of the Salvation and Church Armies tried to provide a loving environment. As one prospective customer said of the former, 'If I had to go any place I would rather go to that Salvation Army than any other rescues (sic), for they do give you plenty of victuals and let you go in and out sometimes'.[14] Some of the smaller homes achieved a high degree of specialisation and expertise. There were those for the unfallen, others like St Cyprien's in London 'for the fallen though not deeply sunk in sin', and maternity homes for unmarried mothers. The alternative was still the workhouse hospital ward. At the point of their greatest expansion, the rescue homes were offering a variety of voluntary social services and probably doing as much for pregnant and troubled girls as for prostitutes.

\* \* \*

The failures of rescue, the constructive half of the formula, hardly slowed down the vigilantes' pursuit of repression. Their partnerships with municipal officials, in fact, often proved an essential condition for the success of a local operation. In surveying these activities against prostitution there is a useful distinction to be made between various kinds of communities, in particular the garrisons, provincial cities and the metropolis. The presence of the army or navy created almost insurmountable obstacles. When the Church of England Purity Society launched an investigation of the garrisons in 1890, Montagu Butler reported to Archbishop Benson, 'The environment of military and naval settlements is an Augean Stable that calls for a Hercules'. At Aldershot and Chatham the troops and their whores tempted official as well as divine wrath by using officers' gardens and church porches for intercourse. Prostitutes were brought into the barracks. Through most of the installations pubs were little better than brothels. Benson threw his weight behind approaches to the War and Navy Departments and interest was roused at the top, in the person of the Commander-in-Chief, the Duke of Cambridge. In 1894 orders went out to some local commanders to assist civil authorities in repressing vice and a dramatic improvement was soon reported in Dover.[15]

At the same time the remarkable anglo-catholic Father Dolling took over Winchester College's St Agatha's Mission in the Landport slums of Portsmouth. Dolling led an interdenominational purity crusade that tackled the city's brothels and pub prostitutes. Just before leaving two years later he capped his work by buying out Landport's last brothel for £250. However, a Home Office comment at that time about the control of prostitution in Portsmouth as a whole concluded, 'They do their best . . . but it is useless to expect much in a garrison town'.[16]

The provincial cities of the north, with their strong nonconformist traditions and sensitive councils and watch committees, responded most readily to social-purity pressure. As we have seen, Manchester's religious leaders were moved by Ellice Hopkins to form a vigilance committee in 1882. Frank Crossley's Society for the Prevention of the Degradation of Women and Children proved that much could be done even without the summary jurisdiction against brothels obtained three years later. When the Manchester police made the mistake of admitting they knew of 402 bad houses in 1882, Crossley made it his first objective to close them. Hunting out brothels was part of defeating the double standard; Crossley said that the appearance of vigilance societies marked 'a distinct step in the rise of woman to her proper place as equal of man'.

Ten years later, after the Society and police had cooperated over hundreds of closures and prosecutions, only three brothels were listed as officially known. While everyone knew there were many more than this, there had been a considerable improve-

ment and Crossley thanked the city fathers for helping invoke
'The Thunder of Sinai'. The Society became an NVA regional
centre in the mid-1890s and while the whorehouses crept back
between peals of biblical thunder, cooperation continued between
city officials and vigilantes, who permanently included Manchester's religious leaders. The cathedral was a citadel of purity
work, with active support over the years from bishops, canons
and deans, the latter post being filled from 1906 by Dr Welldon,
the former headmaster. No wonder Manchester boasted a thriving White Cross movement and cracked down against obscenity
in the pre-war 'great fear' that spread across Britain. At NVA
behest in 1904 the police closed 150 brothels in two hectic weeks.
Shortly before the war, there was some dispute about just how
much prostitution there really was. The professionals had taken
to legally inaccessible furnished rooms. The secretary of the local
NVA, however, insisted that not only had 'the old-time brothel
practically ceased to exist', but that the streets were better and
prostitution had remained diminished over a period of years.[17]

In Sheffield, Leeds and Liverpool the Act of 1885 was enthusi-
astically enforced by the police. Within a few years the number
of brothels known to the Sheffield police fell from 300 to seven
and the Leeds Vigilance Committee was said in 1912 to have
'created . . . a public opinion behind the city council; the police
took action in regard to the houses of ill-fame, and the convictions went up leaps and bounds'.[18]

The social-purity crusade on the Mersey became a major
political issue and resembled the contemporaneous anti-vice
drives in urban America. The agitation here overturned the city's
lax Tory council, which was sympathetic to the brewers, in order
to purge Liverpool's abundant public houses of its prostitutes.
The powerful local temperance puritans were undeterred in
1889 when they failed to get the unreformed watch committee
to order the banning of whores from licensed places. One of the
local divines, the Baptist C. F. Aked, later said of his social-
purity mission, 'The puritanism of the seventeenth century failed
to secure the reign of the saints, but there is no reason why the
puritanism of the twenties should not at least prevent the rule
of the scoundrels'.[19]

It soon became clear that the scoundrels were not limited to
the publicans and the brewers. The able chief constable, William

Nott Bower, was running a system similar to what the Americans called segregation. In 1890 he told a deputation of protesters, 'Our theory in Liverpool has been to try and localise the evil, instead of allowing it to spread into otherwise respectable districts'. Nott Bower insisted that repression was impossible and dismissed the Manchester and Sheffield reductions in known brothels as misleading. The puritans responded by forming a purity party for the November elections. With the help of the Liverpool Temperance Confederation and groups of local liberals, they swept into power, purged the watch committee and issued new instructions to the police. All brothels were to be prosecuted and the police were to oppose the renewal of licences for any premises that served prostitutes. These guidelines remained in force permanently, even after the purity party disintegrated.

The police listed 443 known brothels in 1891, when there were 818 prosecutions. Some keepers paid their fines or took a short enforced holiday and reopened. Nott Bower claimed the 'irrational and irritating' fanatics were pushing vice into respectable neighbourhoods. However, he later admitted, and his successor agreed, that 1890 marked the beginning of 'a very real and visible improvement'. Repression forced many high-class brothels to migrate across the water to Cheshire. The steady reduction in pubs helped clear the streets, as did the increasing willingness of magistrates to convict on perfunctory proof of annoyance. This last development, along with the stricter enforcement of local byelaws against street soliciting, also marked other provincial clean-ups. When Abraham Flexner visited Liverpool shortly before the war, he was told that prostitutes sometimes took their clients to Bootle to ensure tranquillity. While this was hardly a victory for regionalism, it made the streets a less attractive option for inner-city girls.[20]

While purity workers who tried to adopt these political tactics in South Wales met with only mixed success, there was another approach that worked to some effect there and elsewhere. 'Moral moonlighting', as it was called, involved the attempted intimidation of brothel customers by men's patrols. These excursions were something of a minor diversion through northern Europe at the time and it is reliably reported that a Rotterdam patroller with a wooden leg sometimes ended up in a canal.

Judging from the Cardiff clergymen whose lanterns revealed their own parishioners leaving houses of ill-repute, the tactic was not without effect. As Coote noted, 'no houses can survive a fortnight's patrolling in a town of moderate size where men are known'.[21]

The earliest of these patrols sparked the Glasgow clean-up. In the late 1860s spiritually elevated Glaswegians took to surrounding brothels and posting the names of recognised customers on the city walls. This kind of name posting became standard practice in Russia after the revolution. The Victorian patrols caught on throughout the Celtic fringe, in Cardiff, Belfast and especially Dublin, where the thriving White Cross movement was affiliated to the NVA and then organised branches throughout the city and suburbs. There were strict rules here for the workers, who were recommended by their ministers and had to promise not to speak to the women. Their objects were to save men and close brothels. The Dublin police offered advice as well as protection and the two dozen zealots made brothel visits risky for the respectable. One proprietor offered a £1,000 bribe and the keepers allegedly syndicated to share their losses. By 1892 thirty-five bad houses had been put out of business and Mecklenberg Street cleared. The prostitutes reappeared in less respectable districts, a fact of little interest to the Anglo-Irish crusade.[22]

Such tactics could hardly be applied generally in London, though sometimes the vigilantes of Finsbury Park were to be heard singing the Doxology on the steps of a defunct brothel whose clientele had been scared off. It was more than the possibility of anonymity for pleasure seekers that made repression complicated in London. In 1901 C. T. Ritchie, the Home Secretary, told a purity deputation that on these questions 'London stands on a different plane from any other city in the kingdom'.[23] Public opinion was more tolerant and political factors also militated against a hard line. Until the creation of the new tier of borough councils in 1899, the chief responsibility for prosecuting brothels lay with the old parish vestries, who sometimes showed reluctance even after the expediting legislation of 1885 to enter into the reduced expense of pursuing brothels. The Metropolitan police answered to the Home Secretary, who was better insulated from public opinion than were the provincial watch committees. However, he was not completely insulated; strikingly, the great police drives against streetwalkers coincided with peaks of purity agitation.

The first such drive began in 1883. While Harcourt had decided that the general adoption of the Glasgow soliciting law was a necessary sequel to repeal of the CD Acts, London's magistrates had begun to convict streetwalkers more readily. By outlawing 'solicitation to the annoyance of the inhabitants or passengers', the crucial Act of 1839 had always permitted a great deal of discretion. It was open-ended on several points, the most important being whether it was sufficient for a policeman who witnessed annoyance to give the court his account of it without the annoyed party coming forward. While magistrates usually insisted on the elusive corroborative evidence before 1883, at that time they made a significant turnabout to the more repressive interpretation. The Chief Commissioner and the Home Secretary reacted quickly and unleashed the police.[24]

The background to the new judicial and police policy was the touchier public opinion engendered by the white-slave revelations and the thronging of the streets by prostitutes dispossessed from some of London's shuttered pleasure spots. By 1883 a number of vigilance committees had sprung up around town, most led by newly-awakened parish incumbents. The Rev. H. W. Webb Peploe, Vicar of St Paul's, Onslow Square, tried to impose some order on these developments. With the support of the omnipresent Shaftesbury he formed a Central Vigilance Society, inspired by the Societies for the Reformation of Manners. While it was later taken over by the NVA, its early importance was to focus on the government the wish of the parishes for relief from the hordes of prostitutes and undisturbed brothels.

The attempt to get the streets back from the prostitutes ended in disaster in 1887 when Constable Endacott rashly arrested a Miss Cass for soliciting in Oxford Circus. Her indignant protests of innocence produced a furore in the press and in parliament about police tyranny. The force retreated to a low profile and there were two years of near anarchy when observers complained that London was becoming an open whorehouse. Yet by 1889 police policy reverted to the pre-Cass rather than the pre-1883 status quo. Constables were to arrest where annoyance was witnessed, after one warning. This occasionally caused other public-relations disasters as in 1895, when the Oxford anatomy professor was arrested for defending a prostitute in the West End. Still, it became virtually unheard of for the police to wait for a gentleman to complain and in 1900 all the prostitutes convicted for soliciting in Piccadilly were victims of police evidence alone.[25]

After the Cass case the second essential ingredient for an effective street clearing, solid judicial determination to convict, was absent. It was in 1901 that C. T. Ritchie, the police and the magistrates reached the same sort of understanding as their predecessors in 1883. This was a turning point in the social history of the streets; for the following five years marked the most intense clean-up to date. When another alleged false arrest made headlines in 1906 it had only a temporary effect on the drive. Abraham Flexner's observations of pre-war London tell of solicitation by 'stealthy glance or mumbled word', of prostitutes avoiding Bond and Regent Streets by advertising, albeit through sandwich men rather than the modest post-1959 notices.[26] The brazen Victorian harlot was disappearing and the state did not bother to legislate to remove her relatively timid successor from the streets until 1959.

The occasion for the 1901 departure was the new activism of the borough councils. All through the year they had been pressing the authorities about prostitution, while working closely with the social-purity movement. Late in 1901 the Westminster City Council sent a deputation to Ritchie with a mass petition organised by the Public Morality Council asking that the West-End streets be cleared. Not wishing to stir up the police-baiters, the Home Secretary was noncommittal; in fact three days earlier he had met with the chief magistrate and obtained assurances that the bench would be cooperating with the police.[27]

Social-purity leaders had anticipated the new opportunities that would arise with the elected councils and the PMC was Bishop Creighton's way of focusing religious opinion on them and on other public bodies. Creighton was soon ill and his PMC foundering. Sir Joseph Compton Rickett, its nonconformist godfather, called in Coote to become deputy chairman and organiser. By 1901, when Bishop Winnington Ingram took over the chairmanship, the PMC was on a solid basis with over 1,000 members and the federation of virtually every religious denomination in town. The Bishop's devotion to this cause was such that in his thirty-eight-year incumbency he never missed a meeting of the PMC's council or its disorderly houses sub-committee. Thanks to intervention by local vigilance committees and purity-conscious vicars, the results of the first borough council elections had been very satisfactory. The new Watch Committee of the Westminster City Council was in Winnington Ingram's pocket.[28]

Before the coming of the borough councils progress against London's brothels was gradual. In working-class districts the parish vestries believed repression was futile and were reluctant to make pointless expenditures. Even though the Act of 1885 had provided inexpensive summary jurisdiction, it was still common to have to pay agents for the preliminary watching of suspected houses. Only then would the police step in and collect the definitive evidence about the comings and goings that proved a house a brothel.

In the East End Frederick Charrington grew impatient with the inactivity of the local parishes and began one of the typically extravagant campaigns that made him a London legend.[29] In one of his elevated states of mind, Charrington decided to close all the brothels in the East End. The NVA prepared the way in 1886 by obtaining a ruling in the High Court that private persons could take out summonses themselves without bothering to bind over the parish authorities to do so. In the autumn of 1887 Charrington and his helpers from the Tower Hamlets Mission stormed through Whitechapel, Stepney and Shadwell closing up brothels. They concentrated on the dens off the Commercial Road, venturing into places like 'Jack's Hole', where prostitutes and notorious criminals had lived undisturbed for generations. As news of their exploits spread, East-Enders began supplying Charrington with tips for his famous little black book.

Usually the threat of legal proceedings against the keeper or official notice to the landlord was enough to close the houses. When these tactics failed Charrington fell back on exemplary prosecutions. It is reported that 'His name actually excited the same sort of terror as Napoleon in 1813'. Apparently he did not believe in turning the other cheek; on one occasion he was sued for kicking a brothel attendant in the stomach when rescuing a repentant prostitute's possessions. One keeper dropped dead at word of his approach and an unemployed bully was heard to curse him when arrested for stealing nuts.

There was a strange lull in these activities just before and during the appearance of Jack the Ripper, whose murders gripped the East End from August until November 1888. Charrington is one of the few people in a position to have been the Ripper who has never been considered as a suspect. Even Sir Robert Anderson, the CID chief and purity lecturer, was once a leading candidate for the Ripper's mantle. It appears that Charrington was ill during these months, recovering from the effects of his personal ordeal. While there is no evidence to link Charrington with the murders, it is worth speculating on whether his activities in dispossessing Whitechapel prostitutes might have supplied the Ripper with one of his victims. At the height of the panic the police commissioner pointed out that Charrington had forced these women to 'exercise their calling in the streets'. Charrington always invited the prostitutes to his Mission for breakfast and a group photograph but seems to have had little interest in them otherwise. Just after the Ripper terror abated, he launched the second stage in his clean-up. Ultimately he closed over two hundred brothels. While many of them eventually popped up somewhere else, at least he succeeded in stirring some of the East-End vestries into subsequent activity.

Effective work began in south London in 1894, when F. B. Meyer started the most dramatic campaign there since Wat Tyler burnt down the Southwark stews in the Peasants' Revolt five centuries earlier. When Meyer took over Christ Church, Westminster Bridge Road, he decided to reclaim as much of the region as possible. The local Free Church Council helped and the effort gradually gained popularity through the vestries south of the Thames. By the time of the first borough council elections some two hundred brothels had been closed; Meyer's 'Christian stalwarts' then helped obtain sympathetic new councils in Lambeth and Southwark.[30]

The West-End parishes awoke early to their responsibilities, especially because of the keen interest of the vicars in the heartland of vice: St Martin's-in-the-Fields, Trafalgar Square; St James's, Piccadilly and St Anne's, Soho. The activity of the clergy here demonstrates again the new Church-of-England vigour against sexual vice. In 1887 the incumbents of the first two parishes started up a West-End branch of the NVA and over the next thirty years this Charing Cross Vigilance and Rescue Committee was a force for the vicious to reckon with. The vestries used it for intelligence and for the early watching of brothels and they put the archaic system to work by paying rewards to it as a semi-official part of the parish machinery.[31]

A start had thus been made before the great departure of 1899. From then on brothels were able to survive only if the authorities did not know of their existence. The new Westminster City Council's Watch Committee appointed a watcher, received a steady flow of intelligence from the PMC and the Charing Cross Vigilance Committee and closed well over five hundred brothels by 1914. St Pancras Borough Council took a very hard line and reported by 1909, 'The evil has materially decreased here and the possibility of numerous prosecutions has greatly lessened'. Stepney, Fulham and Finsbury followed suit and across the river Meyer's Christian stalwarts helped the authorities close another seven hundred by 1912.[32] In 1905 the *Vigilance Record* paused to ask, 'Is London Becoming Morally Better?' The answer was an enthusiastic yes.

*    *    *

Yet certain qualifications must be registered. To some extent, and not for the first time, improvement masked a relocation of prostitutes. After the night houses had been eliminated in the 1860s and 70s, licensing authorities closed a series of popular but irksome pleasure spots around town, like the Cremorne Gardens in Chelsea and the Highbury Barn. Then in 1878 Alfred Dyer and his brother had a hand in closing the Argyll Rooms, the elegant but notorious dancing emporium that attracted some seven hundred ladies of dubious virtue on a busy night. The unintended consequence of all this was to push more prostitutes on to the streets and to concentrate them in the music-hall promenades. Social-purity workers then pressed the police to clear the streets and music-hall proprietors to cleanse their theatres.

When brothels came under attack in the following decades there were even unseemlier consequences. Poorer prostitutes may well have been driven increasingly to render their services in the open as well as to solicit there. At the height of the London crackdown, in 1905, the number of females charged with having sexual intercourse in the open rose to a formidable 944.[33] The legal onslaught also contributed to the spread of massage parlours, which then as now provided a whole range of sexual services. The main ramifications, though, were to push prostitutes into flats and into the arms of bullies. The appearance of these figures of popular fear, in its turn, lay behind the international movement against white slavery, and the remarkable series of white-slave panics that swept Britain and North America between 1907 and 1914.

To unravel these developments we must first go back to the Act of 1885. Under it, landlords could be held responsible if they knowingly let houses for purposes of prostitution. While it was difficult to prove such knowledge, local authorities and vigilance committees regularly intimidated landlords by sending them formal notice that a house was a brothel. Self-contained flats did not come under the legal definition of a brothel and landlords could not be held responsible for what went on in them. However, respectable property owners became wary about letting even flats to suspect women. Prostitutes on the move as the traditional brothel came under attack thus had a housing problem. Partly to solve it, they paired off with bullies or pimps who posed as their husbands.

This created a new and unsurpassed devil in purity demonology. According to Arthur Lee, parliamentary pilot for the White Slave Bill in 1912, 'The bully was typically the most brutal figure imaginable . . . the most cunning and slippery of all criminals . . . the keystone of the whole structure of commercialised vice'. The prostitute as slave to her bully was the sequel to the prostitute as victim of seduction. While these men could be brutal, the official reaction to Lee's outburst reflects realistic opinion then and now: 'The police do not believe in the wide prevalence of an intolerable system of oppression. Prostitutes like to have a man with them whose presence enables them to get apartments, to have protection from robbery and violence and to have companionship in their off-time'.[34]

While London's chief magistrate, Sir John Bridge, took a more serious view of the phenomenon, it was generally agreed that bullies were proliferating because brothels were being closed and landlords threatened. At the conclusion of one case in 1894

Sir John blasted the vigilance societies whose purifying activities 'drove women into the hands of scoundrels who lived on them, preyed on them and drove them to become thieves. Formerly they were only this in the rarest possible cases, but it was not so now for the vigilance societies had made this sort of crime more common than any other in London'.[35]

With bullies lending commercialised vice a particularly menacing visage, the social-purity movement set out to solve the problem it allegedly had caused. There was little difficulty in working up opinion against those who abetted the selling of sex. Pimps and bullies were not unknown before the 1890s and it was legend amongst West-End vestries that twenty years earlier a Regent Street merchant had formed a vigilance society only to be ruined when prostitutes and their bullies threw up a virtual picket line around his shop. Towards the end of the century, however, more of London's pimps were noticeably foreign, as were the girls they controlled, a part of the problem that could not be blamed on vigilance work. During the 1900s about a quarter of the arrests in London for living off immoral earnings and for prostitution involved foreigners, mostly French, Germans and Belgians as well as Polish and Russian Jews.[36]

In the midst of the controversial mass immigration from Eastern Europe, Londoners did not take kindly to foreign streetwalkers and their ponces. Wildly exaggerated stories abounded about the influx of foreign vice, contributing to the climate of opinion in which the Aliens Act of 1905 was passed. George R. Sims, normally a reliable witness, was convinced that a mysterious central syndicate of foreign bullies systematically divided up the capital into personal provinces. By 1895 an alliance between the parishes and the NVA had emerged to push for legislation that would outlaw living off immoral earnings and send the foreign undesirables home. The West-End vestries were frantic; in 1896 Mr Kitto of St Martin's claimed there were 3,000 foreign bullies in the neighbourhood of Charing Cross and Piccadilly, and Mr Cardwell of St Anne's complained that the situation around Leicester Square was 'notorious and unbearable'.[37]

The government passed a Vagrancy Law Amendment Act in 1898 to deal with the problem. Living off immoral earnings was outlawed, though the Home Office still refused to undertake to expel undesirable aliens. Once again homosexuals got the worst of an outburst of moral indignation aimed at another target, this time pimps. The Tories included one of the most regressive provisions in modern parliamentary history, making it possible to have men convicted for a second time of soliciting other men flogged. The NVA had been pressing for an alteration in the solicitation laws that would bring under their scope men who annoyed women and a provision emerged for punishing men who solicited for immoral purposes in public places. In the aftermath of the Oscar Wilde case it was meant 'to lay hold of a certain kind of blackguard who is unmentionable in decent society'.[38] It was only used against homosexuals and flogging remained fairly common until 1914.

Mr Cardwell called the Act of 1898 a 'crowning victory for the vestries and the vigilance societies'. At the very time it was being passed Coote was looking beyond it. Thirteen years of power and influence had left him with a messianic ambition. It was now time to tackle commercialised vice on a world scale. Coote has left an account of his decision to organise an international movement against white slavery. It happened when he sat down in 1898 to revise the NVA's 'Friendly Warning to Young Women Leaving Their Own Country'.

> ... calling to mind a number of suspicious cases, in which we had been able to do very little, the utter hopelessness of all our methods came over me with a kind of physical oppressiveness. ... Falling rather than leaning back in my chair, I fell into a kind of reverie. Whether it was a Divine Vision, or a day-dream inspired from on High, I know not. ... It had not lasted more than ten or fifteen minutes, but during that time the ideas came as suggestions, and were by me transmitted to paper.[39]

For the last time a Victorian evangelical set out to fulfil a divine moral mission. Coote found peculiarly specific instructions on his paper : tour the Continent to establish national committees against white slavery, hold an international congress in London and then obtain a diplomatic convention on the subject. Coote prayed for £200 from 'heaven's treasury'. His European tour was a triumph and the First International Congress for the Suppression of the White Slave Traffic was duly held in 1899, attended by delegates from forty-five British institutions and eleven nations.

By white slavery Coote and his allies meant any instance of female prostitution abetted by a third party. It might involve one of the professionals brought over from France to take advantage of London's opportunities, or it could mean a virgin drugged and carried off to a brothel. The original aim of the white-slavery crusade was to prevent the movement of women across international borders for purposes of vice. In the mass migration of the time this 'international traffic in girls and women', as the League of Nations later called it, was a significant phenomenon. Yet it is important to remember that just as in the days of the Brussels revelations, only a very small part of the traffic involved white slaves in the most emotive sense of the term. Because this was normally not made clear, the movement against white slavery caught the public imagination, and this time all over the world. On the other hand it would be quite wrong to dismiss the campaign simply as a late-Victorian parody of the classic agitation whose rhetoric it copied, anti-slavery. While British nationals were well protected, female immigrants and others in their European and Asian homelands were sometimes literally shanghaied by procurers, if not driven to prostitution by poverty. Prostitutes away from home were particularly open to exploitation. Believing that commercialised vice itself was exploitative, it was natural for Coote and company to take advantage of public confusion about white slavery in order to strike a blow at pimps and bullies everywhere.

Nobody knew better than Coote that the entrapment of British girls at home and abroad had been eliminated. Supplementing the severe law of 1885, the NVA and the Travellers' Aid Society posted warnings, shepherded nervous travellers to their final destinations and carried out thousands of enquiries for girls going into new situations. Just a few weeks before Coote's vision, the always militant Mrs Chant rhapsodised about the 'revolution' in such provisions.[40]

The occasional cases of entrapment that had surfaced usually involved young entertainers recruited for European or South American *cafés chantants*. It was not until after the First World War that the problem was largely resolved, with warnings from the Variety Artists' Federation and occasional Foreign Office prohibitions to troupes wishing to go to Buenos Ayres. The two girls whom Coote was asked to come and collect by the English consul in Rotterdam in 1887 were not so fortunate. One of them had been instructed, 'If you are cheeky to the gentleman you will get lots of presents. You must ask them to give you champagne, and to buy you gloves and cigarettes'. The other girl was brought home from the local V D hospital. Girls were underpaid, fined and worn down by indebtedness. Yet it is the case that many of these young entertainers refused to return home with Coote, when he was summoned by English consuls through northern Europe.[41]

In 1901 Scotland Yard reported that it was five years since they had received a complaint 'as to any English girl having been procured for immoral purposes for the Continent'.[42] By this time Coote had begun to lay the basis for the first in a series of international conventions. He and his friends were particularly upset by the arrival in London of large numbers of foreign prostitutes, many of whom were stopping off on their journey to destinations beyond Europe. The Jewish Association for the Protection of Girls and Women did an excellent job alerting British social-purity leaders to the presence of some of these alien prostitutes and to cases of entrapment. The Jews had formed their rescue society in 1885 under the guidance of philanthropists from the great old families: Constance Battersea, who was a Rothschild, and two of her relations, Claude Montefiore and Arthur Moro. They established rescue and training homes and put Yiddish-speaking agents to work meeting ships at the London docks. The task was daunting, as between 1885 and 1914 nearly 300,000 Jews escaping the hardships of life in Eastern Europe passed through the port of London.

In 1898 one of the officials of the Jewish Association received word that a group of girls had been procured for immoral purposes and was about to sail for Cape Town on the *S.S. Tonic.* The police raced to the Royal Albert Docks but there was nothing they could do. The law required warrants for the arrest of procurers. The score of girls were all known to the police as prostitutes and they and their bullies waved farewell as the ship sailed.[43] Coote started his agitation to prevent scenes like this. The Jewish Association pushed him ahead, picking up a large share of the expenses for the 1899 international congress and helping plan out the nature of the struggle.[44] Once the white-slavery flag was raised, purity workers instinctively felt that commercialised vice itself, with its army of pimps and bullies, would come under fierce attack.

# 8

# The International Crusade against the White-Slave Traffic

HAVELOCK ELLIS complained in 1912 that 'During the past ten years one of those waves of enthusiasm for the moralisation of the public by the law has been sweeping across Europe and America'.[1] While the pursuit of the obscene and education for chastity were part of the phenomenon, white slavery was the issue that caused the greatest sensation and evoked the most response in official circles. Social purity advanced because it was concerned with the health and abundance of the race in an age of imperial mission and military rivalry. Purity and preparedness, however, were not the whole story. The Dutch were largely out of international adversary politics and in 1911 they rushed through a morals law that punished white-slave traders and persons who exposed any article which 'offends decency', and this law raised the age of consent to twenty-one.

The injection of the partly symbolic old bugbear of white slavery into the social politics of the western world suggests that particularly sensitive factors were at play, including fears generated by the changing role of women, domestic and international migrations and rapid urban and industrial growth. Coote and company could hardly have chosen a more explosive issue around which to organise their attack on commercialised vice. Bunting held that success was guaranteed by Coote's 'insight that the whole of the respectable world would be brought into line'.

In the short run the British leaders wanted an international treaty banning the procuring of any woman to go abroad for prostitution. Once their propaganda achieved momentum, they believed that opinion would be created for agreements that were impossible in 1899, including one limiting state regulation. Coote said that the Butlerites' old nemesis would be undermined 'by the natural law of progression'.[2] With state-sanctioned vice still so well entrenched around the world, however, it was prudent to proceed one step at a time. Like Josephine Butler's self-styled 'new abolitionists', this newest of liberation movements saw itself as in the tradition of anti-slavery. Bunting argued by analogy that it had been the slave trade rather than slavery itself that had come under attack initially. Therefore, he continued, 'it occurred to Mr Coote that there were immense numbers of private individuals and societies and governments who could not be induced to Mrs Butler's primary condition . . . and that these people could be got together in a . . . movement to do away with the horrors of "middle passage", the recruitment, the purchase and sale and transport of these girls from one part of the world to another.'[3]

Mrs Butler responded cautiously, sensing that the issue could help her as it had twenty years earlier. She wrote to an old friend, 'I have had letters abroad from friends telling me of the immense zeal and interest which the conference (Mr Coote's) is arousing, Miss Humbert sees it as such a contrast to the little interest taken in our direct Federation work, which is much more difficult to arouse. . . .' With the convening of the 1899 Congress her doubts increased. The French delegation was led by Senator Beranger, known to his countrymen as 'father prude' for his outspoken leadership of the anti-obscenity forces in France. More to the point, he was a staunch regulationist and his committee included Le Père du Lac, a Jesuit anti-Dreyfusard whom Josephine called 'a dreadful man'.[4] While the Dutch, Swiss and Swedish delegations were staunchly abolitionist, the Germans were not. This appeared to be an unstable coalition that would accomplish little of importance.

As it turned out, by avoiding the issue of regulation, the national committees established at and after the 1899 Congress obtained the financial support of governments and the patronage of royal families and leading politicians across the Continent. In addition to the flood of new measures for the protection of women, the Butlerites were indirectly helped. The French repealers admitted as much and the Dutch abolition of state regulation in 1913 was probably expedited by the white-slavery issue. Most of the national committees came to oppose state regulation and on the motion of the Germans the 1913 Congress resolved against state brothels.

In 1899 an International Bureau was established in London to coordinate the movement and work for a diplomatic convention. It was the NVA executive in another guise, with delegates co-opted from the national committees. The British National Committee was composed of two delegates from each of twenty social-purity, religious and women's societies. Bishop Talbot was the first president of the International Bureau and the British National Committee. Both could do much while avoiding the abolitionist quagmire. The international traffic was admittedly cruel, after all, even to the professionals caught up in it and its dimensions were remarkably wide.

* * *

By the late-nineteenth century the steamship and the telegraph had made prostitutes nearly as migratory as when they followed medieval markets, fairs and armies. The white-slavery offices established in most European police departments after the international convention of 1902 also used modern technology. In St Petersburg the Russians showed Coote a rogue's gallery of one hundred photographs of known traders in 1906 and the German police had one hundred and fifty. These commercial travellers were easier to photograph than to arrest. The laws against procuring were insufficient and the police were usually one step behind.

Most observers agree that the traditional brothel was becoming unpopular with prostitutes, and this, as much as the clients' demand for variety, accelerated the turnover in recruits. The actual pattern of the traffic was dictated by social, political and economic factors. Looking at supply, it is hardly surprising that the largest proportion of females came from regions of endemic poverty and even starvation. Until the League of Nations inherited the work of the International Bureau, the movement focused on Europe and emphasised the 'white' in white slavery. By 1887, however, from his new outpost in Bombay, Alfred Dyer was reporting on the substantial traffic in Chinese girls, purchased from their parents, who were shipped through Shanghai, Hong Kong and Singapore to wherever Chinese men and Europeans were found in Asia and Australia. Dyer's reports were strikingly confirmed in detail by the League of Nations investigation of 1934.[5] By then much had been done to solve the problem that caused Dyer to start a Bombay Midnight Mission and get himself beaten night after night. This was the appearance of European prostitutes in all the ports of Asia following the 1869 opening of the Suez Canal; they came largely from Austria, Rumania, Russia, Greece and France—the sources of supply for West as well as East that were of most concern to the International Bureau.

Greek prostitutes predominated amongst Europeans plying the trade in the Middle East. In one of the fanciful *exposés of* 1912, a Salvation Army leader and a crusading Australian senator claimed that marauding Arab raiders kidnapped Greek girls from their islands and sold them into prostitution. We do know that in 1910 the Alexandria Society for the Suppression of the White Slave Traffic helped nearly a thousand Greek girls without resources and two years later Greece passed legislation forbidding girls under the age of twenty-one from going abroad without a special permit.[6]

French prostitutes were also on the move because procurers here thrived under state regulation. A prominent lawyer on the French National Committee claimed in 1904 that in the previous quarter-century 4,000 French girls had gone into Sultan Abdul Hamid's harem. The information that Coote brought back from Buenos Ayres, notorious for its brothels, in 1913 is probably more reliable. French prostitutes comprised twenty-five per cent of all those registered there. Others were probably suffering in clandestine prostitution; for there are legal cases on record in France at the time of real coercion, including the trial in 1908 of a gang of fifty people who trapped girls and held them at gunpoint before sending them abroad or to the provinces.[7]

We knew most about the Jewish sources of supply because Jewish philanthropy was at the forefront of the efforts against the traffic. The investigations of the London-based Jewish Association for the Protection of Girls and Women, which became the headquarters for a worldwide network of committees, and the fieldwork of German-Jewish social workers in Southern and Eastern Europe, are amongst the most interesting materials extant on the history of prostitution in the period. Speaking of Jewish involvement in commercialised vice, the Chief Rabbi of Britain told the Jewish International Conference on the traffic in 1910 that 'we can trace this deplorable change directly to the recrudescence of active Russian persecutions in 1881'.[8] This was certainly part of the story for the more than four million Jews crowded into the towns of the pale of settlement in the western Russian empire. Official anti-semitism meant economic deprivation, a condition of life shared too by the bulk of the Jews in the neighbouring Hapsburg provinces of Galicia and Bukovina, and in Rumania.

Moral indifference is the handmaiden of poverty. Jewish procurers appeared in Eastern Europe to take advantage of the girls who drifted into prostitution or to prepare snares for the many who were anxious to start a new life anywhere else. Certain traditional features of Jewish life abetted the procurers. Abandoned wives were not entitled to a divorce and the economic prospects of those posted a divorce by husbands who had emigrated to raise money were little better.

Traditional marriages amongst the unemancipated were open to abuses. Couples could marry, much as they did in medieval Christian Europe, without the presence of a religious dignitary and there was no guarantee that any marriage would be registered with the civil authorities. Procurers were known to go through the traditional ritual and then take their legally unmarried and largely unprotected partners off to a domestic or foreign brothel. A report by the Polish National Committee in 1927 says these women were 'the most tragic figures among the victims of the traffic'. Since their mates were not legally married either, there was nothing to prevent them from repeating the process. The report tells of one agent who sold a dozen wives to brothels.[9] While such diabolical fraud was comparatively rare, there were some notable cases of entrapment. In 1892 twenty-two men were convicted in Lemberg for procuring girls from small Galician towns with promises of jobs as servants, and selling them to brothels in Constantinople, Alexandria and points east of Suez. The Austrian consul in Constantinople had rescued sixty of them from virtual imprisonment the year before.[10]

From the evidence available, it is possible to see Jewish prostitution in perspective. Typically, in Cracow during the first decade of the century where Jews constituted thirty per cent of the population, they accounted for sixteen per cent of the registered prostitutes. In 1914 the secretary of the Jewish Association reported, 'In all my enquiries in different countries I have unfortunately had to admit that there are many Jewish traffickers and that there are many Jewish victims. But I have found that they are not in a majority anywhere, although the numbers are certainly much larger than they should be'.[11]

Jewish reformers responded actively to this development. In 1905 members of the socialist Jewish Bund in Warsaw attacked their co-religionists' vice district, killing eight pimps and injuring another hundred. The cossacks had to be called in to restore order. In Cardiff at about the same time, members of a Jewish vigilance committee got themselves charged with assault during their attempts to purify the streets.[12] The unsavoury situation was described by Shalom Asch in his *God of Vengeance*, first performed under the direction of Max Reinhardt in Berlin in 1910. This publicised a problem that not everyone was anxious to talk about.

Bertha Pappenheim, the German social worker and feminist, pinpointed the dilemma : 'If we admit the existence of the traffic our enemies decry us; if we deny it, they say we are trying to conceal it'. In an age of the new ritual murder trials it made some sense not to give your enemies ammunition. However, the argument prevailed amongst philanthropists and social workers at the 1910 Jewish International Conference that it was necessary to risk publicity by seeking to join national committees and by sectarian field work. The Jewish Association in London led the way, promoting local committees around the world and distributing financial support. No individual did more than Bertha Pappenheim, described by Martin Buber as 'a woman in whom passion and intellect were most felicitously combined'.[13] She left her base in Frankfurt to do preventive work with her unemancipated sisters in Galicia and the Balkans. Earlier in her life she had been the 'Anna O' of the seminal *Studies in Hysteria* by Freud and Josef Breuer. As such she was the first patient in the history of psychoanalysis. While the work of the International Bureau ultimately resulted in a series of hysterical white-slave panics, the problems Bertha Pappenheim and her colleagues uncovered were all too real.

The chief dumping grounds for the international traffic were Buenos Ayres, as we have seen, and Egypt and Constantinople. All were regulationist and thoroughly corrupt. This meant steady demand and little trouble for procurers who chose to supply the clandestine brothels. Bribery and corruption also opened the

United States to domestic and international commercialised vice. Traders in Egypt and Constantinople had the additional advantage of the inefficient legal system of capitulations, which meant that foreigners came under their own national laws enforced by their own creaky consular courts.

Sex ratios were another factor of considerable importance in the market for prostitutes. Where the pattern of migrations provided a surplus of males, as in parts of South America, prostitutes redressed the balance. Buenos Ayres was only the tip of the South American iceberg. On their tours Coote and Samuel Cohen, secretary of the Jewish Association, found European prostitutes through provincial Argentina and Brazil. The absence of women was also behind the traffic to Alaskan and South African minefields and Michigan and Wisconsin timber camps. It is interesting that when the Women's Christian Temperance Union tried to create a second 'Maiden Tribute' in 1887 around the revelation that women were lured to the lumber camps and virtually held captive, it failed to have much impact.[14] After the beginning of the international movement, which radiated from the NVA offices in London, American politicians like those of other nations would be moved to act.

\* \* \*

The International Bureau's first priority was to have the subject included in the corpus of international law. It was not lost on the delegates to the London Congress of 1899 that the first Hague Peace Conference was meeting simultaneously. The Earl of Aberdeen, who became NVA president in the following year, was one of the leaders of the International Crusade for Peace. There were grandiose ideas about what might be accomplished and Beranger looked forward to an 'International Union for the common protection of human life, in fact, even property'.

It proved as difficult to reach an effective international agreement about sex as it did about war. While the International Bureau hoped Britain would take the lead and summon a conference, the government hesitated on the grounds that there was not enough evidence to show that new legal departures were required. Besides, Britain was in the midst of the Boer War. The French always showered the white-slavery movement with attention in order to demonstrate the human face of state regulation.

G

In 1902 delegates from sixteen European nations assembled in Paris under Delcassé, the Foreign Minister, and drafted the first minimal agreement. The British delegate was none other than Thomas Snagge, then a judge, who had done so well in Brussels in 1881. When the convention was ratified two years later, it bound the signatories to establish a central authority to collect and communicate information about white slavery; to have ports and stations watched for procurers; to supervise employment agencies who sent women abroad; and to instruct officials to collect information leading to the detection of the traffic.

This required no controversial domestic legislative departures about state regulation and it was not everything that even the cautious International Bureau desired. The gap between the diplomats and the voluntary workers was partly closed in 1910 when delegates went back to Paris to draft an initial convention on obscene publications, another evil now the subject of international cooperation, and to amend the one on white slavery. This time it was agreed to adjust domestic laws, if necessary, to punish the procuring of girls under the age of twenty, even if the victims gave consent, and the procuring of any woman by force or fraud; these acts would be criminal even if committed across national borders and would be extraditable.[15]

The tensions between the national committees continued. The French and Germans bickered at the triennial congresses about whether the traffic to South America went through Le Havre or Hamburg. As the Germans became abolitionist they ganged up with the Dutch against the French. At the sparkling 1913 Congress back in London, attended by royalty, dignitaries and volunteers from twenty-four nations, the Germans introduced a successful resolution against licensed brothels. The Dutch had been trying since 1908 to commit the movement to repeal, when the trial of the cruel white-slave gang already described took place in Paris. The brothel-keepers who had bought some of the girls for local use came to court as top-hatted spectators. Dr De Graaf, the Dutch Butlerite, shouted, 'It was Mr Coote, our venerable Secretary, who gave us this good advice: "Let us make concessions, let us work together, union will come later." But now we have done with concessions. Too late, no more concessions'.[16] The French were free to ignore the resolution and the diplomats did not resolve against regulation itself until it was already dead in France, when the United Nations took over the work after the Second World War.

While the first two conventions failed to address the institutional and social causes of the traffic, they evoked considerable activity and some of it was worthwhile. By the time the war stopped the work and the traffic there were about twenty functioning national committees. At a meeting of the British National Committee in 1906, the Earl of Lytton put Coote's role in perspective and compared English to continental approaches: 'Mr Coote is the life and soul of the whole movement . . . in organising any work on the Continent, one has to go first to headquarters . . . and having secured official cooperation, everything goes quite smoothly forward. In England the contrary is the case. These movements spring forward by the force of public opinion'.[17] Coote travelled tens of thousands of miles to bring the weight of British opinion to bear on foreign officials. Only in the United States, Canada and Holland did volunteer workers seize the initiative and remain relatively autonomous, as in Britain.

Many of the other committees were quasi-governmental, relying on public money and official direction. In Germany, Coote's first stop in 1898, the breakthrough came when his clerical contacts immediately interested the Empress. Soon, though, men and women from Catholic, Jewish and relatively right-wing philanthropic and voluntary societies connected with the Evangelical Church were surprisingly united in the effort. The German National Committee became the close ally of a special imperial police office and it was used to communicate with foreign sources and for other tasks. Coote's visit to Spain in 1902 led to a very effective committee formed with royal patronage by the decree of King Alfonso. In 1914 Coote helped the Portuguese Prime Minister initiate a committee under his own chairmanship and at that time the Hungarian National Committee was chaired by Count Tisza, the prime minister.[18] With such support there was considerable willingness to fulfil the spirit of the agreements. In regulationist countries it was a noncontroversial way to demonstrate a progressive attitude.

It was more difficult to organise in the receiving areas, where official support was slower to compensate for the absence of any endemic tradition of voluntary work. The Balkan Wars disrupted the efforts of the Jewish Association in Constantinople, where the authorities allegedly were only concerned to keep Turkish girls out of the trade. Conditions were terrible. In the Galata district prostitutes were kept in cages facing the street, a feature not unusual in Asian vice. In 1914 Coote helped US Ambassador Henry Morganthau launch a national committee in a meeting at the American Embassy, though the war cut short its efforts. By 1912 early work in Egypt was in disarray and the treasurer of the Alexandria Committee was in jail for embezzlement of its funds. Coote went back to reorganise and Lord Kitchener, the Viceroy, proved a great help. New committees emerged with the membership of diplomats and native officials in Port Said, Alexandria and Cairo. Occasional convictions began to take place and even 'The Beautiful Julot', the legendary French procurer, was arrested.[19]

The International Bureau's first real initiative in Argentina involved one of those extraordinary but fully confirmed incidents which demonstrate that the most lurid forms of white slavery were an occasional reality. In 1910 one Vizar, a Polish immigrant, married a Cardiff girl and in the following year he took her to Argentina on the pretext of visiting his brother. Once there Mrs Vizar was sold to a brothel for £250 and threatened that if she tried to leave her infant daughter would be harmed. An English ship's engineer who visited the house reported her plight to the English Seamen's Mission and she was rescued in a spectacular police raid. Mrs Vizar returned home, divorced her treacherous first husband and married an Arab seaman from the cosmopolitan Cardiff dock area, and placed her little girl in an orphanage. All this came to light in 1927 when she tried unsuccessfully to regain custody of the girl.[20]

After Mrs Vizar's escape, Coote and Samuel Cohen went out to Argentina to shore up the defences. The Argentine National Committee had accomplished little. The local Jewish Committee was struggling against the apathy of the settled West-European and German community, which was not anxious to acknowledge the fact that hundreds of prostitutes filtered in with the 100,000 Jewish immigrants from Eastern Europe who landed between 1890 and 1914. The two local committees shared the services of the figure who actually inscribed the prostitutes for licensed work. From 1903 he spent a few hours each day at the public *Dispensario* licensing and placing rescue leaflets in all the registration books. While he kept underage prostitutes off the rolls, he could hardly do anything about clandestine prostitution or the conditions that persisted in the licensed houses. After his extensive tour, Samuel Cohen said about these conditions, 'I am of the opinion that most of these women had led a life of prostitution before going to South America, and that they went voluntarily. I feel sure, however, that false representations were made to them'. They were often unable to extricate themselves from debt, and the same was true of the artistes in the South American *cafés chantants*.[21]

The two London investigators agreed that Buenos Ayres was not as irredeemably evil as they had expected to find it. Conditions were better than in the late nineteenth century when the city had achieved its unenviable reputation. A few months after their departure the Argentine government passed its first legislation against procuring, which protected females under the age of twenty-one. Coote was described in the debate as the 'self-denying apostle of a holy cause'. The *Buenos Ayres Standard* claimed that 2,000 procurers withdrew one-and-a-half million pesos from their bank accounts and left 'as if fleeing from an earthquake'. At the same time the International Bureau despatched to Buenos Ayres Mrs Lighton Robinson, one of the NVA's travelling secretaries; there, in her relentless search for white slaves, she met and boarded every passenger ship to land in the port between 1913 and 1931.[22] While the international traffic was far from dead in South America it was past its peak. The war interfered with Coote's acceptance of an official invitation to Brazil where the government passed age-of-consent and anti-procuring legislation in 1915. The fears generated by the opening of the Panama Canal in the previous year brought Chile into the movement. South America was open to European moral opinion and to the persistent entreaties from those NVA offices in the Strand.

\* \* \*

In Europe elaborate steps were being taken to safeguard women from procurers for the overseas vice markets. The British government fulfilled the first requirement of the 1902 convention by establishing as the central authority a special bureau at Scotland Yard. It collected intelligence, much of it from the voluntary organisations, and stepped up police measures against procurers. While prosecutions rose after 1902 the requirement of warrants limited what could be done. On a typical occasion in 1903 an NVA worker in Victoria Station spotted the notorious Tilly, a French actor and bully, with a Belgian prostitute in tow. At the approach of the vigilant lady Tilly ran off and was probably out of town by the time the warrant was obtained. On the Continent the same voluntary intelligence and redoubled police work was evident. Where domestic laws on procuring did not measure up to the 1910 convention they were changed.

The signatories also met their undertaking to do something about registries that sent women abroad. In fact, despite the longstanding efforts of the NVA, Girls' Friendly Society and other groups to protect servants, the issue became something of a rage.[23] In 1904 the NVA turned down a scheme of Stead's to open a chain of sixty employment bureaux through London, and another, by Alfred Harmsworth, who wanted Coote to do the enquiry work for a Domestics' Bureau established by his *Daily Mirror*. Regulation was the goal, and it came through local bye-laws in London and where NVA chapters were strong. An Act of 1913 prohibited the employment abroad of artistes under the age of fourteen and mandated special licences for those under sixteen. A number of nations joined Greece in requiring mayoral or parental permission for the emigration of underage girls. After the 1906 Triennial Congress in Paris, Clemenceau, then French Interior Minister, ordered strict regulation of *cafés chantants*.

Everywhere measures were forthcoming to protect females and curb commercialised vice. The expansion of travellers' aid work was indicative of the climate at the time. There were already extensive arrangements for protecting anxious and inexperienced travellers in 1903, when Coote launched an ambitious force of paid and unpaid port and station watchers called the International Guild of Service for Women. Always interested in pushing the slave-trade analogy, Bunting later wrote that 'in the course of transport of these girls from one part of the world to another, they must all go through the narrow neck of the railway stations and ports, and if you can catch them there you will be able to do what our naval cruisers did in stopping the Arab dhows—you catch the freight in transit and so put a stop to the traders' business'.[24]

Hitherto the primary concern of travellers' aid workers had been to protect the innocent. Now the International Guild sought also to intercept prostitutes and send them home. Like so much else in the white-slavery campaign, there was a basic ambiguity about what was going on. However, Coote's report to the Home Secretary on the six-month pilot project that initiated the Guild is clear enough. His team of ladies in the London termini and the ports of Dover, Hull and London had participated in 2,500 cases. While there was plenty of help for innocents abroad, the workers spent much of their time at the points of arrival or later in the streets trying to persuade foreign prostitutes to leave England.

Coote asked for an officially controlled and supported staff 'ostensibly for the purpose of rendering first-aid to the foreign women as they arrive, but really judiciously to ascertain for what purpose they come....' The government was not interested in supporting the work. While the Aliens Act of 1905 gave magistrates discretionary power to repatriate foreign prostitutes, that power was used sparingly at first. There were good arguments for foreign prostitutes and Chief Commissioner Henry advised, 'As there must always be prostitutes, it is perhaps less demoralising to have foreign than Englishwomen and if you get rid of the former, their places will be taken by Englishwomen. The foreigner is more amenable to control....'[25]

The new travellers' aid work caught the imagination of the public and of women's groups. The NVA soon had the cooperation of virtually all the railway and steamship companies in London, where it put nearly fifty women on permanent duty. In many of the provincial ports the city fathers and local vigilance committees cooperated in the effort. The Hull branch of the NVA was reorganised in 1902 by Lady Nunburnholme, whose husband owned a shipping line. With financial support from the city its agents were first to board all passenger ships that landed in the port. They were undeterred when one of their number fell into the sea and was nearly lost in the fog. In Sunderland, where the mayor was a member of the NVA regional centre, special watch was kept for the regular arrivals of the *S.S. Venus* from Bergen. In Liverpool the Lord Mayor and foreign consuls welcomed trained ladies from London in 1907 who were on permanent duty at the landing stage to meet the steamers from

Ireland and help foreign women in transit from Europe to the United States. The Travellers' Aid Society resented these intrusions and tried to keep the NVA out of Southampton, but to no avail. Foreign governments and national committees sent delegates to London for instructions and by 1910 travellers' aid work through Europe was coordinated by a secret telegraphic code, common armbands and international conferences.[26]

The little army of workers gave some aid and comfort to the emigrants on their way to America. Hull, Liverpool and London were all important trans-shipment points for the North-European migration and it was not unusual for young women to travel unaccompanied or for groups of children to travel in charge of the eldest. The International Bureau was also concerned with conditions in steerage, which one worker described in 1890 as 'a forest of iron poles on which the hammocks, sometimes a thousand in number, are all slung in three layers, for men, women and children, together, with no possible privacy or decency, spreading a moral contagion. . . .'[27] Partly because of social-purity pressure, conditions were somewhat improved by 1914, with steerage on the newer ships broken up into compartments.

The fact remains that much of the port and station work was a waste of time. Once Coote failed to get official support for his Maginot Line to stop prostitutes at the borders, the obvious motive for meeting boat trains and ships was lost. Occasionally cases of entrapment were uncovered or whores were prised from their pimps at Dover. But many of the 35,000 persons aided by the International Guild through 1914 were similar to the American woman who had come to England for the coronation of George V and called on the workers at Liverpool to help her find her lost luggage.

The constant use of the term 'white slavery' and the permanent search for victims had predictable consequences. Through Britain and North America it finally generated a series of hysterical panics. In 1907 Coote honoured an invitation to help launch the US National Vigilance Committee in New York. While he was travelling in the east, the first in a series of revelations about commercialised vice broke in Chicago. The subsequent North American campaign was marked by the same ambiguity over the meaning of 'white slavery' as the British one. Sometimes it referred to cases like that of the woman in 1913 who was alleged to have been pricked in a Newark, New Jersey, cinema with a needle filled with South American 'woorale' poison. Other times it meant the wretched plight of prostitutes recruited from the growing urban slums mostly by immigrant procurers, who were figures of fear in America as in Britain.

By 1914 it was claimed that over one billion pages had been written on white slavery in North America. By then absurd drugging and abduction reports had become endemic. In this climate of opinion the Progressive opponents of segregated vice districts and urban corruption made significant gains. Before the war over fifty cities abandoned segregation for repression. In addition to the Mann Act, the famous US federal law against procuring, forty-two states passed their own so-called white-slave measures.[28]

In Britain the social-purity lobby's attempt to push its long-delayed measure against procurers, bullies and brothel-keepers through the overburdened parliament of 1912 was the immediate occasion for the great panic. During the debates on the white-slavery bill one MP claimed his constituents were much more concerned about this issue than the insurrectionary Irish Home Rule crisis. The curious hysteria was long in the making. Coote's vision and all the subsequent publicity had made white slavery a familiar topic of conversation and opened a pandora's box of repressed fears.

In an age of female emancipaion it was comforting for men to subscribe to the white-slave myth, with its connotation of female helplessness, because it symbolised the simpler days before women demanded personal and political rights. As adolescents became the objects of increased social control it was natural for parents to give credence to the same myth. For generations fear of the city, adolescent fantasy and an element of real entrapment had generated white-slave stories from girls. While the actual abuse had virtually disappeared there were good reasons why Coote's campaign evoked a torrent of such tales. Many reported abductions and druggings were connected with contemporary novelties that had both frightening and stimulating facets, the dark cinema and the powerful motor car. Then too the white-slave story had to do double duty because the larger myth of which it was a part, that young women who engaged in sex had been seduced, lay in ruins. Seductive women were a recognised fact of life by the 1890s. It was no longer so easy for girls and women to take refuge from the guilt of sexual activity or desire in the notion that they were at the mercy of seducers. Once Coote set the white-slave trader stalking through the land, this figure was pressed into service to fill the psychological role of the Victorian seducer. Frederick Bullock, the head of Scotland Yard's special new white-slavery bureau, wrote during the panic of 1912 of girls whose employment opened them to seduction or who received immoral proposals:

> To all such instances it has become fashionable to attach the stigma of the white slave traffic; but is it not reasonable to suppose that with the modern desire for independence and liberty of action which has become so characteristic of women, it is not only the man who is to blame for some of the deplorable consequences which follow in the search for a free and uncontrollable life?[29]

These factors made the pre-war scare more endemic than that of 1885, when the working classes absorbed most of the shock. On both occasions, though, propaganda and rumour fuelled the panic and feminists politicised it. By 1910 England was being deluged with articles, plays and books on the theme; the Canterbury Music Hall even staged *The White Slaves of London*. It was an international rage. Italians were treated to *The White Slave*, a five-act melodrama about a local girl trapped in Buenos Ayres, with a verse prologue read by Gabriele D'Annunzio's son. In the following year the Swiss and Danish National Committees gave their sanction to the first film on the subject. When commercial interests followed with *White Slave 2* and *White Slave 3* the committees backed off, concerned that 'vicious instincts' might be aroused.[30] This sort of film arrived in Britain after the war and helped perpetuate the myth through the interwar period. In the meantime, the issue was taken up by the suffragists. Moderates like Millicent Fawcett and militants like the Pankhursts and Alison Neilans, their supporter and then secretary of the LNA, agreed that the vote was wanted to purify society. Suffragists were handed this symbolic issue of violation and victimisation and they found it irresistible.

Once the International Bureau was well under way the social-purity lobby went shopping with a grocery list of proposals for the further protection of women from the various modes of

violation, including abduction, seduction, rape, incest and juvenile prostitution. After years of official opposition the Incest Act
was obtained in 1908 with the parliamentary help of Donald
Maclean.[31] There were almost more bills in parliament for
raising the age of consent to eighteen and abolishing the 'reasonable cause to believe defence' than one can keep track of. Bishop
Winnington Ingram's advocacy of these measures made him a
suffragist; speaking of one of the PMC efforts in 1914, he told
the Lords, 'If I had a million women's votes behind me I should
carry this bill into law'.[32]

It was the worst possible time to raise controversial issues
which split the government. The Liberals were embroiled with
their complex social welfare programme, with the constitutional
crisis over Lloyd George's budget and the Parliament Bill and with
Irish Home Rule and votes for women. In 1909, however, the
Home Office pledged support for some relatively uncontentious
steps to strengthen the law against bullies, procurers and brothel-
keepers. These proposals had 'originated in the office of the
Jewish Association in 1905'. Anxious to close the loopholes in the
law dealing with commercialised vice, that group's approach to
Coote and Bishop Winnington Ingram had resulted in the formation of a conjoint committee that met at Montefiore's home to
draft proposals. The Home Office found them helpful and
promised to help with what one of the civil servants called 'a
useful little bill'.[33]

As the prewar domestic crisis deepened the Liberal Party's
managers hardly had their thoughts on bullies and their accomplices. While the government had promised to provide time for
the so-called Criminal Law Amendment (White Slavery) Bill
once it was introduced by a private member, something more
urgent always intervened. When the measure was blocked in
April 1912 by a coalition of Tories and libertarians reminiscent
of the one that had dogged the great Act of 1885, social-purity
leaders did not know where to turn. Fate then struck in the
form of an iceberg: W. T. Stead went down on the *Titanic*. It
seems fitting that he was accompanied by fifty-six per cent of the
third-class women passengers and hardly any of the better off.
Inspired by his gallant martyrdom and reminded of his earlier
sacrifice, the bill's supporters decided to push ahead at all costs.

By June a 'Pass the Bill Committee' under Mrs Bunting, a

leader in rescue work, was coordinating the activities of the suffragists, women's liberal associations, religious bodies and purity institutions. With hundreds of petitions pouring in the government made time for the measure; but it was slashed up in committee. The clause to permit constables to arrest suspected procurers without a warrant was rendered useless; the one to root out prostitution from flats by punishing the person in charge of the building was deleted; about all that was left in was the provision to flog men on a second conviction for living off immoral earnings.

That summer and autumn, along with the London dockers' strike and the militant suffragists' attacks on pillar boxes and golfing greens, fears of white slavery reached epidemic proportions. According to Frederick Bullock, 'a remarkable manifestation of anxiety was exhibited in regard to the dangers run by women and girls in the streets of London, for which there was in fact no justification or foundation. All sorts of stories, sensational and wholly improbable, were repeated from mouth to mouth of sudden disappearances, abductions and attempts to entice and allure innocent girls. . . .'[34] In addition to the fuel supplied by the 'Pass the Bill Committee' and the daily press, there was even a new rag called *The Awakener* begun by a Men's Society For Women's Rights. Fake nurses were said to be on the prowl in department stores, a Hampstead hairdresser's daughter was carried off in a motor car and girls were being chloroformed in the streets.

In mid-October Reginald McKenna, the Home Secretary, promised an influential deputation he would get the bill through, though it was agreed that the regulation of flats would have to be sacrificed. Feeling ran high in the House that such a provision would lead to mass evictions of prostitutes from their homes and their further victimisation by bullies. The debates on the later stages of this White Slave Bill in November, attended by up to four hundred MPs, remind one more of Cromwell's or Mussolini's parliament than of Asquith's.[35] There was wild talk of black pimps crowding the London streets. Support for flogging came from all sides. Will Crooks, the Labour MP who was an avid supporter of James Marchant's movement, said he would happily flog bullies himself. Colonel Lockwood, a long-time parliamentary spokesman for the NVA, observed, 'If Romilly's daughter had been exposed to the horrors of white slavery, he would be for flogging'. They were debating a punishment then reserved for prisoners who attacked warders, and for homosexuals. When they were flogged under the Act of 1898, they usually received fifteen strokes with a birch or a whipcord; it was not supposed to draw blood but it usually did.

McKenna reported that in the previous twelve months there had been twenty-three such floggings and that the Court of Criminal Appeal had responded by stating that fifteen strokes were too few. As usual, homosexuals had been getting the worst of the moral storm. The only question was whether flogging would be allowed at the first or the second offence for living off immoral earnings. While the Commons voted for the former, the government reimposed its whips to restore the clause to its original form, reserving the punishment for second offenders. McKenna then redeemed his pledge to obtain provision for the arrest of suspected procurers.

With the passage of the Act the panic largely disappeared, though the fears underlying it remained dormant. In 1913 the 5,000 girls of London's telephone exchanges were given official warnings to watch out for drugged chocolates and similar dangers. *Justice* condemned the Commons for 'one of those displays of hysterical puritanism with which it is periodically affected'.[36] Josiah Wedgwood, later to be a member of the first Labour government, insisted that the bill was 'thrust through the House by almost terrorisation of members. . . .' Yet this was a measure most MPs were more than willing to accept. In contrast to votes for women, it gave the politicians the opportunity to do something for the weaker sex that implied they were still weak.

One of the Pankhursts' most astute allies, Mrs Billington-Grieg, was disgusted by what she described as a 'campaign of sedulously cultivated sexual hysterics'. Describing the panic, she wrote that the Pankhursts had 'set women on the rampage' with 'the silly notions of the perfection of women and the dangerous fellow notion of the indescribable imperfections of man'.[37] The Women's Social and Political Union had made its contribution and now it moved from the issue of man as abductor to man as polluter. However, militants like 'General' Drummond, who lectured widely on white slavery, were only part of the outcry.

Mrs Billington-Grieg quoted Coote as regretting and discounting the 'many painful stories [that] have been in circulation respecting the decoying and drugging of young women'. He had really started the whole thing with his ambiguous movement. Nevertheless, he now had what he wanted. In 1913 prosecutions for living off immoral earnings rose by fifty per cent while those for procuring multiplied by five. A few weeks before the war the NVA claimed that the threat of the lash had cleared London of most of its foreign pimps.

* * *

While the First World War interrupted the traffickers and their opponents, it is remarkable how quickly the adversaries reverted to their prewar activities and attitudes. Arthur Balfour, the urbane Foreign Secretary, told the League of Nations Assembly in 1921, 'This kind of traffic is the most abominable stain upon civilisation which it is possible to conceive. We all know that during the war the material conditions under which the world lived made that traffic impossible. The war is over, and if all the reports that reach us be true, the traffic is again raising its abominable head'.[38] Thus the League of Nations took over the work of Coote, who had died in 1919, with an emotive flourish that left nothing to the Victorian pioneers.

The surveys of the League, the Jewish Association and the International Bureau, which stayed in existence with its national committees to promote the work at Geneva, show that along with the reappearance of the professional peripatetic prostitute there were some special problems. Chinese children were bought openly for the vice dens of Asia; Russian women escaping the revolution were sometimes unlucky enough to end up in the brothels of northern China and Manchuria; some immigrants caught in transit who failed to reach the United States before the imposition of the strict quota system in 1920 were to be found in Cuban houses of ill fame; the German Railway Station Mission claimed in 1922 that some of the 90,000 German girls who sought work in Holland after the war had gone 'to the bad'; the ravages of war on the eastern front had made the economic plight of the Jews worse than before and commercialised prostitution re-emerged amongst them in Poland and Rumania. Yet while there were these particularly unhappy developments, the

League concluded that most of those trafficked knew what they were doing. French whores following the holiday trade to North Africa must have substantially outnumbered Russians trapped in Manchuria, and the like.[39]

Interwar cooperation between the League of Nations and the older voluntary groups made real inroads against the resurgent European traffic. Two more international conventions were agreed and that of 1933, which was signed by twenty-five nations before the war, stipulated that it should be illegal to procure any female for prostitution abroad, consent notwithstanding. Most of the signatories brought their legal codes into line and took additional steps to protect troupes of entertainers and emigrants. Within a year of achieving power Mussolini decreed stiff penalties against procurers. National committees were active in the poorer continental nations where the traffic was still a problem. In Hungary, for example, a national network of lecturers and local committees emerged to advise and assist girls who were migrating to Budapest and abroad. In deference to the League's Advisory Committee on trafficking, France and Hungary banned the inscription of foreigners in their brothels.

The delegates to the 1927 International Jewish Conference on the problem, in London, agreed there was still much room for improvement and the title of Bertha Pappenheim's *Labour of Sisyphus*, written two years later, bears this out. However, a remarkable case in Buenos Ayres in 1930 seems to have permanently dislocated the Jewish traffic to that centre. Early one May morning the police arrested 400 members of the Zwi Migdal, formerly known as the Warsaw Society. This was a Jewish burial club begun early in the century by disreputable figures denied normal participation in the religious life of the community. By 1930 Zwi Migdal had its own synagogue and cemetery and most of its members seem to have been leading honest lives but some were trafficking in Polish prostitutes with the help of passports purchased locally. Samuel Cohen was in Buenos Ayres at the time and his investigations led to the arrests. No evidence of a major white-slave organisation emerged at the trial; a few of the suspects were deported as undesirables and a few others were convicted of procuring.[40]

Despite the fact that most of the members of Zwi Migdal were blameless, it is unlikely that the knowledgeable Jewish

Association would have been willing to hand the fascists useful propaganda in 1930 if there had not been good reason to believe this case was a key to the South American traffic. Afterwards Cohen declared that 'the traffic of Jewish women to Buenos Ayres from Europe has largely ceased and the traffickers have become almost inactive'. Measures taken at the source of supply also helped. Cohen had toured Eastern Europe and left behind a string of local preventive committees while the Polish government had instituted strict regulations regarding the emigration of young females. By 1937 the Jewish Association claimed that the 'organised traffic has largely ceased', though most likely it ended only with Hitler.[41] Meanwhile, after eighteen years of watching ships at Buenos Ayres, Mrs Lighton Robinson retired in 1931 on the grounds that the work was no longer essential. While the inscription of foreigners persisted until Péron closed the tolerated houses, entrapment was at an end in the most notorious of the western white-slave centres.

In Britain there was little trafficking of any kind, though the murders in the 1930s of the infamous pimp, Max Kassel, and of 'French Fifi', an equally notorious prostitute, were allegedly tied in with a 'marriage traffic' in which French prostitutes entered into alliances of convenience with British husbands before being set up in West-End flats. The NVA assisted girls who migrated from Ireland and from the distressed areas of Wales and the north-east in search of work. Its aides in London's railway and coach termini helped well over 50,000 people between the wars. Many more were assisted by the dozen or so affiliated societies, which included the older semi-autonomous regional centres. Under Edith Rose, who received an O.B.E. for her long efforts, the Liverpool Society For The Prevention of the International Traffic assisted about a thousand Irish travellers annually in the 1930s. Rescue workers agreed these girls were particularly vulnerable because of their innocence; on the other hand there were many sad cases of unmarried Irish girls sent to England to have their babies.

After the socially liberating experience of 1914–1918 Dr Helen Wilson, a leading feminist, claimed that 'now the girls are not frightened . . . because they know how to take care of themselves'.[42] In fact the migrations generated by the long interwar British slump brought to the surface a steady stream of familiar white-slave scares. None had the intensity of the prewar explosion nor of the remarkable outbreaks in provincial France in the 1960s and early 1970s.[43] However, the NVA expended a great deal of energy debunking the stories because they worked to discredit the belief there was any commercialised vice, and because they were scaring young girls in the distressed areas from leaving home to take up the Ministry of Labour's Juvenile Transference Scheme.

While the League of Nations enquiry on the traffic in 1927 minimised the role of entrapment, the very fact of the celebrated investigation reactivated the old myth. The subject was taken up in literature and film. For example, across the pages of Evelyn Waugh's *Decline and Fall*, published in 1928 as his first novel, there moves a League of Nations white-slavery investigator and the memorable Margot Metroland, owner of Anglo-South-American Enterprises. The year before, when the British Board of Film Censors refused a certificate to *The White Slave Traffic*, an import made with the consultation of the German National Committee, the London County Council deemed the subject important enough to provide special permission for screenings. The misguided social worker who produced *Night Patrol* in 1930 had less luck. Its sequence on the drugging and spiriting abroad of a provincial girl was deleted by the censor and Bernard Shaw claimed this was done to avoid scaring off domestics who were needed in the capital.

By the time these film curiosities appeared, the NVA was finding it impossible to stem the tide of reports about pinpricks and numb thighs on provincial transport systems and in cinemas. One widespread tale concerned the haglike old lady who asked for help crossing the street and then bagged her prey with the aid of a 'dope ring', a hollowed-out piece of jewellery fitted with a needle and filled with quick-acting curari poison. The outlandish campaign of commandant Mary Allen, former head of the wartime women's volunteer police force to root out gangs of 'human fiends' in London and elsewhere, did not help. A learned exchange of correspondence in *The Times* of 1932 concluded that it was almost impossible to use hypodermic needles in the way claimed; but this was lost on a public fascinated a few years later with reports on 'Heinrich the Satyr', credited with sending over 4,000 European girls to their doom in South

America, and by the appearance of Albert Londres' sensational but largely unsubstantiated *Road to Buenos Ayres.*[44]

The police and the NVA were never able to verify an incident. The reports proved irrepressible because thousands of girls who left home to seek their fortunes broke contact with their families, some to avoid sending money home, others because their parents had opposed their going off. The *News of the World* helped parents to get back in touch with some of these girls, as did the NVA. Typical was the Jarrow girl whom the NVA found working as a hairdresser in Kentish Town after entreaties by the constituency MP. While she promised to write home the NVA files are filled with cases of girls who refused.

The social-purity coalition of feminists and puritans began coming apart between the wars. Its final victory for the protection of women was the Criminal Law Amendment Act of 1922, the last piece of legislation on the subject. It lengthened to nine months the period during which a victim of statutory rape could lodge a complaint and it limited the 'reasonable cause to believe' defence to men of twenty-three years or younger. This peculiar provision was the cost of passage and it was the result of a compromise arranged by Sir Arthur Steel-Maitland, the Tory politician and supporter of the PMC. Dozens of purity and women's societies pressed for the deletion of the hated clause and most of all this was a partial victory for the newly enfranchised ladies. Mrs Gertrude Gow, an old figure in the NVA and women's work, wrote to a political contact that if the bill failed it would emerge 'as a party cry against the government— you can have no idea how strong feeling is on this question'.[45]

While old hands like Mrs Gow continued to work with the vigilance societies, there was continuous tension between these institutions and the Butlerites. The latter now had their own school for rescue workers in Liverpool and working through the British National Committee, they began to infiltrate the national committees in Egypt and India with workers who went out to lecture the natives on Josephine's single standard of chastity. Frederick Sempkins, a former Indian police official who succeeded Coote, was driven to despair. Closer to home the feminists and suffragists wanted to liberalise and equalise the solicitation laws and they had little interest in the PMC's continued intelligence work for the borough councils. Social purity no longer spoke with a more or less unified voice on prostitution. But it was still aligned behind Victorian standards of sex expression and able to exert considerable influence on behalf of those standards.

# 9

# The Pursuit of the Obscene

IN Britain and throughout the West during the three or four generations before the war, concern about the corrupting influence of obscenity and indecency developed parallel with anxieties about the white-slave traffic. Normally judicious individuals believed that society was being swamped by the erotic. In his presidential address to Josephine Butler's Federation in 1882, Emile de Laveleye, the well known Belgian economist, offered a stark judgment that was shared by no less a figure than Cesare Lombroso, the leading criminologist of the age. 'Civilised countries,' according to Laveleye, were suffering from 'an inundation of immorality . . . a contagion of satyriasis . . . which infects alike our books, our journals, engravings, photographs, etc., and extends from our fine art exhibitions down to our allumette boxes. And this rising tide of pornography . . . threatens family life itself, the very foundations of society.'[1]

The renewed interest in suppressing the obscene in Britain during the 1880s naturally developed from the anti-sexual politics of the period. As the NVA's *Pernicious Literature* explained, it was quite impossible 'that such a society as the National Vigilance Association, which soon after its formation incorporated the existing Society for the Suppression of Vice, should not repeatedly have attacked this form of impurity'. In fact inexpensive obscene books and prints and objectionable periodicals and newspapers were becoming increasingly widespread. There was, however, an important common factor accelerating anxieties about this development and explaining the appearance of anti-obscenity movements throughout the West; it was the diffusion of these wares amongst the poor at a time of rapid social change and in a frightening new urban landscape. Thus the American Anti-Vice Society movement, with its Progressive orientation, has been described as 'a response to deep-seated fears about the drift of urban life in the post civil-war years'. Under the lead of Adolf Stöcker, the influential court pastor and pioneering anti-semite, Germany was organised by 'Morality Leagues' during the 1880s and 1890s, a period notable for the development both of its economy and of a sense of despair about modern civilisation.[2]

While there was nothing new about urban problems in Britain in the 1880s, it was the decade in which squalor was rediscovered and socialism was reborn. With compulsory education in force since 1870, the diversions of the poor were obvious objects of scrutiny as potential sources of incivility and dissidence. Vigilance societies commonly called attention to the dangers of indecent literature 'scattered broadcast among the slightly educated'. Ivan Bloch advised that to reduce immoral literature, 'Take a proper care for a genuine popular culture'.[3]

Social-purity leaders recognised this. Lord Kinnaird for example, an indispensable lifetime bankroller of purity causes, was President of the Football Association from 1890 to 1923. The Pure Literature Society, one of the evangelical Kinnaird family's numerous interests, had distributed £63,000 worth of books by 1889. In that year the National Home Reading Union was established and by 1914 it had a membership of 50,000 with the Earl of Aberdeen, President of the NVA, as its leading patron. Even the music halls might be seen to have a positive side when it came to building a popular culture. Mrs Chant, for instance, was not against them but wanted to advance their didactic potential. Speaking of the famous Albert Chevalier and his 'My Old Dutch', she told an audience in 1895,

> Think of what they owed to men like Mr Chevalier for making songs like that which had just been sung that expressed the finest sentiments in the human heart. . . . Think of 'Mrs Enery Awkins', 'Knocked em in the Old Kent Road' and others which had taken the place of the boozy, fighting, hateful songs which too often in former years were the songs supposed to belong to the music halls.[4]

Yet while some of the purity workers took positive steps to create a popular culture in their own image, the balance of their work was overwhelmingly negative. Most of Mrs Chant's allies had an obsessive hatred for the halls. Vigilance committees hardly stopped with the cleansing of working-class entertainment. They broke fresh ground by proceeding against serious art and literature. After 1900 they generated an unparalleled inquisitorial climate in which there was a rush to self-censorship. The NVA and the PMC served as funnels directing religious, feminist and respectable opinion to the Home Office and local government and their voice was very powerful. As Bishop Winnington Ingram explained in 1911, when the ecumenism of social purity had far transcended the nonconformist conscience,

> When I want to put down any objectionable thing, we send a strong deputation to the LCC. I speak first, the Roman Catholic Bishop speaks next, the Jewish Rabbi speaks next, a leading Nonconformist Minister speaks next, so that we have a united front, backed up by the Salvation Army.[5]

The rich fruits of this tactic can be traced through literature, art and popular entertainment from the aftermath of 'The Maiden Tribute' until organised religion lost its commanding influence after the Second World War.

In the cat-and-mouse pursuit of the indecent, vendors of cheap wares had taken advantage of the demise of the Vice Society to return in force. Coote put his new machinery into motion in 1886 with pensioned policemen employed as private detectives and fanatical informers used to supply intelligence. Amongst the latter was Maurice Gregory, the well-known Quaker secretary of the Gospel Purity Association. Gregory patrolled town and country, covering quack advertisements and shop windows where risqué pictures were sold with his own gummed posters which warned, 'Having eyes full of adultery, and that cannot cease from sin, where will you spend eternity?' On one occasion a riot ensued when he threatened a shopkeeper that he was taking some photographs to the NVA for legal action. Working with people like Gregory was an embarrassment and Coote's cooperative relationship with the police was much more significant.

Taking the lead from public opinion, Chief Commissioner Charles Warren issued new instructions in 1886 for the strictest possible enforcement of the law against the sale of indecent wares. Arrests rose from eight in 1885 to fifty-four in the following year and the street sale of dirty pictures was finally eliminated. The NVA acted as an intelligence service for Scotland Yard and prosecuted some cases as well. On one occasion in 1889 when Coote obtained a warrant against a major supplier of photographs, it took four hours to load up cabs with the evidence. In the following years the trade was said to be 'so hampered . . . that it is most difficult in London to obtain either pictures or books'.[6]

While efforts against local outlets usually paid off, supplies from abroad were still largely free to flow in. The Home Office discovered that even MPs and diplomats bought erotica from overseas sellers and on one occasion Lord Halsbury, the Lord Chancellor, indignantly complained he had been posted an unsolicited copy of Sade's *Justine*. From 1890 when Dr Warre, Headmaster of Eton, complained to the Prime Minister, Lord Salisbury, that his students were receiving parcels of pornography from Paris, the Home and Foreign Offices kept the crisis under constant review. While US postal authorities could open suspect materials, this was considered an invasion of privacy in Britain, where the procedure was for the Home Secretary to sign warrants authorising the post office to intercept the post from specific traders.

This had little effect and when the school pornography epidemic spread to Winchester and Wellington in 1894 a storm broke out. Britain's next generation of leaders were at risk. For the first time Asquith at the Home Office issued double warrants to stop orders and cheques to the dealers as well as parcels from them and British ambassadors in Europe were instructed to put pressure on local officials. The young Horace Rumbold later ambassador to Berlin, persuaded the Dutch government to make illegal arrests of the Amsterdam culprits and the same thing happened in Belgrade. In 1899 and 1902 the NVA had Senator Beranger prosecute and convict the most famous international dealer of them all, Charles Carrington. Despite the diplomatic offensive, however, the public schools continued under siege.[7]

One of the primary objectives of the social-purity movement was to sweep the streets of the erotic so that people would forget they had sex organs. The parading of prostitutes was largely beyond their control; but they could do something about objectionable billboards and those omnipresent handbills and posted advertisements for quack venereal remedies. These notices were considerably milder than in the eighteenth century, when the virtues of Leake's Patent Pills were extolled with a graphic account of how they cured the clap that one John Morris contracted in France. Yet the actual advertising of late-Victorian products like Dr Paterson's Famous Female Pills, a purgative sold mostly as an abortifacient, was enormous. In the mid-1880s even the YMCA's *Monthly Review* carried notices for the Electropathic Battery Belt to aid nervous debility. They were placed conveniently a few pages after the advertisements for White Cross lectures, which could bring on the symptoms.

Coote claimed he was able to collect sixty quack handbills in a few hours along the Strand for use in the debates on the 1889 Indecent Advertisements Bill. When the issue was long settled and the bills were banned, Lord Braye said,

> If any historian deals with this matter he will be considered certainly as going beyond the possibility of truth. To mention the fact would not obtain credence that all over the high roads and even the by-roads in the country parts of England only twenty years ago, these advertisements could be tolerated. And they were more shocking, inasmuch as they were the only advertisements placed on the posts and gateposts all over the country. . . .'[8]

New taboos were established quickly.

The Indecent Advertisements Act was the only legislation to deal directly with indecency between 1857 and 1959. Written by the NVA's legal sub-committee and introduced with the support of the medical profession, it prohibited the posting up or distributing of advertisements relating to complaints or infirmities arising from sexual intercourse. Within a few months the streets were cleared. There were, however, a series of loopholes. Shopkeepers put the actual items, rather than descriptions, in their windows. Advertisements were still permitted in newspapers, though the NVA went to work behind the scenes and ultimately got them banned from the respectable press. There was also nothing about birth control in the Act.

There was little advertising for contraceptives at the time and the question of including birth control in the bill did not arise. Naturally the social-purity forces held that birth control was deeply immoral. In 1878 the Vice Society had sent Edward

Truelove, Bradlaugh's radical friend, to jail for publishing birth-control tracts. As late as 1934 Bishop Winnington Ingram told the Lords, '. . . when I hear of 400,000 [contraceptives] being manufactured every week, I would like to make a bonfire of them and dance round it'.[9] This memorable outburst was on behalf of the PMC's perennial measure to ban the advertising of birth control, a demand that started up very soon after 1889. When advertising reached some of the women's sewing magazines early in the century, social-purity leaders as well as the British Medical Association became frantic. However, the NVA and the police were limited to pot shots at the birth controllers and over the years they sent many of them to jail for publishing obscene libels. Marie Stopes said that the Leeds Vigilance Association's action against Dr Allbutt in 1886 slowed down the acceptance of con-traception in medical circles. Yet while there was *ad hoc* harass-ment, governments resisted all attempts to ban advertising. This is one of the areas in which Coote fell short of Comstock.

While birth control was considered a private matter, Coote remained in the foreground over questions of public indecency. Take the saga of Zaoe the acrobat and Paula the snake charmer. These two ladies performed at the Royal Aquarium, the London attraction open day and night with animal acts, high diving, acrobatics and the like. Early in 1890 Zaoe was placarded through London in an acrobatic pose with bare arms and legs while Paula appeared in a tank surrounded by reptiles. Coote had been waiting for an opportunity to cleanse the city of sinful billboards and this was it. He sent the prominent B. F. C. Costelloe from the legal sub-committee into court to invoke the new Act. While it did not apply, the magistrate agreed the Zaoe poster was indecent and he sent a policeman along to ask the Aquarium manager to alter it. Captain Molesworth replied, 'I am willing to have the lower limbs of Zaoe's picture enveloped in artistically designed unmentionables provided the Vigilance Society will pay the cost of printing and posting the same'.[10]

Coote decided to go to the sympathetic licensing committee of the new London County Council. By the time of the hearing in October, Molesworth had sold a quarter-of-a-million copies of the Zaoe photograph, which became the most famous poster of the century. Speaking for London's religious leaders, Coote told the committee that Zaoe's indecency was without parallel. Councillor Frederick Charrington and his colleagues agreed and it was made a condition of the licence renewal that the poster be withdrawn. Captain Molesworth can hardly have been too aggrieved, having made a fortune, but there is an important aftermath to the story. The London bill posters immediately formed a secret committee for self-censorship and entered into an agreement to withdraw any placards of which the NVA disapproved. Soon the arrangement extended to the provinces and ultimately it came to include cinema posters as well. Early victims included corset and lingerie displays as well as ghoulish faces and bloodstains. By 1900 so many posters had been condemned that the theatre managers and printers demanded and received a voice on the committee. The bill posters cooperated with the PMC until the late 1940s and this was but the first of a series of arrangements for formal self-censorship that emerged in the period.[11]

From the beginning it was clear that the vigilantes would not overlook serious art. In 1885 *Seeking and Saving*, Ellice Hopkins' journal, discovered yet another form of female degradation, the posing of nude models. This was the beginning of a long struggle against undress which extended to Zaoe and the living statuary of the music halls. The CEPS worked behind the scenes and for the first time the Royal Academy excluded 'indecent studies' from its students' annual show.[12] This kind of foolishness did not last for long in the studio. In 1890, however, the prudes ran for the figleaves when an exhibition of 160 of Jules Garnier's illustrations of the works of Rabelais opened to large crowds at the Waterloo Gallery.

The Rabelais case is a good index of public opinion. An art exhibition had never before been closed and the government refused to have anything to do with the case. However, Coote and Dr Henry Lunn, a Methodist veteran of the Dublin midnight patrols, had no trouble in obtaining a search warrant under the Act of 1857 despite the fact they could produce no specimen of the offensive material. With the help of the police they carted off a load of paintings, twenty-two of which were ordered to be destroyed. The hearing over the destruction order and the subsequent NVA prosecution of the exhibit's organisers were farcical. The NVA was represented by Mr Bodkin, later one of the most reactionary Directors of Public Prosecutions, and Mr Besley, who insisted on calling Rabelais 'a lewd and filthy priest' and expressed satisfaction to learn that Garnier was dead. Counsel for the defence knew the case was hopeless. Some of the nude figures had less than innocent facial expressions and were in suggestive poses. He pointed out that it was not the intention of the Campbell Act or the Hicklin judgement to prosecute serious works of art. In fact the issue had been settled in the previous two years by the cases against Henry Vizetelly, Zola's publisher. Wishing to avoid a diplomatic incident, the government interceded to rescue the paintings and with the approval of the NVA they were ceremoniously crated and returned to France.[13] This became a useful precedent for closing public exhibitions and later victims included a particularly horrid exhibit of syphilitic wax models and a showing of D. H. Lawrence's paintings.

One Home Office official called the first conviction of Henry Vizetelly in 1888 'epoch-marking'. It was the modern departure for using the law of obscene libel against serious literature and there was to be a long and distinguished catalogue of victims before the Act of 1959 made literary and scientific merit a defence. By 1888 Vizetelly had built up an impressive list of European authors which included Zola, Maupassant, Flaubert, Dostovesky and Tolstoy. Zola's *Nana* was published in 1885 in slightly expurgated form and had done so well that *La Terre, Pot Bouille* and other titles were issued. In May 1888, Samuel Smith, the Liverpool MP who was the NVA's chief spokesman on obscenity, told the Commons in a special debate that Zola's 'novels were only fit for swine'. While Smith was a fanatic, Zola was a popular target. Tennyson used the same metaphor about 'Zolaism' in 1886: 'Feed the budding rose of boyhood with the drainage of your sewer'.

When the government refused to proceed against the Zola novels, Samuel Smith and the NVA started their own prosecution. The Attorney General then changed his mind, took over the case and sent the Solicitor General into court assisted by the young Asquith. While Frank Harris offered to pay Vizetelly's legal expenses if he fought on, the old man wisely pleaded guilty and escaped with a fine, promising to withdraw the three Zola novels and not publish anything similar. Six months later he was to pay more dearly. Not satisfied with the withdrawal of the most celebrated novels, the NVA asked the government to suppress more of Vizetelly's list. This time Coote responded to an official refusal with an omnibus case against four publishers and booksellers, including Vizetelly, whose guilty plea failed to keep him from a three-month prison sentence for publishing titles by Zola, Maupassant and Paul Bourget.

In court B. F. C. Costelloe explained the origins of the case. The advertising circulars 'afforded ample proof that the books were intended not for a select literary class, but for the common market'. Before the trial Vizetelly had informed Coote he would expunge any objectionable passages. The puritans wanted exemplary punishment. With the ruined and sick publisher in jail, the *Vigilance Record* commented, 'We trust that his imprisonment may not unduly affect his health'.[14]

A little later *Truth* observed,

> Mrs Grundy has had a good year and her holiday is well deserved. She has created such a scare in literary circles as has not been known within the memory of man, for since the prosecution of Mr Vizetelly, every author is compelled to write with the fear of some pestilent association of busybodies before his eyes; she has spread terror in thousands of respectable homes, for a young man may well be afraid to walk abroad with the girl of his heart unless he has first obtained leave from the local vigilance committee.[15]

The only consolation for Coote's enemies was the intense embarrassment caused him by the revelation that the *Vigilance Record*'s wholesaler was publishing works every bit as indecent as those condemned. This was John Kensit, the fanatical head of the Protestant Truth Society. Before meeting his martyrdom in 1902 when a Roman Catholic threw a metal file through his head after a rally in Liverpool, Kensit kept 'the ritualistic traitors in the protestant church' at bay with such foul and grisly old anti-Catholic favourites as *The Awful Disclosures of Maria Monk* and *The High Church Confessional*. This temporary embarrassment aside, however, the Vizetelly case had made the NVA famous.

Lady Isabel Burton thus naturally turned to Coote for assistance in 1891 after she had set fire to her late husband's irreplaceable manuscripts of Arab erotic folklore. Together they went through Sir Richard's surviving manuscripts to 'mark out any sentences, or words to which exception could be taken'. They bowdlerised reprints of his works. They collected and burnt, at the cost of £1,500 to Lady Isabel, one of his books said to be doing incalculable harm in the universities; it was probably the translation of a sixteenth-century book of sex instruction, whose author, a Tunisian sheikh, had written 'I swear by Allah that it is necessary to know this book. It is only the shameless boor and the enemy of science who will not read it, or make fun of it'. This nasty little partnership did not even end with Lady Isabel's death; as one of her literary executors Coote was given supervision over Sir Richard Burton's publications.[16]

In the short run the literary pendulum swung in the liberal direction. However, Frank Harris's comments of 1894 about the politics of literary prudery placed the situation in long-term perspective : 'In France, the artist and man of letters is supported by the organised opinion of his fellows, while the bourgeoisie is unorganised and comparatively innocuous—a helpless pullulating mob. In England, on the other hand, Grocerdom is organised in conventicle and church and rancorously articulate, especially on those subjects with which it is wholly incompetent to deal, while the men of letters who have done something in their past of freedom for England's honour are unorganised and powerless'.[17] Grocerdom referred to the purity party on the London County Council, who were lumbered with the epithet because Charrington used a grocer as an informer. As the fortunes of the party on the LCC demonstrate, if London was not Paris, neither could it be moulded into the new Jerusalem.

\*　\*　\*

The election of the first London County Council provided the social-purity movement with the opportunity to exercise the same kind of pressure in the capital as it did in the provinces. The licensing of nearly four hundred music and dancing halls was delegated to London's new parliament and the membership of the Theatres and Music Halls Committee was most promising. Among the twenty-one councillors were a solid half-dozen active supporters of the NVA, including Charrington and John McDougall. Known as 'MuckDougall' and the Grand Inquisitor, McDougall was a prominent Methodist who later became chairman of the LCC. In the 1890s he was one of the most publicly

reviled men in town. Captain Verney, MP, was another committee member vocal about his intention 'to level up the morality
of Piccadilly'. His purity work and other activities were cut short
in 1891 when he was sent to prison for conspiring to ruin a young
girl.

Militant Christians had long despised the music halls. To the
Salvation Army they were 'fortresses of Beelzebub' and to Charrington they were 'music hells'. Almost everyone agreed that the
songs and variety entertainment at the halls were much less suggestive and crude than they had been in the 1850s and 1860s,
a period when they had in turn offered mixed audiences much
improved fare over the gross obscenities of the earlier all-male
song and supper clubs. The entrepreneurs of the highly capitalised
new establishments believed that respectability was essential for
profits. When the Middlesex bench of licensing magistrates manifested a temporary interest in the fare in 1879, the proprietors
approached Richard Cross, the Home Secretary, admitting they
had trouble controlling comic singers 'who are by universal practice when upon the stage in the habit of introducing impromptu
words in their songs'.[18] They made the impossible suggestion
that he appoint a censor with powers to fine purveyors of un-
licensed material. But the improvements did little to placate the
puritans. The suggestiveness of Marie Lloyd more than undid the
lessons of the songs praised by Mrs Chant. There was insidious
sexual innuendo in the songs and gags, prostitutes in the promenades and drink in the auditorium. The ladies of the British
Women's Temperance Association thus had two reasons to join
the attack.

Once Charrington's struggle with Lusby's was disrupted by a
court injunction, the focus of attention shifted to the West End.
Wishing to avoid accusations of class bias, Charrington began a
mission to the fallen in 1886 at the Alhambra, Pavilion and
Criterion. Omnibuses of chanting zealots plying their way west
from the Tower Hamlets Mission became familiar sights to
Londoners. The 1889 campaign was launched at a great prayer
meeting organised by Hugh Price Hughes and chaired by Bishop
Temple. It is worth looking for a moment at how Hughes'
Methodist connexion formed a network of well-placed busy-
bodies capable of disrupting London's entertainment. Percy
Bunting was treasurer of Hughes' West London Mission;

Bunting's wife Mary and his sister, Mrs Sheldon Amos, were leading Christian feminists active in the NVA, British Women's Temperance Association and numerous other causes. Mrs Bunting's brother, George Lidgett, sat on the Theatres and Music Halls Committee with McDougall, his son-in-law.

When the proprietors attended the committee they discovered that half-a-dozen councillors had forsaken their quasi-judicial function to collect evidence and prosecute. Exception was taken to dozens of songs and impromptu gags. McDougall complained about an objectionable ventriloquist and high kicking at the Rosemary Branch, and a fifteen-year-old acrobatic act at the Trocadero that included a song about a girl sitting on a man's knee. 'The Bewitched Curate' at the Canterbury, describing a churchman gazing at a girl's legs, helped the purity caucus carry the committee. Three halls had their licences revoked, including the Royal Aquarium which was punished for harbouring prostitutes. Six others were relicensed subject to an undertaking that they would take better care to maintain propriety. While prudery reigned in the committee, common sense ruled the Council. Lord Rosebery, its first chairman and later Gladstone's successor as Liberal prime minister, looked upon the proceedings with horror. The full LCC restored the three licences subject to promises of better behaviour. The precedent was set at once; while licences were virtually never revoked for indecency, proprietors had to answer for improper entertainment and conditions were sometimes put on renewals. In 1890 the LCC established a panel of twenty-three inspectors to scrutinise the nature of the performances and the conduct of the audiences, especially the women.[19]

Social-purity leaders were satisfied with the compromise that put the proprietors under official supervision. The greatest entrepreneur among them, Oswald Stoll, instituted house fines for anything unauthorised. When an official inspector or a vigilante reported something amiss a cautionary letter from the chairman of the licensing committee usually sufficed to get the abuse corrected. The monitoring system was credited with furthering the decline of music-hall bawdry; G. W. E. Russell, the NVA member who was on the licensing committee and was also a minister in the Liberal government of 1892, compared this work by the LCC with the great parliamentary victories of 1885 and 1886.[20]

With the issue of the prostitutes unresolved the status quo did not last for long. Besides, in late 1893 Charles Morton, who had pioneered the music halls when he opened the Canterbury Hall next to his Lambeth public house in 1851, introduced living statuary at the beautiful Palace Theatre in Cambridge Circus. These were scenes from art or history posed by partially draped men and women. Admiral Nelson's Lady Emma Hamilton may well have devised them. While she was at Naples, where her husband was ambassador, Goethe saw her pose as Venus and Diana of the chase and wrote, 'She lets her hair down, takes a couple of shawls and presents such a variety of poses, gestures, expressions, etc. that one finally wonders whether one is dreaming'.[21] Living statuary, also known as *tableaux vivants*, appeared in some of the early Victorian song and supper clubs like the famous Coal Hole, where the poses were more daring than anything staged later by Charles Morton. The LCC inspector sent to view the very first series in 1893 reported,

> The tableaux vivants . . . are a new departure. Some of them are very clever representations of pictures and statuary to which the most severe could not object, but several are of a classical nature, represented by apparently semi-nude, or nearly nude women. The last one, 'Aphrodite', was apparently quite nude, except for a scarf over the loins. I say *apparently* because in every case I observed that the body, arms and bosom were completely clothed in very delicate close fitting fleshings which when a warm light was thrown on them, appeared like nature.[22]

For the social-purity forces, simulated nudity was as evil as nudity itself. In 1894 when a girl in Boston posing in 'The Birth of the Pearl' was scalded to death by a fountain of hot water, it was considered a divine warning. That year they began a struggle to clothe living statues and cast the harlots from the halls. By autumn their efforts were the most topical subject in London, and the most controversial as well, judging from the 175 letters in the *Daily Telegraph*'s 'Prudes on the Prowl' series. In August Lady Henry Somerset, President of the British Women's Temperance Association, initiated the public debate by criticising the new form of nudity and evoking a response in religious circles and from the women's magazines. As the *Women's Signal* noted,

'If pure art is the aim of the representations, why exhibit only a Venus, leaving a Hercules or Adonis in the shade?' Advocacy in the Theatres and Music Halls Committee was left to Coote, though one of the leaders of the Liverpool purity party was in town to assist. Speaking as usual for London's religious establishment, Coote obtained from Charles Morton a promise that any pose found objectionable by the LCC would be withdrawn. On this basis the licence was renewed.[23]

When the storm had first blown up, Richard Roberts, the chairman of the committee, had persuaded the Palace to withdraw the most controversial representation, 'The Moorish Bath'. However, the committee majority and the purity advocates did not always agree about what was objectionable. When Coote and Miss Reed, head of Lady Henry's Purity Department, showed up again in 1896 to register a complaint, they met with complete disaster. Coote took exception to a pose at the Palace called 'The Source', which portrayed a nude woman lying across some rocks with a spring running under her. Since all discussions on these subjects were veiled, the councillors easily mistook Coote's objection to mean that the scene alluded to urination. For once great fun was had at his expense and he was thoroughly humiliated. At the same time Miss Reed's mistaken insistence that Madge Ellis had posed at the Oxford Theatre with bare legs was so scandalous that it resulted in a lawsuit and a £300 settlement.[24] *Tableaux vivants* were now safe until the puritans mobilised on a wider scale in the following decade.

Meanwhile the tireless Mrs Chant, who edited the *Vigilance Record,* was spearheading the attack on the promenades. Inspired by an all-day prayer meeting held simultaneously with the 1894 hearing, she and her supporters explained to the committee what its inspectors had already confirmed. The promenades in the Empire Music Hall in Leicester Square as well as those elsewhere were crowded each night with prostitutes who paid nothing to enter and were on friendly terms with the attendants. There was great mirth when Mrs Chant described how she had been accosted in the Empire while disguised in her best evening dress. The committee ruled that relicensing would only be on the conditions that no drinks be sold in the auditorium, meaning that a number of lounges would have to be screened up, and that the promenades be filled in with fixed seating. The first stipulation

H

was part of the LCC's long-term policy and had been foisted on a series of other theatres. The Empire's management bluffed that it would close up and throw some seven hundred people out of work, and attempted unsuccessfully to prove in court what virtually was true, that there had been an illegal conspiracy forged at the Buntings' home between the plaintiffs and members of the quasi-judicial committee.[25]

The LCC's upholding of the ruling caused a sensation. Winston Churchill devoted ten pages in his *My Early Life* to an account of how he led an assault of his fellow Sandhurst cadets and gentlemen armed with walking sticks on the canvas partitions that were erected to separate 'the temples of Venus and Bacchus'. His first public speech was made on the rubble. While more permanent partitions followed, within two years the LCC permitted the Empire to pull out the seats and reopen the promenades to strollers. This was largely because prostitutes came anyway and could not be barred if they were orderly. Mrs Chant and company had been thwarted.

While promenades were forbidden in theatres constructed after 1889, prostitutes remained settled in those of some of the older theatres until the First World War; it was 1916 when the London vigilantes finally dislodged them. One official of the PMC told the Theatres and Music Halls Committee at that time that he had been solicited four times in one evening at the Empire. With stories circulating that the famous theatre was a source of venereal disease, the LCC finally ruled that licences would not be granted to any theatres where prostitutes congregated. The Empire gave up its promenades, as Oswald Stoll's theatres had already done.[26] With a fine sense of occasion, the Empire staged *Lady Be Good* on the night it closed in 1927 to make way for a cinema.

As the anti-obscenity forces gained strength before the war, they had considerable success imposing their standards on music-hall entertainment and they forced local authorities to take another look at living statuary. In 1907, when Bishop Winnington Ingram mounted one of his interdenominational deputations to the LCC asking for a ban on the familiar poses, artistes like the popular 'La Milo' were no more or less undraped than their predecessors fifteen years earlier. Yet public opinion was now such that the full LCC resolved, 'The continuance of living statuary is undesirable'.[27] While this did not end the genre it shortened its life in London, and provincial vigilance committees and town councils followed suit.

As always something else libidinous sprang up to torture the puritans. This time it was the craze for oriental dancing that developed after Maud Allan's sensational appearance in 1908 in her Dance of Salome with loose Greek gown and John the Baptist's head. The LCC explained to complainants that Maud Allan had such high patronage they dare not touch her. Less cowed watch committees in the north at least banned John the Baptist's head and Maud's imitators did not enjoy her relative immunity. F. B. Meyer forced an indecent dance about Adam and Eve, 'The Dawn of Love', off the London Palladium stage in 1911, the same year that he led the successful resistance to the Jack Johnson versus Bombardier Wells prize-fight. LCC inspectors and vigilantes scrutinised traditional music-hall fare more closely than ever in these years and soon provincial towns too were passing new regulations against stage indecency. Marie Lloyd was constantly pestered and she was the only major star not invited to perform at the famous 1912 command performance for the King and Queen. Ambrose Thorn was warned by the LCC to omit a song about a harem and Dusty Rhodes had to delete from another about a courting couple the lines, 'He shoves his arm round her neck, he shoves it round her neck. Then he shoves it. . . .' The music-hall stage bore the imprint of three decades of effort by social-purity workers. But it was never fully divested of its spirit, as the new Birmingham theatres' inspectorate discovered in 1917 when it spent much of its time bringing charges of indecency against the entertainers.[28]

* * *

In 1911 Coote went to see Austin Harrison, editor of the *English Review*, about a piece he had published called 'A Platonic Marriage'. Like almost everything else to which exception was taken in these years it was inoffensive. The enraged Harrison refused to withdraw the number and invited prosecution. Coote naturally had the issue banned at W. H. Smith's and Harrison wrote in the following number :

Literature as an art is today literally in the power of a group of well-meaning molly-coddles banded together under the name of the Vigilance Society, whose deliberate corporate purpose is to act as informers to the police. They are permitted to tyrannise over the whole literary world of England, to terrify publishers who are timorous people, editors and authors, to set themselves up with impunity as the rightful tribunal of literary censorship until they have created a state of irritation in English letters which has become intolerable. It is unEnglish and vile that libraries, bookshops and bookstalls should actually refuse to sell a book or magazine because of some backstairs warning by the Vigilance Society people.[29]

While this frustrated outburst sums up the situation in literature, it does not do justice to the breadth of the anti-obscenity agitation, which was dealing with every medium that might harbour a hint of the erotic : music-hall entertainment, plays, films, public statues and waxworks exhibits, mutoscopes, illustrated newspapers, seaside postcards and finally real pornography. It was the most sustained outburst of its kind and it was part of an international phenomenon. When delegates from sixteen nations met in Paris in 1910 to amend the white-slavery convention, they also drafted the initial agreement on the trade in obscene publications. Beranger had obtained inclusion of the subject at the conference, where the tasks of defeating the traffic in females and the traffic in smut were considered allied objects in the modern struggle for morality. The signatories agreed to establish central authorities to collect and share information, on the model of the white-slavery offices, and they undertook to try culprits even if their crimes were committed in other countries. There had already been considerable activity. Beranger had obtained amendments to the French censorship laws, though his threat of an anti-hissing league failed to win stricter control of the stage. From 1910 efforts were accelerated, with a new law in Holland, a special clean-up ordered by the Italian Prime Minister, and regular raids carried out by new police bureaux through Europe.

The common fear of the obscene was grounded, once again, in the popular association between purity and preparedness, reinforced by the realisation that norms for artistic expression and personal behaviour were changing. In Britain the birth rate was falling, militant suffragists were initiating a virtual sex war, and in 1909 a Royal Commission had begun considering reform of the divorce laws. St Loe Strachey expressed common anxieties in his attack of that year on H. G. Wells's *Ann Veronica*, a novel about an emancipated girl:

> The loathing and indignation which the book inspires in us are due to the effect it is likely to have in undermining the sense of continence and self-control in the individual which is essential to a sound and healthy State. . . . Unless the citizens of a State put before themselves the principles of duty, self-sacrifice, self-control and continence, not merely in the matter of national defence, national preservation and national well-being, but also of the sex-relationship, the life of the State must be short and precarious. Unless the institution of the family is firmly founded and assured, the State will not continue.[30]

Strachey's review of 'A Poisonous Book' shows how the fear of the obscene spread in Britain to a degree unparalleled since the French Revolution. From the beginning of the century revitalised social-purity institutions led by Coote, Bishop Winnington Ingram and the progressively influential James Marchant had been promoting this fear along with that of white slavery. They were joined by the British Medical Association, anxious for an absolute ban on the advertising of quack remedies and contraception; the Headmaster's Conference, which established a committee on indecent literature in 1902 under Edward Lyttleton; women's societies and municipal governments, who vied with one another to declare their cities pure.

When the Liverpool magistrates began a crackdown on naughty postcards in 1906 but found the law inadequate, they proposed new legislation and rallied the support of sixty other towns. In the following year Hull obtained clauses written by the local NVA branch which made possession of indecent material illegal and punishable by stiff fines. As the chief constable declared, 'The feeling in Hull runs very high against indecency of any sort or kind'. In Manchester, where the Vigilance Association had prompted the seizure and destruction of 25,000 copies of Balzac's works in 1905, the chief constable made the immortal claim three years later that his jurisdiction was known by some as 'the holy city'.[31]

At first the authorities and the vigilantes were absorbed with actual pornography or the many forms of indecency for the masses. In 1901 the Chief Commissioner of the Metropolitan Police ordered another sustained crackdown on obscene books and prints and five years later he reported they were virtually unobtainable. Magistrates would always condemn the grossly obscene. There was a problem, however, with borderline indecencies. In cases of photographs and illustrations, convictions were not always guaranteed unless pubic hair was showing.

The indecent drove purity workers to distraction. Naughty mutoscope scenes became a rage at the turn of the century; arcades and gutted shops were filled with the machines and they attracted the poor of all ages. A craze for picture postcards developed at the same time and by 1908 800 million postcards had been handled by the post office. Some moralists considered naughty cards more dangerous than the Germans, though they might have found some consolation in the fact that German postal authorities handled nearly twice as many. Canon Rawnsley, a stalwart of the Manchester NVA who made this his special interest, claimed the 'bathers postcards' were the worst, with the 'amatative little child golliwogs' a close second. Reproductions of living statuary and of nudes by Raphael, Corregio and Velasquez were also considered particularly demoralising. As if this avalanche of undress and seaside innuendo were not enough, the cheap illustrated papers, filled with advertisements for everything from VD remedies to French pornography were selling 400,000 copies a week by 1902.

The vigilantes and the police acted where they could. By 1902 after the Newcastle NVA branch secretary helped obtain a conviction of a mutoscope manager for showing 'The Artist's Model : Special Extra', other managers in the north-east either closed down or withdrew their most daring offerings. It was not as easy in London, where the police wanted to proceed against the arcades on Tottenham Court Road but were advised by the public prosecutor that it was a waste of time. Yet after public protests by the PMC in 1902 the sexiest exhibitions were withdrawn. In the previous year the Mutoscope Company had offered to submit all its plates to the Home Office for comment, an offer characteristically refused because it was tantamount to precensorship. Here was another industry that did not want to be pestered by prosecutions. However, the demands of the social-purity movement were so severe that there was continual friction with those whom Samuel Smith called the purveyors of 'filthy animated pictures'.[32] At the same time newsagents all over the country were being hauled before magistrates for exposing lewd postcards, but with no discernible effect. It was necessary to alter the law to make the indecent as liable as the obscene.

Under severe pressure the Home Office considered this and all the other controversial points at issue before turning the whole question over to a Joint Committee on Indecent Advertisements and Lotteries in 1908. The mixed nature of the enquiry did not prevent a thorough airing of the whole issue of obscenity and the speedy issuing of comprehensive recommendations : there should be diplomatic initiatives to stop the postal trade in pornography; the advertising of contraceptives should be banned and the 1889 Act extended to newspapers; a summary jurisdiction for dealing with obscene libel would clear up the borderline cases by taking them out of the hands of juries; looking ahead, genuine works of art and literature should be exempted from the law.

The appointment of the committee caused a great stir in the purity camp. The leaders of London's purity and rescue societies had been meeting, strange as it sounds, to consider what to do about the undraped statues astride the BMA's new Strand offices. Now fourteen secretaries expanded this task force into a permanent group to press for new legislation, the Conference of London Societies Interested in Public Morality.[33] James Marchant began a Forward Movement and soon his National Council of Public Morals had the support of Strachey and other leading figures in journalism and publishing.

The government ordered legislation to be drafted roughly on the lines recommended. While waiting for parliamentary time to be found for the controversial subject, social purity demonstrated it would not go along with the exemption of serious literary works. Some of the celebrated backstairs threats and private prosecutions were undertaken by freelances not unlike those who operated in the 1960s and 1970s. For example, after Strachey's condemnation of *Ann Veronica*, the Rev. Herbert Bull, who worked with the Manchester NVA, had no difficulty in using

*The Spectator* to raise a large guarantee fund for his own use. Refusing Coote's offer of cooperation because the NVA was too cautious, he began work on his own blacklist of ninety-eight titles. Another individual, who was dismissed as a lunatic when he tried to convince the police that the personal notices in *The Pelican* printed with defective type were actually secret messages to homosexuals, succeeded in getting destruction orders against W. H. Smith's for selling indecent periodicals. Such people are always about; before the First World War they could exert influence.[34]

Mr Bull instructed his supporters in the White Cross that John Long and John Lane were the most offensive publishers. At the cost of £1,000 the NVA had sent Donald Maclean into court in late 1908 to suppress *The Yoke*, published by Long. This 'sex novel' by Hubert Wales was on the theme of incest and it was the very year Maclean helped obtain legislation on the subject. The prosecution was popular and a few months later Bull's threats made Long withdraw another novel. Attention then turned to John Lane, whose adventurous Bodley Head had published *The Yellow Book* and works by Oscar Wilde. Lane submitted after two policemen visited to tell him that an unnamed party had taken exception to *The Song of Songs*, the story of an immoral woman by the internationally-known Hermann Sudermann. The book was withdrawn.

During this inquisition the NVA and the authorities obtained destruction orders against Ivan Bloch's scholarly *Sexual Life of Our Times; Droll Stories* yet again; *Tom Jones* and Nietzsche's works. Public libraries around the country responded to the climate of opinion; Canon Lambert of the local NVA said at the meeting of the Hull Library Committee that banned *Ann Veronica*, 'I would just as soon send a daughter of mine to a house infected with typhoid or diphtheria as put that book into her hands'. The greatest stir of all was caused by the Circulating Library Association's announcement in 1909 that Mudie's, Smith's and the other great members were imposing precensorship on all books they distributed. Arnold Bennett complained, 'The atmosphere of this island is enough to choke all artists dead'.[35]

In this sort of environment vulnerable parties fell into line. James Marchant was able to tell the first International Moral Education Congress in 1908 that a Newsagent's Federation and a Postcard Trader's Association had been formed to clean up noxious papers and cards. The editor of the postcard industry's trade paper placed these efforts in an interesting light: 'The Postcard Trader's Association is anxious to save the trade from the same fate that overtook the valentine, which reached the lowest depths of vulgarity a few years ago—and died'. This meant precensorship committees of stationers and dealers in all the great seaside restorts. By 1914 they had rejected a quarter of the manufacturers' 7,000 designs.[36]

The same impulse was behind the West-End theatre managers' petition to the King in 1912, after the report of the Joint Committee on Stage Censorship, asking that the Lord Chamberlain's controls be retained. The film industry was badly exposed and in the same year, with the cooperation of the Home Office, it designed an enduring plan for voluntary precensorship to be administered by a British Board of Film Censors. The rigid chief examiner of plays, George Redford, became its first president.

While the anti-obscenity crusade was triumphant in the private corridors of power and in the provinces, there was still no new general legislation. The Joint Committee's report had virtually ruled out giving the postal authorities additional powers to stop mail, though in 1908 a new law was passed against sending or receiving obscene wares through the post. Behind the scenes the government continued its struggle against foreign traders. However, the affair of the pubic hair in 1907 proved just how difficult it was to make the kind of diplomatic progress the Joint Committee anticipated. Scotland Yard had wanted the Paris police to stop the posting of the *Illustrated Artistic Encylopaedia*. The Entente Cordiale notwithstanding, the Chef de Sureté responded gravely that pubic hair was not obscene in Paris. A new cluster of double postal warrants had more effect and by 1911 Charles Carrington wrote a pathetic letter to Reginald McKenna, the Home Secretary, explaining that his business was being ruined.[37]

In 1912 McKenna was besieged by two formidable deputations and promised to introduce legislation during that session. One was led by Bishop Winnington Ingram and the Earl of Aberdeen and the other, called 'a remarkable phenomenon' by McKenna, came from Marchant, who arranged for St Loe Strachey to act as spokesman for a group of leading publishers, editors, newsagents and booksellers, including C. P. Scott of the *Manchester Guardian* and A. G. Gardiner of the *Daily News*.

While the Home Office had a bill in hand it was never introduced. For one thing, it attempted to define indecency and most such formulations simply break down in practice. Legal advisers pointed out that indecency as 'obscene, disgusting or grossly offensive' subsumed the greater offence under the lesser; an undersecretary advised that the exemption of serious literature 'would raise a great storm in the House'.[38] In the end the government was let off the hook when the social-purity movement concentrated all its attention on the White Slave Bill after Stead's drowning; success over white slavery was followed by a great release of tension and the fear of the obscene diminished. Yet during this last purity campaign of national dimensions the machinery for a long aftermath of prudery had been established.

\* \* \*

Between the wars D. H. Lawrence wrote, 'The greatest of all lies in the modern world is the lie of purity and the dirty little secret. The grey ones left over from the nineteenth century are the embodiment of this lie. They dominate in society, in the press, in literature, everywhere, and naturally they lead the vast mob of the general public along with them'.[39] Lawrence believed the grey ones of the National Council of Public Morals had been responsible for the banning of *The Rainbow* in 1915 and a complaint by the PMC in 1929 was one of the factors leading to a heavy-handed police raid on an exhibition of his paintings. After the war social-purity institutions could no longer generate mass movements as they had in 1885 and 1912. However, they did retain their status as important pressure groups, concentrating on officialdom the cumulative weight of the grey ones and fighting an effective rearguard action against more open standards of sex expression until the twentieth century was nearly half over.

To seek out the indecent and to distinguish the pure from the impure, the PMC relied on an auxiliary of stage and screen spotters, a full-time film critic, a stern film committee always chaired by a leading Methodist, an equally forbidding stage committee and a literary panel anxious to commit to the flames anything compromised by a relationship with adult life. The Bishop's helpers and the NVA also sifted and transmitted complaints from old ladies in the country, provincial vigilance committees, church dignitaries and religious and social groups. Representatives of sixty organisations sat on the PMC in 1930; Bishop Winnington Ingram's memorial to Stanley Baldwin in 1935 on 'The Tendency of Present-Day Films, Plays and Publications' was supported by 260 institutions. Through the 1920s the NVA and the PMC talked about amalgamation and established a short-lived Joint Readers' Panel. Frederick Sempkins and Samuel Cohen agreed that the PMC, which had seized the initiative, should be allowed the lead in questions of obscenity. An imperfect division of labour emerged amongst the members of the British National Committee, with the other major groups devoting themselves to the protection of women and rehabilitation of prostitutes.[40] After Sempkins retired in 1940, the NVA and the PMC shared the services of a secretary for vigilance work until shortly before the NVA was wound up in 1953.

Because social purity had done its work so well before 1914, the direct policing of the obscene in the twenties was largely out of its hands. The film industry censored itself, the recommendation of the Joint Committee on Stage Plays in 1912 to abolish the Lord Chamberlain's censorship had been ignored and public authorities were diligent about obscene books. Relations were cordial with the individuals responsible for precensorship and for the state's legal policy. In 1925 the chief examiner of plays had said the puritans were 'very insistent and capable of extremely articulate pressure'. The following year his boss, the Lord Chamberlain, gave the PMC the privilege of regular access and protest. The Bishop of London's comments in 1936 on his friendship with the film censors are most revealing: 'Dear old T. P. O'Connor used to come down and have lunch with me when he had a doubt about a film. Then there was Mr Shortt, and now Lord Tyrrell'. In fact Lord Tyrrell was on the executive of the International Bureau at the time and he later became President of the NVA. In 1930 the PMC even reached an accord with Will Hays, the powerful industry censor who was reducing American films to infantilism; the PMC became Hays' official source about British reaction to American films.[41]

As for the public officials with whom the social-purity lobby dealt, William Joynson Hicks, Tory Home Secretary from 1924 to 1929, was a staunch puritan and anti-communist; Frederick

Sempkins, who got to know him well, wrote Joynson Hicks was 'greatly concerned with the bolshevik element in literary and artistic circles'.[42] Thomas Inskip, Tory Solicitor General or Attorney General for eleven years between 1922 and 1936, was another fervent evangelical who actively supported purity causes. The Director of Public Prosecutions between 1920 and 1930 was Archibald Bodkin, who had been the NVA's favourite counsel; in 1923 he drafted draconian legislation empowering police searches for the simple possession of obscene literature that was thrown out by parliament as a threat to civil liberties. The Tories had no monopoly on prudery. J. R. Clynes, the Labour Home Secretary, sanctioned the absurd raid on D. H. Lawrence's paintings while he and Ramsay MacDonald successfully withstood pressure for the official dissemination of birth-control information.

Despite their basic sympathies with Victorian standards, the authorities had to strike a balance with changing mores. Social purity hardly had everything its own way and even Frederick Sempkins found it necessary to disarm some of the hoarier schemes devised by the Bishop's colleagues. Purity was to the fore after Joynson Hicks' celebrated suppression of Radclyffe Hall's *Well of Loneliness* in 1928 and the subsequent destruction order against Norah James' *Sleeveless Errand*, a Joycean tale deemed both indecent and blasphemous by the PMC, which called it to official attention. At that point the PMC suggested a simple bill to suppress anything promoting promiscuity and Sempkins complained, 'The idea seems to be fantastic. I could put up a good case for that matter against permitting jazz bands, moonlight or silk stockings'.

Despite the court successes, the authorities refused to accede to the PMC's request to proceed against Aldous Huxley's *Point Counter Point* in 1929. The overall state of judicial opinion had to be considered and as Sempkins noted 'The magistrates are no longer willing to convict in cases where a conviction could most easily be obtained in Mr Coote's day'. In 1937 Bishop Winnington Ingram complained with frustration, 'I took in twenty-one filthy books to one Home Secretary and told him to read them and see what he could do about them. To the last Home Secretary but one I took in about a dozen filthy periodicals. Are we to wait for Mussolini or Hitler to come and put these down?

What is the good of a National Government if they cannot do it, we asked?'[43]

The Bishop's standards were very high. In an average year like 1931 over one hundred complaints were lodged with the various authorities and many were acted upon. Over the years the Lord Chamberlain and the film censor deleted scores of sexy, sacriligious and violent scenes at the behest of the PMC. The film censor was particularly accommodating. After a deputation from the Bishop in 1930, Edward Shortt warned the trade to cut out erotic and sordid scenes and the new nauseating sounds. He explained to Winnington Ingram how *Dynamite*, a recent gangster film, had upset him because the clergyman who married a woman and a condemned man the night before the execution reminded him of his father. Out went the sequence for a civil ceremony. And typical of the stream of complaints to the Lord Chamberlain was the one in 1948 about the seduction of a Salvation Army officer in Mae West's *Diamond Lil*. It, too, was cut out.[44]

The social-purity lobby continued to have a hand in the literary witch-hunts that periodically broke out. There was the right of private prosecution and the serious consideration of all complaints made to the Home Office. Publishers usually never knew who had lodged a complaint and they pleaded unsuccessfully with the government for guidance before publication. When Thomas Inskip, as Attorney General, obtained a destruction order in 1935 against William Heinemann for *Bessie Cotter*, which portrayed life in a Chicago whorehouse, counsel for the defence claimed that if the police had given any intimation of an objection, the book would have been withdrawn. In fact the complaints came from Mudie's Library and the PMC. On this occasion a fellow publisher, Stanley Unwin, claimed, 'The Home Office and the police, to do them justice, are not unreasonable in applying this obscenity law but their hands are often tied'. Three years later the *Daily Mail* reviewer of *To Beg I Am Ashamed*, the rather mild memoirs of a prostitute, sent his prepublication copy to the PMC, which forwarded it to the Home Secretary. This led to a police threat to the publishers, Routledges, and the withdrawal of the book before distribution.[45] With the assistance of the vigilantes, repression worked in a variety of ways.

Though the devoted Winnington Ingram retired in 1939 his

successors at the helm of the PMC continued to take their
responsibilities as seriously as the tall and influential Bishop had
in his thirty-eight years of guarding London's morals. By tradition the chairmanship had come to devolve upon the incumbent
bishop. After a decade of work, Bishop Wand said in 1955 that
he 'regarded the chairmanship of the Council as one of the most
important duties of his office'.⁴⁶ Officials still treated the multitude of complaints with the respect due to organised religion's
moral watchdog. In the early 1950s the arrival of American
girlie magazines like *Razzle* and *Caress* were causing a good
deal of concern and hundreds of prosecutions were launched
between 1950 and 1952 with the usual temporary results. Chief
Inspector Black of the Scotland Yard Vice Squad confirmed
the role of George Tomlinson, who had been the PMC's busy
secretary since 1940 : 'The Chief Inspector was good enough
to say that the nationwide campaign against indecent literature
had been due entirely to the secretary's interview with the public
prosecutor'.⁴⁷

Initiatives from this legacy of Victorian moral rearmament
got the authorities moving on children's horror comics in the
1950s, kept contraceptive slot machines at bay for a time and
British Rail toilets as free from graffiti as humanly possible, and
even stopped at the borders Danish Dandy Chewing Gum, which
had indecent pinups on its wrapper. The PMC played its part
in the puzzling 1954 'purge' when Sir David Maxwell-Fyfe, the
Tory Home Secretary, sanctioned five major prosecutions in the
last blanket onslaught on serious literature. There is no doubt
that Maxwell-Fyfe was sympathetic to the aims of the PMC,
since he addressed its annual meeting the year before. The publications committee lodged a complaint with the public prosecutor
about *The Image and The Search*, whose theme was nymphomania. It became one of the five objects of legal attack; interest-
ingly enough, two juries failed to convict.

The puritans of the PMC were out of touch, a fact not surprising with Mrs Neville Rolfe still scrutinising books for them
up to her death in 1955. New members included Sir Cyril Black,
a leading Baptist who was to carry on his own campaign against
obscene literature, at considerable personal expense and trouble,
right into the 1970s. With the exception of the 1954 outbreak
the authorities mostly ignored the PMC's complaints about

literature, despite the fact that Tomlinson screened many of his constituents' crankiest complaints.

Nothing reveals the dead end of social purity better than the self-styled 'anti-nudity' campaign. Living statuary had finally given way to the real thing in the early 1930s with static poses and semi-nude dancing in reviews. The Lord Chamberlain ruled that nudity would be permitted in the theatres under his control under special conditions: no movement, dim lights and redeeming artistic merit. When Winnington Ingram protested in 1934 he drew a rebuke from Marie Tempest, the well-known entertainer, who wrote to *The Times*, 'I see the Bishop of London is protesting against the scantiness of costumes worn on the stage. ... I have memories of Mrs Chant's crusade and the wave of indignation and disgust that was aroused in every decent-minded person by that prurient, prying and self-righteous campaign'.[48] Miss Tempest recalled how she had wept when she had to appear in tights for the first time forty years earlier; but she concluded that the public no longer cared about stage nudity.

The arrival of the American striptease in 1937 caused even more alarm. The Lord Chamberlain's strategic meeting with representatives of seven hundred local authorities failed to stop it, as did provincial prosecutions. Then one night in Hull early in the war Phyllis Dixey introduced the famous performance in which she disrobed behind an expensive ostrich-feather fan. In most locales she was tolerated as long as she remained still while undressed. She usually succeeded, although a rat fell on her in Chatham, a V-2 rocket cut out over a theatre, and audiences shot peas at her. After Dunkirk the striptease was banned from London's West-End theatres, only to surface in private night clubs like the El Morocco, which advertised 'the most daring cabaret of all time' along with an official air-raid shelter. The PMC succeeded in getting these clubs reformed at about the same time as it secured the appointment of special police to stop love-making in public air-raid shelters during the all-clear.

With stage nudity settled into the Windmill Theatre after the war, vigilantes attended every one of the hundreds of 'revuedevilles' to report to the Lord Chamberlain on whether any nudes had broken his rule by moving, or whether dancers' breast covers were too revealing. On one occasion in 1951 Tomlinson got the

BBC to stop comedians from alluding to the Windmill; four years later, after a typical protest to the Lord Chamberlain about the 'Paris by Night' review, Marqueez was 'revealed after discarding the final scarf wearing breast coverings the size of saucers in place of the rosebud tips previously worn'.[49] In the meantime, while the striptease had returned to theatres under LCC authority, Gypsy Rose Lee's 1952 tour led to a ban in those houses on disrobing on stage. This was a ban the PMC enforced. Thus the Victorian purity movement wound down with its last loyalists in front row seats keeping Phyllis Dixey 'under the closest examination' and scrutinising the breast covers of Pauline Penny and Peaches Page.

# Epilogue

SINCE the belated demise of Victorian social-purity institutions in the 1950s and 60s, a number of celebrated successors have appeared on the scene. But the exploits of Mary Whitehouse, Lord Longford and the Festival of Light appear to have produced more smoke than fire when measured against those charted above. Not since the 1930s has a Bishop of London, with prominent Roman Catholic, nonconformist, Jew and salvationist in tow, been able to obtain instant results from the authorities. While many of the leading anti-pornographers continue to draw sustenance from a rigorous Old Testament Christianity and Mrs Whitehouse claims to have detected a significant new religious revival, the fact remains that increasing apathy towards the Christian religion has undermined their natural social constituency and thereby their ability to influence public policy and levy private blackmail.[1] One can plainly see the meagre results of the Festival of Light's two most ambitious projects of the 1970s, 'Operation Newsagent' and the 'Nationwide Petition for Public Decency', the latter a joint effort with Mary Whitehouse's National Viewers' and Listeners' Association.[2]

As the public has grown less tolerant of private vigilantes influencing the tone of public moral standards, the law has been adjusted accordingly. After Sir Cyril Black launched a private prosecution against *Last Exit to Brooklyn*, Roy Jenkins, then Home Secretary, rushed through legislation in 1967 removing the right of a private person to take out a summons for a destruction order. When the Lord Chamberlain's stage censorship was ended the following year, it was arranged that private actions would be permitted only with the sanction of the Attorney General. By 1976 the judge in the rare common-law prosecution of a film was outspoken in court about the need to limit such actions and in the following year the head of the British Board of Film Censors concurred.[3]

Yet while the new permissiveness is self-evident and sustaining its advances, and the moral vigilantes find their legal options circumscribed or under attack, the fact remains that at the time of writing hard-core pornography cannot be legally sold or exhibited in Britain. The lag between what is permitted there, and in the United States and parts of Western Europe, is due in part to the opinion-forming forays of Britain's celebrated purity advocates.

In the realm of sex education Mary Whitehouse and her allies have managed to salvage something as well. It is true that guest lecturers from the Family Planning Association annually provide thousands of schoolchildren with the kind of explicit and morally unadorned information that would have shocked the pioneer experts of the Alliance of Honour or the British Social Hygiene Council. The Longford Report went so far as to condemn BBC film material for school sex education as virtually pornographic.[4] The new sex educators, however, have hardly had things all their own way. Anti-pornographers have stiffened local resistance to the introduction of explicit materials into the schools. In 1975 one expert estimated that only about 30 per cent of local authorities provided for sex education; approaches varied to a startling degree and included the familiar nurturing of venerophobia, now augmented with films of giant magnified VD germs.[5]

In its heyday social purity had derived its power from the alliance between puritans and feminists, many of whom were puritans themselves. The coalition came apart between the wars as the Butlerites, the prostitutes' friends, squabbled with the repressionists, for whom the equality of the sexes before the law was secondary to removing vice from view. The latter triumphed in 1959 when the Street Offences Act pushed prostitutes out of sight, at the risk of conviction for soliciting on police evidence alone. It was not until 1976, more than three-quarters of a century after the misleading Vagrancy Act of 1898, that a Home Office working party proposed that the law be made more equitable by classifying 'kerb crawling' by men in search of women as a criminal offence. However, real equality was made more remote than ever by the working party's approval of the severe law of 1959, the radical feminists' *bête noire*.[6]

The social-purity alliance had been based on advocacy of a single standard of chaste behaviour and on the politics of protecting females from procurers and seducers. These transitional aims reflected the wish of some men to atone for the abuses of the double standard, and the desire of females to pay men back for such evils as juvenile prostitution. The pursuit of protection and the single standard of purity was also a result of the anxieties attending the early emancipation of women. The abuses are largely corrected and the anxieties worked through. While there is a continuing furore over inadequacies in the rape law, the protection of females is no longer the multi-faceted central issue it was when social purity was at its height. In the mid-seventies responsible opinion, some of it clerical, emerged in favour of reducing the age of consent to fourteen and abolishing the crime of incest. At the same time, though, the award-winning television documentary, 'Johnny Go Home', and evidence from other sources made it clear that runaway teenagers of both sexes were hardly secure from the lures of procurers. The fact that these revelations caused no 'Maiden Tribute' sensation is a measure of our distance from the Victorians.

When the NVA and the British National Committee were short of funds in 1953 and believed that permanent station work was no longer essential, they reorganised as the British Vigilance Association, which had a twenty-year life helping au pair girls and pressing successfully for the stricter regulation of employment agencies. On one occasion in the sixties it helped break up the operations of a London agency trafficking in Irish prostitutes. By then white-slave tales were relatively scarce, though the stubborn story about the old witch-figure who doped girls as they helped her across the road was repeated to this author by a number of older vigilance workers who still gave it credence. Enforced prostitution persists in certain parts of the third world, like India, which have proved impervious to the international efforts begun by Coote and now continued by the United Nations. And British rule did not prevent a cruel white-slavery ring from abducting girls in Hong Kong in the 1970s.[7] Symptomatically, the last series of astonishing panics in the West, in the French provincial cities of Amiens, Orleans and Chalons in the late sixties and early seventies, surfaced where urban growth was significant due to migrations from the hinterland. A reminder of how explosive

the subject once was in Britain can be found at platform seven
of Victoria Station, where a lone travellers' aid outpost run by
the YWCA still advises those in distress.

# Appendices

## THE BRITISH NATIONAL COMMITTEE FOR SUPPRESSION OF THE WHITE-SLAVE TRAFFIC

Below is the institutional membership of the British National Committee in 1910. These members were the core of the social-purity movement at the time. By the 1920s the British National Committee had become something of a clearing house for the discussion of purity questions and apportionment of work.

Associated Societies for the Protection of Women and Children
Church Army
Girls' Friendly Society
International Catholic Society for Befriending Young Girls
Jewish Association (Gentlemen) for the Protection of Girls and
    Women
Jewish Association (Ladies) for the Care and Protection of Girls
London Council for the Promotion of Public Morality (Public
    Morality Council)
London Diocesan Council for Preventive, Rescue and Penitentiary
    Work
London Female Preventive and Reformatory Institution
Metropolitan Association for Befriending Young Servants
National Council of the Evangelical Free Churches
National Union of Women Workers
National Vigilance Association
Rochester Diocesan Association for the Care of Friendless Girls
Salvation Army
Society for the Rescue of Young Women and Children (Rescue
    Society)
Travellers' Aid Society
West London Mission
Young Women's Christian Association
Young Women's Christian Association (International Union)

# APPENDIX B

## THE NATIONAL VIGILANCE ASSOCIATION IN 1886

National Vigilance Association

*Council*
### THE BISHOP OF SOUTHWELL, *Chairman*

†The Archbishop of Dublin
The Bishop of Durham
The Bishop of Bedford
†The Bishop of Brechin
Cardinal Manning
The Lord Brabazon
*Rt. Hon. J. Stansfeld, MP
*Professor Stuart, MP
Rev. Dr Adler
Mrs Adler
*Miss Baker
*C. C. M. Baker
*Miss Bear
†E. B. Benson
*Wyndham A. Bewes
*Miss C. A. Biggs
*Dr Elizth. Blackwell
S. A. Blackwood
W. Bramwell Booth
*Mrs W. Bramwell Booth
*T. L. Boyd
*Mrs Boyd
Mrs Bradley
J. Britten
Rev. G. Brooks
*Rev. R. A. Bullen
*Percy W. Bunting
*Mrs Bunting
Rev. Canon Geo. Butler
*Mrs Josephine Butler
*Mrs Ormiston Chant
†Rev. F. M. Caulfield
F. N. Charrington
*Rev. Dr Clifford

†T. Clarkson
†Rev. E. S. Cole
†H. S. Coleman
†Rev. W. E. Coller
*Miss L. Cooper
*B. F. C. Costelloe
*Mrs Costelloe
*W. F. Craies
Miss Sharman Crawford
†S. Crawshaw
F. W. Crossley
*Canon Donaldson
A. S. Dyer
*Mrs H. Fawcett
*Hon. Mrs Fraser
G. Gillett
†Captain W. H. Goldney, R.E.
†G. A. Gregory
†J. Henderson
*W. Hill
C. Hoe
*Miss Ellice Hopkins
*Rev. J. Horsley
Rev. H. Price Hughes
†W. J. Hutchings
*Miss Janes
Rev. A. W. Jephson
†Rt. Rev. H. W. Jermyn, D.D.
†W. Johnston, MP
*Rev. R. E. Johnston
†H. Kershall
*Edwin H. Kerwin
*A. A. Knight
Mark Knowles

National Vigilance Association—*continued*

*F. T. Laurence
*C. H. Lepper
†Miss B. Leppington
*Miss Lidgett
*Mrs Lynch
†Hon. and Rev. A. Lyttelton
*Miss Mackrell
*Arthur J. S. Maddison
†H. Marshall
*C. T. Martin
*Miss Mason
 Rev. Andrew Mearns
*Rev. Grant Mills
*Haford L. Mills
*Chas. T. Mitchell
*Mrs Mitchell
†Rev. T. Mitcheson
 R. C. Morgan
†Wm. M. Oatts
*J. Ockendon
†W. H. Parish
*Francis Peek
†F. A. Powell
†T. E. Powell
†Rev. Harry H. Pullen
*W. D. Rawlins
 J. S. Rendell
 Admiral Rodd
*C. H. Rowse

 George Russell
*Miss Maria Rye
†D. Rylands
†Sydney J. Saunders
*Mrs A. L. Savory
*Madame la Comtesse Schack
*Wm. Shaen
†W. Slade
 Rev. S. Singer
 Mrs Singer
 Samuel Smith, MP
†J. J. Spraggon
*W. T. Stead
*Miss Steer
 Rev. Dr Stevenson
 Rev. Dr T. B. Stephenson
*Mrs Steward
†H. Tasker
*Ralph Thicknesse
†Miss Thomson
†R. W. Vick
†Mr J. Warren
†W. C. W. Vincent
*Rev. Benjamin Waugh
*Miss Whitehead
*H. S. Wilde
*J. W. Williamson
†Mrs Woodman
†Rev. Canon Wynne

*These are members of the Executive Committee, of which* Mr P. W.
Bunting *is Chairman.* † *Representative members of Local Association.*

HON. TREASURER—FRANCIS PEEK.

Many of these individuals are discussed in the text and can be
traced through the index.

# Notes

Unless otherwise stated, the place of publication of all the material referred to is London.

INTRODUCTION
(pp. 1–7)
1. W. T. Stead, *The Revival of 1905*, 1905, 12.
2. T. B. Macaulay, *Works* 5, 1879, 391.

CHAPTER ONE
(pp. 11–31)
1. David Ogg, *England in the Reigns of James II and William III*, Oxford 1955, 531.
2. *The Sentinel*, March 1888.
3. P. E. H. Hair, ed., *Before the Bawdy Court*, 1972. Christopher Hill, 'The Bawdy Courts', *Society and Puritanism in Pre-Revolutionary England*, Panther ed. 1969, 288–332.
4. Defoe cited first in Anthony Babington, *A House in Bow St.*, 1969, 28; Defoe, *A Poor Man's Plea . . .*, 3rd ed., 1700, 18.
5. John Disney, *An Essay Upon the Executions of the Laws Against Profaneness and Immorality*, 2nd ed., 1710, 47.
6. T. C. Curtis and W. A. Speck, 'The Societies For The Reformation of Manners : A Case Study in the Theory and Practice of Moral Reform', *Literature and History* 3, March 1976, 47–8. John Walsh, 'Origins of the Evangelical Revival', *Essays in Modern Church History*, ed. G. V. Bennett and J. D. Walsh, 1699, 2.
7. *An Account of the Societies for the Reformation of Manners in London and Westminster and Other Parts of the Kingdom*, 1699, 2.
8. Cited in Donald Thomas, *A Long Time Burning*, 1969, 81.
9. See the collection of Stephen's Admonitions at Guildhall Library, An. 2.5.13.
10. *Antimoixeia: Or, The Honest and Joynt Design of the Tower Hamblets for the general suppression of Bawdy Houses, as En-*

*couraged thereto by Public Magistrates*, June 1691, Guildhall Library Broadsides.

11. *The Tryals of such Persons as under the notion of London Apprentices were Tumultuously assembled in Moor-Fields, and other places, on Easter Holiday last, under colour of pulling down Bawdy Houses*, 1668, at Guildhall Library.

12. *A Vindication of a late undertaking of Certain Gentlemen in Order to the Suppressing of Debauchery and Profaneness*, 1692, 7. See also Dudley Bahlmann, *The Moral Revolution of 1688*, Archon edition Hamden, Connecticut 1968, ch. 2; Garnet V Portus, *Caritas Anglicana*, 1912, ch. 2.

13. C. F. Secretan, *Memoirs of the Life and Times of The Pious Robert Nelson*, 1860, 96–100.

14. *The Good Fight of Faith ... Exemplified in a Sermon preached ... at the Funeral of Mr. John Dent*, 1709.

15. On the provinces, the minutes and correspondence in W. O. B. Allen and E. McClure, *Two Hundred Years. The History of the Society for Promoting Christian Knowledge*, 1898.

16. Henry Sacheverell, *The Communication of Sin ...*, 1709.

17. *A Sermon Preached To The Societies For The Reformation of Manners, 15 January 1732*, 1733, 11.

18. Peter Gay, *The Enlightenment*, 2, 1969, 525–8. Gibson cited in W. B. Whitaker, *The Eighteenth-Century English Sunday*, 1940, 64.

19. Josiah Woodward, *A Rebuke to the Sin of Uncleanness*, 1704, passim. See also his *Young Man's Monitor ...*, 1706.

20. Portus, *Caritas Anglicana*, Appendix V.

21. Bernard Mandeville, *A Conference About Whoring*, 1725, 5.

22. *Lord Chesterfield's Letters to his Son*, Everyman ed. London 1929, 25. On this subject see the interesting comments by Keith Thomas, 'The Place of Laughter in Tudor and Stuart England', *Times Literary Supplement*, 21 Jan. 1977, 77–81.

23. Richard Sennett, *The Fall of Public Man*, New York 1977, 23.

24. Jonas Hanway, 'The Character of Mary Magdalene', *Letters Written Occasionally on the Customs of Foreign Nations in regard to Harlots ...*, 1761, at Guildhall Library.

25. Lord Bishop of St Asaph, *Sermon Preached to the Societies ...* 1730, 23–4.

26. *An Account of the Societies ...*, 1699, 22–3. 14 July 1699 Grand Jury Presentments, London Sessions Papers at Guildhall Record Office.

27. J. P. Malcolm, *Anecdotes of the Manners and Customs of London During the Eighteenth Century*, 1, 1810, 234–5. Jeremy

Collier, *Essays Upon Several Moral Subjects*, 3, 1705, 129.

28. Westminster Sessions Papers, Oct. 1725, 4–7, at Middlesex Record Office.

29. W. J. Hardy, *Typescript Calendar of Sessions Books and Orders of Court*, 1729–32, 44–5, 50, 58, 68, 72–4, 87, 92, 105–11, 127, Middlesex County Records. *Grub Street Journal*, 30 July 1730.

30. *The Good Fight of Faith* ... 1709; Malcolm, *Anecdotes*, 2, 21.

31. Cited in *Thoughts on Means of Alleviating the Miseries Attendant upon Common Prostitution*, 1797, 20n.

32. *Grub Street Journal*, 6 Aug. 1730.

33. Hardy, *Calendar*, Oct. 1720, 91.

34. 24 May 1699 Grand Jury Presentments, London Sessions Papers at Guildhall Record Office.

35. Arthur Bedford, *Serious Reflections on the Scandalous Abuse and Effects of the Stage*, Bristol 1705.

36. *A Letter from severall members of the Societies ... to the Archbishop of Canterbury*, 1704; Joseph Wood Krutch, *Comedy and Conscience After the Restoration*, New York 1961 ed., 168–75.

37. Richard Findlater, *Banned: A Review of Theatrical Censorship in Britain*, 1967, 33–4.

38. Jeremy Collier, *Essays*, 3, 154–5.

39. For such a case of attempted sodomy : 16 June 1699 deposition of Joseph Thomas, London Sessions Paper at Guildhall Record Office. On the legal aspects, see H. Montgomery Hyde, *The Other Love*, 1970.

40. *British Gazetteer*, 7 May 1726. Many of the cases are in *Select Trials for Murders, Robberies, Rapes, Sodomy, Coining, Frauds ... at the Old Bailey*, 1 and 2, 1720–1732.

41. *Proceedings of the Old Bayley*, Dec. 1730, at Guildhall Library.

42. *Some Considerations upon Street-Walkers, With a Proposal for Lessening the Present Number of them*, 1737, 2–3, at Guildhall Library.

43. Bishop of Lichfield and Coventry ... *Sermon Preached to the Societies* ... 1724, 15.

## CHAPTER TWO
(pp. 32–50)

1. On the meaning of pornography, Steven Marcus, *The Other Victorians*, New York 1966; George Frankl, *The Failure of the Sexual Revolution*, Mentor ed. 1975, ch. 7.

2. The ballads named are in 'English Ballads', British Museum C 22 f. 6.

3. Thomas, *A Long Time Burning*, ch. 5, for the following.

4. *British Gazetteer*, 14 May 1726.
5. Jeremy Collier, *Short View of the Immorality and Profaneness of the English Stage*, 1698, 7.
6. Jean Jacques Rousseau, *Emile*, Everyman ed. 1972, 299. See also Lloyd de Mause ed., *The History of Childhood*, Harper Torchbooks ed. New York 1975, 47–9.
7. Cited in Michael Ryan, *Prostitution in London*, 1839, 114.
8. Malcolm, *Anecdotes*, 1, 212–13, 354.
9. William Paley, *Principles of Moral and Political Philosophy*, 1785, 249.
10. Robert Isaac and Samuel Wilberforce, *Life of William Wilberforce*, 1, 1838, 79–134, for the following.
11. Paley, *Principles*, 451.
12. Cited in Muriel Jaeger, *Before Victoria*, 1956, 14.
13. John Pearson, *Life of William Hey*, 1822, 119.
14. Sidney and Beatrice Webb, *History of Liquor Licencing*, 1903.
15. *Bishop Porteus Diaries*, entries for 7 Jan. and 1 Apr. 1788 and (nd) Jan. 1790, at Lambeth Palace Library. *Report of the Subcommittee of the Proclamation Society respecting the Improvements which have Lately been Made in the Prisons . . .* 1790, at Guildhall Library.
16. Wilhelm Reich, *Sex-Pol. Essays 1929–1934* ed. Lee Baxandall, Vintage ed. New York 1972, 246.
17. John Bowdler, *Reform or Ruin*, 20th ed. 1798, passim.
18. Ryan, *Prostitution*, 14.
19. On the foregoing, *Report of the Committee of the Society for Carrying into Effect His Majesty's Proclamation Against Vice and Immorality*, 1799; *Report of the Society for the Suppression of Vice* 1825, 5.
20. *Address to the Public From The Society for the Suppression of Vice, Parts One and Two* 1803. Evidence of George Prichard to Police Committee of the House of Commons in *Report of the Society . . .*, 1825, appendix; Ryan, *Prostitution*, 115.
21. Evidence of Prichard in *Report of the Society . . .*, appendix; *Address, Part Two*, 1803.
22. E. M. Howse, *Saints in Politics*, 1953, 120; *Report of The Society . . .*, 37.
23. *Report of the Society . . .*, appendix.
24. Patrick Colquhoun, *Treatise on the Police of the Metropolis*, 1800 ed., 348.
25. Francis Place Papers, B.M. Add. Mss. 27827 f. 50.
26. Letter to the author from the Publicity Branch, Metropolitan Police Office, 6 July 1976.

27. Ryan, *Prostitution*, 197–9.
28. Ronald Pearsall, *The Worm in the Bud*, Penguin ed. 1969, 456.
29. *The Times*, 11 May 1857.
30. On the origins and history of the bill, J. W. Horsley paper to the Church Congress, *Seeking and Saving*, Nov. 1884, *Parl. Debs. 3rd Ser.*, CVIL, 327–30, 1152–3, 1355–6. *Life of John, Lord Campbell, Lord High Chancellor of Great Britain*, ed. Hon. Mrs Hardcastle, 2, 1881, 353, 357.
31. *Seeking and Saving*, Nov. 1884.
32. Ivan Bloch, *Sexual Life in England, Past and Present*, 1938, 659.
33. Letter of Joseph Knight, *Athenaeum*, 29 May 1875; see also the issues for 8, 15 May and 5, 12 June 1875.
34. *Seeking and Saving*, Nov. 1884.
35. Thomas, *A Long Time Burning*, 263–4. As late as 1888 legal advice to the government was that obscenity depended on 'the mode of publication'; H. B. Poland in H.O. 144 A46657C/24 at Public Record Office.
36. *Society for the Suppression of Vice. Abstract of the seventy-sixth Annual Report*, 1879, 5, at New York Public Library; *Seeking and Saving*, Nov. 1884.

## CHAPTER THREE
(pp. 51–71)

1. Fielding cited in Malcolm, *Anecdotes*, 1, 353–5.
2. *Boswell's London Journal*, New York 1950, 49–50, 227, 255, 272–3.
3. *Manners Maketh Man*, 1906, ch. 2.
4. On this subject, Peter Cominos, 'Late-Victorian Sexual Respectability and the Social System', *International Review of Social History* 8, 1963, 18–48 and 216–50.
5. Minute of 25 Feb. 1857, H.O. 45 6628 (OS).
6. *Second Report of the Committee of the Guardian Society*, 1817, passim.
7. Babington, *A House in Bow St.*, 75.
8. Saunders Welch, *A Proposal to Render Effectual a Plan to Remove the Nuisance of Common Prostitutes from the Streets of the Metropolis*, 1758, 8–10; Henry Fielding, *A True State of the Case of Bosavern Penlez*, 1749.
9. *Gentleman's Magazine*, July 1749, also Sept. and Oct.
10. John Wesley, *Works*, 4, 1771 ed., 87–93; Malcolm, *Anecdotes*, 1, 350–51.
11. *Magdalen's Friend*, Oct. 1860; Edward W. Thomas, *Twenty-Five Years' Labour Among the Friendless and Fallen*, 1886.

12. Charles Warren to the Home Office Undersecretary, 22 Mar. 1888 in H.O. 45 9678/A47459/33.

13. On the following, George R. Sims, *Glances Back*, 1917, 14; G. Prichard to Sir George Grey, 29 Jan. 1858 in H.O. 45 6628 (OS); Montague Williams, *Leaves of a Life* 1, 1890, 261–2; Metropolitan Police Division C, Report of 6 Sept. 1874 in H.O. 45 9511/17216.

14. Charles Terrot, *The Maiden Tribute*, 1959, 13–16; Charles Verlinden, *L'Esclavage dans L'Europe Médiévale* 1, Bruges 1955, 513.

15. Frederick Engels, *The Condition of the Working Classes in England*, Panther ed. 1969, 177; Glen Petrie, *A Singular Iniquity*, 1971, 75; NVA *Report of the Executive Committee*, 1887, 6.

16. Hare, *Bawdy Court*, case 533.

17. *Gentleman's Magazine*, Oct. 1747; *Covent Garden Journal*, 25 Jan. 1752; Welch, *Proposal*, 11–13.

18. Babington, *Bow Street*, 100–103.

19. *Gentleman's Magazine*, March 1752.

20. *Report of the Provisional Committee of the Guardian Society ...*, 1816; Talbot in Ryan, *Prostitution*, 118 ff.

21. On the following, J. B. Talbot, *Miseries of Prostitution*, 1844; *Associate Institute for Improving and Enforcing the Laws for the Protection of Women. First Report*, 1846; *Associate Institute ... Remedies for the Wrongs of Women*, 1844, Parl Debs. 3rd Ser., CV, Lords, 25 May 1849, 972–5; CVI, Lords, 14 June 1849, 169–73 and Commons, 27 June 1849, 124–30.

22. *The Gladstone Diaries* 4, ed. M. R. D. Foot and H. C. G. Matthew, Oxford 1974, 20 Jan. 1854.

23. John Fielding, *An Account of the Origins and Effects of a Police ... To Which is added a Plan for preserving those deserted girls in This Town who Become Prostitutes from Necessity*, 1757.

24. 'Sunderlandensis' in *Gentleman's Magazine*, April 1751.

25. Pierre Dufour, *Histoire de la Prostitution*, 7, Brussels, 1861, 66 ff.

26. Jonas Hanway, *Plan for Establishing a Charity House or Charity Houses for the Reception of Repenting Prostitutes to be called The Magdalen Charity*, 1758, 17, at Guildhall Library. On the internal organisation, William Dodd, *An Account of the Rise, Progress and Present State of the Magdalen Charity*, 1761; *Byelaws and Regulations of the Magdalen Hospital*, 1758, 1791, 1816 eds.

27. Colquhoun, *Treatise*, 627; *The Times*, 4 Sept. 1816.

28. William Hale, *Considerations on the Causes and the Prevalence of Female Prostitution*, 1812, 10.

29. *Report of the Committee of the Guardian Society*, 1817; *Report from the Commissioners on the State of the Police of the Metropolis*, P.P., V, 1816, appendix 12, 368–80.

30. Eric Trudgill, *Madonnas and Magdalens*, 1976, 289.

31. They were collected in John Armstrong, *Essays on Church Penitentiaries*, 1858.

32. Rev. T. T. Carter, *Memoir of John Armstrong*, 1858; J. F. M. Carter, *Life and Work of the Rev. T. T. Carter*, 1911; *Life and Letters of William John Butler*, 1897.

33. *The Gladstone Diaries* 3, 1974, XIV.

34. John Blackmore, *The London By Moonlight Mission . . .*, 1860; Thomas, *Twenty-Five Years' Labour*, passim; see also William J. Taylor, *The Story of the Homes*, 1907.

35. *Magdalen's Friend*, May 1860.

36. Arthur Brinckmann, *Notes on Rescue Work*, 1895 ed.; Sarah Robinson, *A Life Record*, 1898, 138; Arthur Maddison, *Hints on Rescue Work*, n.d. 1899, 21–2.

37. *Magdalen's Friend*, April 1860.

38. *Magdalen's Friend*, Feb., Oct. 1862; Arthur Maddison to the Archbishop of Canterbury, 6 April 1883 in Benson Papers, vol. 102, f. 219–20.

39. Derek Hudson, *Munby Man of Two Worlds*, Abacus ed. 1974, 41.

40. Cited in M. Penelope Hall and Ismene V. Howes, *The Church in Social Work*, 1965, 275n–6.

CHAPTER FOUR
(pp. 75–93)

1. Josephine Butler, *Sursum Corda*, 1871, 5–6, at Fawcett Library.

2. Henry Scott Holland, *A Bundle of Memories*, 1915, 228; Dorothea Price Hughes, *Life of Hugh Price Hughes*, 1904, 85.

3. Ellice Hopkins, *Damaged Pearls*, 1885, 22, in White Cross Collection.

4. G. R. Balleine, *A History of the Evangelical Party in the Church of England*, new ed. 1951, 201.

5. *Vigilance Record*, March 1888.

6. Cited in Josephine Butler, *Personal Reminiscences of a Great Crusade*, new ed. 1911, 189.

7. Cited in Helen Ware, 'The Recruitment, Regulation and Role

of Prostitutes from the Middle of the Nineteenth Century to the Present Day' (unpub. Ph.D. thesis, London University, 1969), 167.

8. Benjamin Scott, *A State Iniquity*, 1890, ch. 3.
9. Cited in Ware, 'Prostitutes', 173–4.
10. Butler, *Sursum Corda*, 14.
11. Butler, *Personal Reminiscences*, 6.
12. W. T. Stead, *Josephine Butler*, 1887, 18.
13. Scott, *State Iniquity*, ch. 9; Hans Peter Bleuel, *Sex and Society in Nazi Germany*, New York 1973, 225–9.
14. *Shield*, 1 Nov. 1881.
15. Josephine Butler, *The Voice of One Crying in the Wilderness*, Bristol 1913, 16–17, 30–31.
16. For example, *National League Journal*, Sept., Nov. 1876.
17. *LNA. Sixteenth Annual Report*, 1885, 17–18; also comments of Josephine Butler in *Report*, 1884, 72.
18. *National League Journal*, April 1878.
19. Josephine Butler to Mr and Mrs Clark, June 1876, in Josephine Butler Correspondence at Fawcett Library; *The Sentinel*, June 1886.
20. For the arithmetic, Stead, *Josephine Butler*, 46n–7. G. Morgan, *R. C. Morgan*, 1909, 298–301.
21. Josephine Butler, *An Autobiographical Memoir*, eds. George W. and Lucy Johnson, 3rd ed. 1928, 130.
22. Josephine Butler, *Address in Croydon*, 1871, 6, at Fawcett Library.
23. *Ibid.*, 11.
24. Edward Bristow, 'The Liberty and Property Defence League and Individualism', *Historical Journal* XVIII, 1975, 772–3.
25. Judith Walkowitz, 'We are Not Beasts of the Field : Prostitution and the Campaign Against the Contagious Diseases Acts, 1869–86' (unpub. Ph.D. thesis, University of Rochester, 1974), 355–6.
26. Maurice Gregory, *The Suppression of the White Slave Traffic*, 1908.
27. *British, Continental and General Federation. Fourth Annual Report*, 1878–9, 11–12; *Bulletin Continental*, May, Nov. 1875; Jan., Feb., Sept. 1877.
28. Cited in Butler, *Personal Reminiscences*, 13.
29. Josephine Butler to H. J. Wilson, 14 April 1875, in Josephine Butler Correspondence; Humbert in *British, Continental and General Federation. Fifth Annual Report*, 1879–80, 18.
30. *The Christian*, 19 Nov. 1885. 9 Jan. 1880 Police Report in H.O. 45/9546/59343; Alfred Dyer, *A Prodigal Sect . . .*, 1918.

31. Josephine Butler to Dr Carter, 1 April 1880, in Josephine Butler Correspondence.
32. 'Correspondence Regarding the Immoral Traffic in English Girls to Belgium', in H.O. 45/9546/95343.
33. *Report of the Select Committee of the House of Lords on the Law Relating to the Protection of Young Girls*, P.P., IX, 1881, evidence of Jeffes, ques. 288–90 ff. On the Belgian scandal generally see the *Report*, passim, and Ann Stafford, *The Age of Consent*, 1964, ch. 5.
34. Minute of 6 Dec. 1880 in H.O. 45/9546/53943/41.
35. The investigation is probed in *Six Years' Labour and Sorrow: Being The Fourth Report of the London Committee For Suppressing the Traffic in British Girls . . .*, 1885.
36. Butler in *The Sentinel*, March 1882.
37. Correspondence in H.O. 45/9597/95696.
38. Lawson Tait, *An Analysis of the Evidence in Seventy Consecutive Charges Made Under the New Criminal Law Amendment Act*, Leicester 1894; Albert Moll, *The Sexual Life of the Child*, New York 1913 ed., 227–9.
39. Andrew Mearns, *Bitter Cry of Outcast London*, Humanities Press ed. New York 1970, and the useful introduction by Anthony Wohl.
40. Hartington to Rosebery, 30 May 1883, in H.O. 45/9546/59343G; James Stuart to Samuel Smith, 8 July 1884 in H.O. 45/9547/59343 I.
41. Cited in *The Sentinel*, Sept. 1881.

## CHAPTER FIVE
(pp. 94–121)

1. Ellice Hopkins quoted in F. D. How, *Archbishop Maclagan*, 1911, 223–4. Comment by her biographer in *Prevention*, July 1911. See Rosa Barrett, *Ellice Hopkins*, 1907, for help throughout; also the obituary in *The Guardian*, 31 August 1904.
2. Elihu Burritt, *Seed Lives* (n.d.), 20–21.
3. Sarah Robinson, *A Life Record*; Ellice Hopkins, *Active Service, or, Work Among Our Soldiers*, 1874.
4. Citations from Havelock Ellis, *Studies in the Psychology of Sex* 6, Philadelphia 1913, 315; Mrs. Havelock Ellis, *James Hinton*, 1918, 101; Ellice Hopkins, *Life and Letters of James Hinton*, 1878, 283.
5. Ellice Hopkins to Mr Holland (copy, n.d.), in Benson Papers, 6 f. 375–80; also her *Ladies' Associations . . .*, 1878; *How to Start Preventive Work*, 1884.

6. Ellice Hopkins, *Work in Brighton*, 1877, 39–40.

7. *Seeking and Saving*, July 1883. The data are derived from the periodic lists in this journal.

8. On Plymouth, evidence of Inspector Annis in *Report of the Select Committee of the House of Commons on the Contagious Diseases Acts, P.P.* VIII, 1881, ques. 4885–92; Walkowitz, 'Contagious Diseases Acts', 311–18.

9. *Report of the Manchester Ladies Association for the Care of Friendless Girls*, 1883; E. K. Crossley, *He Heard From God. The Story of Frank Crossley*, 1959, 145 ff.; E. Rendell Harris, *Life of Frank Crossley*, 1899, 240–49.

10. *Seeking and Saving*, July 1883; Sherwin Bailey, 'The White Cross League', *Moral Welfare*, April 1952, 2–4.

11. CEPS (by then called The White Cross Society) *Council Minutes*, 12 June 1891, 24 Nov. 1893, in White Cross Collection.

12. On Cambridge, *Seeking and Saving*, July 1885. For the Oxford membership list, *List of Members, Lent Term 1887*, in *White Cross Ideals* 4 in White Cross Collection. On Talbot, Enid Moberly Bell, *Josephine Butler*, 1962, 162–3.

13. Cited in Pearsall, *Worm in the Bud*, 128.

14. Montagu Butler to the Archbishop of Canterbury, 2 March 1893, in Benson Papers, vol. 120 f. 348–9. For the following, K. S. Inglis, *Churches and the Working Classes in Victorian England*, 1963.

15. Ellice Hopkins, *The White Cross Movement. A Statement of the Bishop of Durham's Movement*, 1883.

16. For these visits, *The Sentinel*, passim. For Edinburgh, Ellice Hopkins, *The Power of Womanhood*, 1900, 112–14. For Dublin, *Vigilance Record*, May 1893.

17. These activities can be followed in *The Sentinel*; see, too, *The Purity Crusade: Its Triumphs and Consequences*, 1885 in Fawcett Library.

18. Guy Thorne, *The Great Acceptance. The Life Story of Frederick Charrington*, 1912, passim.

19. *The Purity Crusade*, 17; *Six Years Labour and Sorrow*, 49–51.

20. Ellice Hopkins to Mrs Benson, 12, 24 April 1885, in Benson Papers, vol. 25 f. 352 ff.

21. Cited in Raymond L. Schults, *Crusader in Babylon. W. T. Stead and the Pall Mall Gazette*, Lincoln, Nebraska, 1972, 12.

22. Mrs Booth in *War Cry*, 18 July 1885; Harold Begbie, *Life of William Booth* 2, 1920, ch. 4.

I

23. Archbishop of Canterbury to James Stuart, 26 Sept. 1885, in Benson Papers, vol. 25 f. 395.
24. Of the many accounts, Ann Stafford, *The Age of Consent*, 132ff.
24a Police denials are in H.O. 144/A40202C.
25. *Pall Mall Gazette*, 6 July 1885.
26. Cited in Schults, *Crusader in Babylon*, 140, 146.
27. *Pall Mall Gazette*, 11 Aug. 1885.
28. See note 17 above.
29. *Justice*, 11, 18 July; 1, 22, 29 Aug. 1885.
30. Bishop Lightfoot to Percy Bunting, 7 Sept. 1885 in Percy Bunting Correspondence.
31. Hector France *En 'Police Court'*, Paris 1891, ch. 3.
32. *War Cry*, 15 Aug. 1885.
33. *Parl. Debs.* 3rd Ser. CCC, 31 July 1885, 770–71.
34. Hyde, *The Other Love*, 134; F. B. Smith, 'Labouchere's Amendment to the Criminal Law Amendment Bill', *Historical Studies* 17, 1976, 165–73.
35. *Shield*, 5 Feb. 1881; Scott, *State Iniquity*, 224.
36. Loose in the *Minutes of the Travellers' Aid Society General Committee*, 1885–93, at Fawcett Library.
37. W. A. Coote, *A Romance of Philanthropy*, 1916, 121.
38. Josephine Butler to Miss Priestman, 9 Sept. 1891, in Josephine Butler Correspondence.
39. *Saturday Review*, 6 April 1895.
40. Coote, *A Romance of Philanthropy*, 20–25; see also the obituary in *The Times*, 28 Oct. 1919.
41. NVA *Executive Council Minutes*, 30 May 1893.
42. *Malthusian*, Aug. 1889; *Vigilance Record*, Feb. 1888.
43. Bewes in *Vigilance Record*, July 1914.
44. Memorandum by Godfrey Lushington for Asquith, 18 August 1893, in H.O. 45/9739/A55202. See the comments of H. P. Hughes on the judicial unpopularity of the new law, in *Social Christianity*, 1890, 161–2.
45. Millicent Fawcett to W. T. Stead (n.d.) in Fawcett Autograph Collection, vol. 8 part B; NVA *Report of the Executive Committee*, 1887, 7.
46. NVA *Executive Minutes*, 1 Dec. 1896.

## CHAPTER SIX
(pp. 125–153)

1. Dr Abraham Flexner, *Prostitution in Europe*, New York 1914, 41n–2; see also Paul Thompson, *The Edwardians*, 1975, ch. 5.

2. *Truth*, 24 Oct. 1889; Edward Lyttleton, *The Training of the Young in the Laws of Sex*, 1900, 3–4.
3. See Joseph F. Kett, 'Adolescence and Youth in Nineteenth-Century America' in *The Family in History* eds. Theodore K. Rabb and Robert I. Rotberg, Harper Torchbook ed. New York 1971, 100–102.
4. R. A. Spitz, 'Authority and Masturbation', *Psychoanalytic Quarterly* 21, 1952, 490–527; E. H. Hare, 'Masturbatory Insanity : The History of an Idea', *Journal of Mental Science* 108 (1962) 1–25.
5. Samuel Solomon, *A Guide to Health, or Advice to Both Sexes* (n.d.).
6. Havelock Ellis, *Studies in the Psychology of Sex* 1, Philadelphia 1913, 255.
7. Bound in the *Annual Reports of the Moral Reform Union* in Fawcett Society.
8. On France, Angus McLaren, 'Doctor in the House : Medicine and Private Morality in France, 1800–1850', *Feminist Studies* 2, 1975, 43.
9. On the following, Ellice Hopkins, *On the Early Training of Boys and Girls*, 1882; *Grave Moral Questions*, 1884; *Village Morality*, 1885; Barrett, *Ellice Hopkins*, 176–8.
10. See Elizabeth Roberts, 'Learning and Living—Socialisation Outside School', *Oral History* 3, 1975, 20–1.
11. *Prevention*, Jan. 1911.
12. On the early attempts, Stead, *Josephine Butler*, 58n; *Monthly Review and Young Men's Christian Journal*, Aug. 1885. On Varley, Henry Varley (son), *Henry Varley's Life Story*, 1916.
13. W. Y. Fullerton, *F. B. Meyer*, 1929, 151.
14. Varley, *Lecture to Young Men*, 1884; *Christian Commonwealth*, 1 Oct. 1885.
15. *The Nonconformist Conscience Considered as a Social Evil and A Mischief Monger—By One who has had it*, 1903, 95.
16. Edward Lyttleton, *Memories and Hopes*, 1925, 28.
17. George R. Parkin, *Edward Thring, Life, Diary and Letters*, 2, 1898, 91, 153–62.
18. Edward Lyttleton, *Causes and Prevention of Immorality in Schools*, 1883, 10–11.
19. *Schoolmasters' Committee Minute Book*, 28 Oct. 1884, in White Cross Collection.
20. Edith Lyttleton, *Alfred Lyttleton*, 1917, 18.
21. Edith Lyttleton, *Causes and Prevention; Mothers and Sons*, 1892; *Training of the Young in the Laws of Sex*, 1900.

22. Havelock Ellis, *Psychology of Sex* 1, 164; on Lyttleton, vol. 6, 53.
23. Ellice Hopkins, *A Practical Suggestion*, 1895, in White Cross Collection. Lightfoot in Barrett, *Ellice Hopkins*, 183.
24. *Monthly Review and Y.M.C.A. Journal*, Aug. 1885–Feb. 1886.
25. Rev. Frizell to the Archbishop of Canterbury, 23 Jan. 1890 in Benson Papers, vol. 70, f. 203–5; *House of Laymen of the Province of Canterbury. Report of the Committee on Purity*, February 1890, in Benson Papers, vol. 102, f. 156–60.
26. CEPS *Executive Committee Minutes*, 23 July 1885; *Women's Total Abstinence Union. Annual Report*, 1893.
27. *On Guard*, May 1894; also Church of England Young Men's Society, *Winter Prospectus and Calendar*, 1887, in Fulham Palace Papers, Box 198.
28. *Continence* (n.d.) in Association for Moral and Social Hygiene Sexual Purity File, Box 49, at Fawcett Library.
29. Havelock Ellis, *The Task of Social Hygiene*, 1927 ed., 244–5.
30. *Free Church Year Book*, (1902) 166, 182, 188; (1903) 249; (1904) 228.
31. NVA *Executive Minutes*, 26 March, 7 June, 28 Oct. 1901; 27 May, 29 July, 28 Oct. 1902; James Marchant, *A Great Moral Crusade in Chatham*, 1902.
32. *The National Purity Crusade. Its Origins and Results*, 1904, 6–7.
33. *The Wel-Care Story* (n.d.) 4–5, in London Diocesan Council for Wel-Care Collection at County Hall.
34. Scott Lidgett in *Alliance of Honour Record*, April 1913; Anderson in *Ibid.*, Jan. 1911. Membership tally in *Ibid.*
35. *Prevention*, July 1911.
36. Arthur Marwick, *Women at War, 1914–1918*, 1977, 39–40, 81–2, 115–27; Magnus Hirshfeld, *Sexual History of the World War*, New York, 1934, 26. On the patrols see also *Sixth International Congress on the Suppression of the Traffic in Women and Children*, 1924, 174–183.
37. *White Cross . . . Society. Fortieth Annual Report*, 1922–3. The Alliance membership tally is in *Honour* and *Chivalry*.
38. On Jones, White Cross . . . *Executive Committee Minutes*, 11, 17 Feb. 1921; T. Miller Neatby, M.D., *The Adolescent and Moral Education*, Alliance of Honour, 1931.
39. William Kent, *Testament of a Victorian Youth*, 1938, 151–2.
40. Mary Scharlieb, *Reminiscences*, 1924, 222.
41. W. G. Macpherson, *History of the Great War. Medical Services. Diseases of the War* 2, 1923, ch. 3. The figure is in

*Report of the Joint Committee on the Criminal Law Amend-
ment Bill and the Sexual Offences Act, P.P.*, 111, 1918, que. 470.
42. *Royal Commission on Venereal Disease, P.P.*, XVI, 1916,
60–61.
43. Cited in Alex Comfort, *The Anxiety Makers*, 1967, 146–7. On
these and other activities described below, see the *Annual
Reports* and *Health and Empire.*
44. On the films, files S1³, S1Q, S10B, NVA Collection; *Shield*,
Dec. 1919–Jan. 1920.
45. *Report of the Joint Select Committee on the Criminal Law
Amendment Bill, P.P.*, VI, 1920, ques. 2325, 2333.
46. Shorthand notes on Deputation to Rt. Hon. Neville Chamberlain, 26 July 1923, in MH 55/191, Public Record Office.
47. The whole story is in MH 55/203.
48. Undated memoranda (1931) and comment of Walter Green-
wood, 30 Oct. 1930, in MH 55/198.
49. *Health and Empire*, Dec. 1931.
50. *Fifth Imperial Social Hygiene Congress*, 1931, 376.
51. *Sex Education in Schools and Youth Organisations*, Board
of Education Pamphlet 119, 1943.


CHAPTER SEVEN
(pp. 154–174)
1. From the Judicial Statistics for England and Wales, Parliamentary Papers.
2. Ellis, *Tasks of Social Hygiene*, 271.
3. *Royal Commission on the Duties of the Metropolitan Police,
P.P.* L, 1908, ques. 6952–8; L1, ques. 40317–86, 40453–87;
*Joint Select Committee on the Criminal Law Amendment Bill
...*, 1918, que. 185, evidence of Sir E. Blackwell.
4. Josephine Butler to Miss Priestman, 5 Nov. 1894, Josephine
Butler Correspondence.
5. Alfred Dyer, *The Glasgow System for the Repression of Vice*,
1884. Comments by Josephine Butler in LNA *Annual Reports*,
1882, 56–7 and 1884, 70–71.
6. *Vigilance Record*, July 1887.
7. A. Brinckman, *Notes on Rescue Work*, 1895 ed., introduction;
Maddison, Hints on Rescue Work, 14.
8. Coote, *Romance*, 30–35.
9. NVA *Executive Minutes*, 29 March 1892.
10. Developments can be followed in the annuals, *Salvation Army
Social Work; Church Army Blue Book; Free Church Year*

*Book; Midnight in Piccadilly. Annual Reports of the Rescue Work of the West London Mission.*

11. The data are in Maddison, *Hints on Rescue Work*, 3. On training and recruiting workers, *Seeking and Saving*, Oct. 1889, Jan. 1890; *National Union of Women Workers. Report of the Conference of Rescue Workers*, 1897; *Salvation Army Social Work*, 1908–9, 57; *The Wel-Care Story*, 4.

12. Madge Unworth, *Maiden Tribute*, 1949, ch. 10, for the Salvation Army. Lucy Colson, *A Simple Handbook for Beginners in Rescue Work*, 1906, for the Church Army.

13. Bishop of London's Visiting Committee, Homes and Refuges. Reports in Box 198, Fulham Palace Papers (Mandell Creighton).

14. *War Cry*, 5 Aug. 1885

15. Montague Butler to the Archbishop of Canterbury, 23 Nov. 1890 in Benson Papers, vol. 102, f. 151–4. Notes on the Moral Condition of the Garrisons and Seaports . . . 9 Nov. 1892, in vol. 112 f. 146–54; also the correspondence in vol. 128.

16. Minute of 27 Feb. 1896 in H.O. 45/9740/A55536.

17. On Manchester, Harris *Frank Crossley*, 145 ff. and appendix; *The Sentinel*, May, April 1883, April 1886; NVA *Executive Minutes*, 26 Nov. 1901, 29 July 1902; James Marchant, *The Social Evil*, 1914, 203–6.

18. Archdeacon Madden cited in *Vigilance Record*, March 1912.

19. *Free Church Year Book*, 1896, 194.

20. On Liverpool, *Vigilance Record*, Aug. 1890–Aug. 1893, passim; Sir William Nott Bower, *Fifty-Two Years A Policeman*, 1926, 141–4 and ch. 10; Nott Bower to the Watch Committee, Westminster City Council, 11 Dec. 1901 in H.O. 45 10123/B13517; Evidence of Sir Leonard Dunning in *Royal Commission on . . . Police*, 1908, que. 39544 ff; Flexner, *Prostitution in Europe*, 315–19.

21. NVA *Report of the Executive Committee*, 1887, iv.

22. *The Sentinel*, June 1892, June 1894; *Vigilance Record*, March, April 1888, April 1890, April 1891, April 1892, May 1893.

23. Notes of Deputation from the Westminster City Council, 17 Dec. 1901, in H.O. 45/10123/B13517/35.

24. Robert Storch, 'Police Control of Street Prostitution in Victorian London : A Study in the Contexts of Police Action' (unpublished paper).

25. Police Memorandum, 21 Nov. 1901 in H.O. 45/10123/B13517.

26. Flexner, *Prostitution in Europe*, 318.

27. See the files in H.O. 45/10123/B13517.

28. *London Council For The Promotion of Public Morality Annual*

*Report*, 1901; NVA *Executive Minutes*, 27 March 1900. Also on the election, John Henry Cardwell, *Twenty Years in Soho*, 1911, 61–2.

29. *East London Observer*, 11, 25 Feb., 3, 17, 31 March, 14 April, 24 Nov., 1 Dec. 1888. Thorne, *Charrington*, 157. Chief Commissioner to the Home Secretary, 25 Oct. 1888 in H.O. 45/ 9798/B5239.

30. *Purity and Temperance Work of the Central South London Free Church Council. Reports*, 1899/1900–1906/7; James Marchant, *The Cleansing of a City*, 1908, 49–59. *Prevention*, April–June 1912.

31. NVA *Executive Minutes*, 3, 17 May 1887; *Charing Cross Vigilance and Rescue Committee Annual Report*, 1898, in Fulham Palace Papers, Box 198. Cardwell, *Soho*, 20.

32. These figures are in the annual reports of the borough councils, available at the B.M., Guildhall Library and Westminster City Library.

33. *Royal Commission on ... Police*, 1908, Appendix, Return C.

34. Arthur Lee to Reginald McKenna, 7 July 1912, and Minute, in H.O. 45/10576/17846.

35. Cited in *St Anne's, Minutes of the Vestry*, 11 Oct. 1894, at Westminster City Library.

36. *Royal Commission on ... Police*, 1908, Appendix, Return C.

37. Sims in *Cleansing*, 106–23. Kitto in *The Sentinel*, June 1897. Cardwell in *St Anne's, Minutes of the Vestry*, 1 Aug. 1895.

38. *Royal Commission on ... Police*, 1908, Report, 117.

39. Coote, *A Vision and its Fulfilment*, 1913, 21.

40. *Vigilance Record*, Aug. 1898.

41. NVA *Executive Minutes*, 19 July, 26 Sept. 1887, 20 Sept. 1888.

42. Special Report on the Traffic in Girls, 21 May 1901, in Mepol 2/558.

43. *Ibid.*

44. *Report of the Jewish Association for the Protection of Girls and Women*, 1899, 10–11, in Montefiore Collection.

## CHAPTER EIGHT
(pp. 175–199)

1. Ellis, *Task of Social Hygiene*, 286–7.

2. Cited in *Vigilance Record*, Jan. 1930.

3. *Vigilance Record*, Jan. 1910.

4. Josephine Butler to Miss Forsaith, 11 April 1899, and to Mr Cope, 13 June 1899 in Josephine Butler Correspondence; *Storm Bell*, May, June 1899.

5. *The Sentinel,* Dec. 1887, Aug. 1892, March–July 1894.
6. Mrs Archibald MacKirdy and W. N. Willis, *The White Slave Market,* 1912, ch. 2; *Vigilance Record,* May 1910.
7. *Vigilance Record,* April 1904, June 1908; *Fifth International Congress for the Suppression of the White Slave Traffic,* 1913, 42–3.
8. *Report of the Jewish International Conference on the Suppression of the Traffic in Girls and Women,* 1910, 94, in Montefiore Collection.
9. *Memorandum and Subjects by the Polish National Committee for the Suppression of the Traffic in Women and Children,* Warsaw 1927, in NVA Collection, file S 74.
10. *Vigilance Record,* Sept. 1891, Jan. 1893.
11. Bruno Blau, 'The Jew as a Sex Criminal', *Jewish Social Studies* 13, 1951, 321–4. Comment by Samuel Cohen in *Report of an Enquiry Made in Constantinople on behalf of the Jewish Association...,* 1914, in Montefiore Collection.
12. *Vigilance Record,* June 1905; Chief Constable to Lord Mayor Illfyd Thomas, 28 Sept. 1908 in H.O. 45/10354/119817.
13. Dora Edinger, 'Bertha Pappenheim (1859–1936). A German-Jewish Feminist', *Jewish Social Studies* 20 (1958), 180–86.
14. David Pivar, *Purity Crusade. Sexual Morality and Social Control, 1868–1900,* Westport, Connecticut, 1973, 135–9.
15. On the treaties, *Vigilance Record* and H.O. 144/536/A48032.
16. *International Congress,* 1913, 90–113.
17. Cited in *Vigilance Record,* March 1906.
18. Coote, *Vision,* 35–9, 105–7; *Vigilance Record,* April 1914, Sept. 1915.
19. *Report of Enquiry Made in Constantinople...,* 1914; *Vigilance Record,* April 1912, April, July, Oct. 1914; NVA *Executive Minutes,* 30 Jan., 27 Feb. 1912.
20. NVA Collection, case file 49, box 116.
21. Jewish Association... *Report of the Secretary on his Visit to South America,* 1913, in Montefiore Collection.
22. NVA Collection, files Col and ColK; *Vigilance Record,* Oct., Nov., 1912.
23. NVA *Executive Minutes,* 30 Nov. 1897; 29 July 1902; 27 Oct., 24 Nov. 1903; 14 Nov. 1904; 31 Jan. 1905; 28 April 1908.
24. *Vigilance Record,* Jan. 1910.
25. Coote, 'Report of Six Months' Work' in *Vigilance Record,* Feb. 1904. Minute of Chief Commissioner E. R. Henry, 14 Nov. 1905 in Mepol 2/558.

26. See the abundant material in *Vigilance Record* and NVA *Executive Minutes.*
27. *Vigilance Record*, Feb. 1890; *International Congress*, 1913, 128–71.
28. Comments of Ernest Bell in *Prevention*, April–June 1913; Comments of J. Bronson Reynolds in International Abolitionist Federation, *Report of the Portsmouth Conference*, 1914, 82–102; Roy Lubove, 'Progressives and Prostitutes', *The Historian* 24, 1962, 300–330.
29. 'White Slave Traffic', memorandum by Frederick Bullock, 12 June 1913, in Mepol 2/1312.
30. On the white-slave films, NVA Collection, file S1L.
31. *Vigilance Record*, Dec. 1908.
32. Cited in Ware, 'Prostitutes', 466.
33. *Report of the Jewish Association . . .*, 1912, 9, 17; NVA *Executive Minutes*, 30 June, 28 July 1908; Minutes of W. P. Byrne, 3, 11 May 1911, in H.O. 45/10576/178486.
34. Bullock, 'White Slave Traffic'.
35. *Parl. Debs.* 4th Ser. XLIII, 1, 5, 12 Nov. and 11 Dec. 1912.
36. *Justice*, 9 Nov. 1912.
37. Teresa Billington-Grieg, 'The Truth About White Slavery', *English Review*, 14, 1913, 428–46.
38. *Vigilance Record*, Oct. 1921.
39. *League of Nations. Commission of Enquiry into Traffic in Women and Children in the East . . .*, 1934; *Vigilance Record*, Sept. 1922; NVA *Annual Report*, 1936; *Official Report of the Jewish International Conference on the Suppression of the Traffic in Girls and Women . . .*, 1927, passim, in Montefiore Collection.
40. NVA Collection, file ColJ.
41. *Report of the Jewish Association . . .*, 1937, 21.
42. Helen Wilson in *Joint Select Committee on the Criminal Law Amendment Bill . . .*, 1918, que. 1282.
43. Edgar Morin, *The Rumour of Orleans*, 1971.
44. NVA Collection, files S1e, S1q, S127, S127A, S109C, S109E.
45. Mrs Gow to Col. Leslie Wilson, 22 June 1922 in H.O. 45/11084/430126.

## CHAPTER NINE
(pp. 200–228)

1. *National League Journal*, Nov. 1882.
2. Paul Boyer, *Purity in Print. The Vice-Society Movement and Censorship in America*, New York 1968, 3–5. R. J. V. Lehman,

254 Notes to pages 201–214

'Art, Society and Law in Wilhelmine Germany: The Lex Heinze', *Oxford German Studies*, 1973, 86–113.

3. Ivan Bloch, *The Sexual Life of Our Time*, 1903, 739.

4. Cited in Martha Vicinus, *The Industrial Muse*, 1974, 275.

5. *Vigilance Record*, Dec. 1911.

6. Memorandum of 10 Aug. 1886 in H.O. 45/9546/88645; *Vigilance Record*, September 1890.

7. This can be followed in H.O. 144/A46657D and H.O. 144/238/A52539B.

8. Lord Braye in *Vigilance Record*, July 1907. See also A. Fessler, 'Advertisements on the Treatment of Venereal Disease', *British Journal of Venereal Disease*, 25, 1949, 84–7.

9. *Parl. Debs.* 5th Ser., XC, Lords, 13 Feb. 1934, 815.

10. *Daily News*, 28 May 1890. See also *Honi Soit Qui Mal Y Pense. The Life of Zæo*, in Theatre Museum, Victoria and Albert Museum.

11. NVA *Executive Minutes*, 30 Dec. 1890, 2 June 1891; Cyril Sheldon, *History of Poster Advertising*, 1937, ch. 3.

12. Rear-admiral Ryder to the Archbishop of Canterbury, 12 Feb., 2 June, 3 July 1885, in Benson Papers, vol. 27.

13. Coote, *Romance*, 94–101. Minute by G. Lushington, 4 Nov. 1890, in H.O. 45/9724/A52071.

14. Memorandum by H. Cuffe, Assistant D.P.P., 2 Nov. 1888 in H.O. 144/A46657/41, and minute thereon. NVA *Executive Minutes*, 30 April 1889; *Vigilance Record*, June 1889; Coote, *Romance*, 43–7.

15. *Truth*, 8 Aug. 1889.

16. Coote, *Romance*, 108–11; Alex Craig, *The Banned Books of England*, 1937, 52–3.

17. Cited in *The Sentinel*, Feb. 1894.

18. Music-Hall Proprietors' Association Memorial to the Home Secretary, M & D 3/64, at Middlesex Record Office.

19. The proceedings are in PC/Ent/2, LCC Licensing Sessions, *Printed Papers* 1, 1889–93; see also LCC *Minutes*, 18 Oct. 1889; *Minutes of the Inspection Sub-Committee*, 1890–6 at County Hall.

20. *Vigilance Record*, Dec. 1892.

21. Bloch, *Sexual Life in England*, 297.

22. Report of Q. Holyoake, 24 Nov. 1893, in LCC *Presented Papers*, vol. 104.

23. *Vigilance Record*, Sept.–Dec. 1894.

24. In PC/Ent/2 ... *Printed Papers* 2, 1894–7, 27 Jan. 1897.

25. Mrs Ormiston Chant, *Why We Attacked the Empire*, 1894.

26. See the comments by Archibald Allen in *Joint Select Committee on the Criminal Law Amendment Bill* . . ., 1918, ques. 2192–2215; *Vigilance Record*, Aug., Sept. 1916.

27. Report of G. A. Blackwell, 16 Jan. 1907, in LCC *Presented Papers*, vol. 81; LCC *Minutes*, 25 June 1907, 1372–6.

28. *Vigilance Record*, June, Aug., Dec. 1917.

29. NVA *Executive Minutes*, 31 Jan. 1911; *English Review* 7, 1911, 530 ff.

30. Cited in Samuel Hynes, *The Edwardian Turn of Mind*, Oxford 1968, 294.

31. NVA *Executive Minutes*, 20 Sept. 1905. Evidence of the chief constables of Liverpool and Hull at the *Joint Select Committee on Lotteries and Indecent Advertisements, P.P.,* ix, 1908; *Vigilance Record*, March, Dec. 1907.

32. *Vigilance Record*, Feb. 1902; PMC *Annual Report*, 1902.

33. *Vigilance Record*, Nov. 1908, March 1909; NVA *Executive Minutes*, 26 Sept., 28 Nov. 1911.

34. NVA *Executive Minutes*, 4 Jan. 1910; White Cross . . . *Executive Council Minutes*, 11 Nov. 1909. Minute by Chief Commissioner Henry, 11 July 1904, in Mepol 2/460.

35. Anthony Hugh Thompson, *Censorship in Public Libraries in the United Kingdom During the Twentieth Century*, 1975, 1–5; Arnold Bennett, *Books and Persons*, 1917, 181 ff.

36. *Vigilance Record*, Aug. 1908, March 1914.

37. Charles Carrington to Reginald McKenna, 7 Dec. 1911, in H.O. 45/10510/124433.

38. Memorandum of Guy Stephenson, 19 March 1912 and minute of 3 April 1912, in H.O. 45/10930/149778/42 and 44.

39. D. H. Lawrence, *Sex, Literature and Censorship* ed. Harry T. Moore, 1955, 219.

40. S. Cohen to F. Sempkins, 10 Oct. 1928, in NVA Collection file S88B; Sempkins to H. Tryer, 11 April 1929, in file S88T.

41. Findlater, *Banned*, 129–31. Bishop of London cited in Neville M. Hunnings, *Film Censorship and the Law*, 1967, 138; PMC *Annual Report*, 1930, 17–18.

42. Sempkins to Marquess of Aberdeen, 16 Jan. 1929, in NVA Collection, file S88U.

43. Sempkins to Howard Tryer (PMC), 8 July 1927 and to Miss Alexander, 17 April 1934 in NVA Collection, files S88T and H; Bishop of London, *London as it Should Be*, 1937.

44. *London Public Morality Council. Meeting of Executive Committee*, 24 April 1931, in NVA Collection, file S1R; PMC *Executive Minutes*, 29 April 1948.

45. On *Bessie Cotter, Manchester Guardian* 11 April 1935. On the 1938 case, PMC *Annual Report*, 1938.
46. PMC *Executive Minutes*, 29 Sept. 1955.
47. PMC *P.P. and P. Sub-Committee Minutes*, 23 Jan. 1952.
48. *The Times*, 5 Jan. 1935.
49. PMC *Executive Minutes*, 15 Feb. 1955.

## EPILOGUE
(pp. 229–232)

1. For Mary Whitehouse's latest views, see her *Whatever Happened to Sex*, 1977.
2. David Tribe, *Questions of Censorship*, 1973, 178–87.
3. For the latest on this, *The Guardian*, 16 May 1977.
4. *Pornography. The Longford Report*, 1972, ch. 17, 21.
5. *The Guardian*, 24 April 1975.
6. *Report of the Working Party on Vagrancy and Street Offences*, HMSO 1976.
7. *The Traffic in Persons. The System in Hong Kong*, Anti-Slavery Society, July 1975.

# Bibliography

ARCHIVAL MATERIAL

*Fawcett Library* (scheduled for removal to the City of London Polytechnic):
National Vigilance Association Collection, including records of the NVA, International Bureau for the Suppression of Traffic in Persons, British National Committee, and British Vigilance Association (1953–69). While a number of the purity periodicals (see below) are housed here along with minute books, case files, correspondence, etc., the NVA *Annual Reports* are scattered and can be seen only in series at the British Museum.
Travellers' Aid Society Records.
Josephine Butler Correspondence.
H. J. Wilson Papers.
Millicent Fawcett Autograph Collection.
Ladies National Association Records (from 1915, the Association for Moral and Social Hygiene).


*Greater London Record Office:*
Public Morality Council Collection.
London Diocesan Council for Wel-Care Collection.
Minutes of the London County Council.
Minutes of the Theatres and Music Halls Committee.
Presented Papers of the Theatres and Music Halls Committee.
Licensing Sessions, Series PC/ent/2.


*Guildhall Record Office:*
London Sessions Papers.


*Middlesex Record Office:*
Middlesex Sessions Papers.
Westminster Sessions Papers.
Music and Dancing Licences, petitions.

*Westminster City Library:*
Minutes of the Westminster City Council.
Records of the Vestries of St Martin's-in-the-Fields, St Anne's Soho
and St James's Piccadilly.

*Public Record Office:*
Home Office Papers, H.O. 45, H.O. 45 (OS) and H.O. 144 (with
permission).
Metropolitan Police Papers, Mepol 2.
Ministry of Health Papers, MH 55.
Registers of Applications to the Director of Public Prosecutions.

*Lambeth Palace Library:*
Archbishop Benson Papers.
Bishop Porteus Diaries.
Fulham Palace Papers : Temple and Creighton.

*Church House, Dean's Yard, London:*
White Cross Collection : records of the Church of England Purity
Society (known as the White Cross after about 1890); tracts,
reports and pamphlets otherwise unavailable.

*Free Church Federal Council:*
Minutes of the National Council of the Evangelical Free Churches
and its subcommittees.

FREE CHURCH YEAR BOOKS

*Church Army:*
Manuscript Lecture for Rescue-work Trainees.
Miscellaneous publications on rescue work.

*British Museum:*
Francis Place Collection. Add. Mss. 27824–8.

*University of Chicago Library:*
Percy Bunting Correspondence.

*West London Mission*

ANNUAL REPORTS

*London Library:*
Montefiore Collection. *Reports of the Jewish Association for the*

*Protection of Young Girls* as well as many other publications of the International Bureau and the anti-white-slavery movement.

*Sources in Provincial City Libraries:*
Minutes of the Sunderland City Council.
Minutes of the Cardiff Borough Council.
*Birmingham and Midland Counties Vigilance Association. Annual Reports* (1887–94); *Occasional Papers.*
*Hull Vigilance Association. Annual Reports* (1927–9).
*Manchester and Northern Counties Branch. National Vigilance Association. Annual Report* (1899–1900), and miscellaneous publications.
*Manchester Ladies Association for the Protection of Girls and Women. Annual Reports.* (1883, 1889, 1890.)
*Annual Reports of the Albion Hill Home.* Brighton City Library.


UNPUBLISHED THESES AND PAPERS

Helen Ware, 'The Recruitment, Regulation and Role of Prostitutes from the Middle of the Nineteenth Century to the Present Day', London University Ph.D. thesis, 1969.
Judith Walkowitz, 'We are Not Beasts of the Field : Prostitution and the Campaign Against the Contagious Diseases Acts, 1869–86', University of Rochester Ph. D. thesis, 1974.
Robert Storch, 'Police Control of Street Prostitution in Victorian London : A Study in the Contexts of Police Action'.
Penny Summerfield, 'The Effingham Arms and the Empire : Working Class Culture and the Evolution of the Music Hall'.


PERIODICALS EXTENSIVELY CONSULTED

*Alliance of Honour Record; Honour* from 1915.
*Le Bulletin Continental,* British, Continental and General Federation.
*Chivalry,* Alliance of Honour.
*Deliverer,* Salvation Army.
*Health and Empire,* British Social Hygiene Council.
*Magdalen's Friend*
*Malthusian,* Malthusian League.
*National League Journal,* Working Men's League for Repeal.
*On Guard,* Young Men's Friendly Society.
*Pioneer of Social Purity,* Social Purity Alliance and Moral Reform Union.

*Prevention*, National Council of Public Morals.
*Seeking and Saving*
*Sentinel*
*Shield*, Ladies National Association.
*Stage*
*Storm Bell*
*Vanguard; White Cross* from 1894, White Cross Movement.
*Vigilance Record*, National Vigilance Association.
*War Cry*, Salvation Army.
*Y.M.C.A. Monthly Review.*

OFFICIAL PUBLICATIONS

*Parliamentary Debates*
Parliamentary Papers as cited.
Judicial Statistics in the Parliamentary Papers.

SELECT LIST OF BASIC SECONDARY SOURCES†

Bahlmann, Dudley, *The Moral Revolution of 1688*, Archon ed. Connecticut 1968.
Barrett, Rosa, *Ellice Hopkins. A Memoir*, 1907.
Begbie, Harold, *Life of William Booth*, 2 vols, 1920.
Boyer, Paul S., *Purity in Print: The Vice-Society Movement in America*, New York 1968.
Brown, Ford K., *Fathers of the Victorians*, Cambridge 1961.
Bullough, Vern, *The History of Prostitution*, New York 1964.
Cominos, Peter, 'Late-Victorian Sexual Respectability and the Social System', *International Review of Social History* 8 (1963), 18–48, 216–50.
      'Innocent Femina Sexualis in Unconscious Conflict', in Martha Vicinus ed., *Suffer and Be Still*, Bloomington 1972, 155–72.
Coote, William A., *A Romance of Philanthropy*, 1916.
      *A Vision and its Fulfilment*, 1913.
de Mause, Lloyd, *The History of Childhood*, Harper Torchbooks ed. New York 1974.
Dufour, Pierre, *Histoire de la Prostitution*, 2 vols, Brussels 1854.
Evans, Richard J., 'Prostitution, State and Society in Imperial Germany,' *Past and Present* no. 70 (1976), 106–27.
Findlater, Richard, *Banned. A Review of Theatrical Censorship in Britain*, 1967.
Freud, Sigmund, *The Sexual Enlightenment of Children*, Collier ed. New York 1963.

Foxon, David, *Libertine Literature in England, 1660–1745*, 1964 reprint.

Frankl, George, *The Failure of the Sexual Revolution*, 1974.

Fryer, Peter, *The Birth Controllers*, 1965.

*Mrs Grundy*, 1963.

Fullerton, W. Y., *F. B. Meyer*, 1929.

Hair, P. E. H., *Before the Bawdy Court*, 1972.

Hare, E. H., 'Masturbatory Insanity : The History of an Idea', *Journal of Mental Science* cviii (1962), 1–25.

Harrison, Brian, 'Underneath the Victorians', *Victorian Studies* xi (1967), 239–61.

'For Church, Queen and Family : The Girls' Friendly Society 1874–1920', *Past and Present* no. 61 (1973), 107–38.

Hall, M. Penelope and Howes, Ismene V., *The Church in Social Work*, 1965.

Haller, John S. and Robin H., *Physicians and Sexuality in Victorian America*, Chicago 1974.

Harris, J. Rendel, *Life of Frank W. Crossley*, 1899.

Henriques, Fernando, *Prostitution and Society*, 3 vols, 1962, 3, 8.

Hollis, Patricia ed., *Pressure From Without in Early Victorian England*, 1974.

Hunnings, Neville March, *Film Censorship and the Law*, 1967.

Hyde, H. Montgomery, *The Other Love*, 1970.

Hynes, Samuel, *The Edwardian Turn of Mind*, Oxford 1968.

Inglis, K. S., *Churches and the Working Classes in Victorian England*, 1963.

Jordan, E. K. H., *Free Church Unity: A History of the Free Church Council Movement 1896–1941*, 1956.

Kern, Stephen, *Anatomy and Destiny*, New York 1975.

Koss, Stephen, *Nonconformity in Modern British Politics*, 1975.

Marcus, Steven, *The Other Victorians*, New York 1966, London 1967.

May, Geoffrey, *Social Control of Sex Expression*, 1930.

Moberly Bell, Enid, *Josephine Butler. Flame of Fire*, 1962.

Morin, Edgar, *The Rumour of Orleans*, 1971.

Parent-Duchatelet, A. J. B., *De La Prostitution dans La Ville de Paris*, 2 vols, 3rd ed. Paris 1857.

Paulson, Ronald, *Hogarth. His Life, Art and Times*, 2 vols, London and New Haven, Connecticut 1971.

Pearce, S. B. P., *An Ideal in the Working. The Story of the Magdalen Hospital*, 1958.

Pearsall, Ronald, *The Worm in the Bud*, 1969.

Pearl, Cyril, *The Girl in the Swansdown Seat*, 1955.

Petrie, Glen, *A Singular Iniquity. The Campaigns of Josephine Butler*, 1971.

Pivar, David J., *Purist Crusade. Sexual Morality and Social Control*, London and Westport, Connecticut 1973.

Portus, Garnet V., *Caritas Anglicana*, 1912.

Quinlan, Maurice, *Victorian Prelude*, 1941.

Radzinowicz, Leon, *History of English Criminal Law*, 3 vols, 1948–55.

Rolph, C. H., *Books in the Dock*, 1969.

Rosen, Andrew, *Rise Up Women*, 1974.

Ruitenbeek, Dr Hendrik, *The New Sexuality*, New York 1974.

Sandell, R. and Wiggins, A. R., *History of the Salvation Army*, 4 vols, 1947–68.

Schults, Raymond L., *Crusader in Babylon. W. T. Stead and the Pall Mall Gazette*, Lincoln, Nebraska 1972.

Searle, G. R., *The Quest for National Efficiency*, Oxford 1971.

Spitz, R. A., 'Authority and Masturbation', *Psychoanalytic Quarterly* 21 (1952), 490–527.

Stafford, Ann, *The Age of Consent*, 1964.

Stuart, James, *Reminiscences*, 1911.

Taylor, Gordon Rattray, *The Angel Makers*, 1958.

Thomas, Donald, *A Long Time Burning. The History of Literary Censorship in England*, 1969.

Thomas Keith, 'The Double Standard', *Journal of the History of Ideas* 20 (1959), 195–216.

Thorne, Guy, *The Great Acceptance. Life of Frederick N. Charrington*, 1912.

Trudgill, Eric, *Madonnas and Magdalens. The Origins and Development of Victorian Sexual Attitudes*, 1976.

Unsworth, Madge, *Maiden Tribute. A Study in Voluntary Social Service*, 1949.

Varley, Henry (son), *Henry Varley's Life Story*, 1916.

Vicinus, Martha, *The Industrial Muse*, 1974.

Webb, Sidney and Beatrice, *The History of Liquor Licensing in England, Principally from 1700–1830*, 1903.

Whyte, Frederick, *Life of W. T. Stead*, 2 vols, 1925.

Winnington Ingram, A. F., *Fifty Years' Work in London*, 1940.

Wilberforce, Robert Isaac and Samuel W., *Life of William Wilberforce*, 5 vols, 1838.

†Unless otherwise stated, the place of publication is London.

# Index